Cherokee Archaeology

Cherokee Archaeology

A STUDY OF

THE APPALACHIAN SUMMIT

By Bennie C. Keel

THE UNIVERSITY OF TENNESSEE PRESS

KNOXVILLE

Library of Congress Cataloging in Publication Data

Keel, Bennie C.   1934-
  Cherokee archaeology.

  Based on the author's thesis, Washington State University,
1972, entitled Woodland phases of the Appalachian summit
area.
  Bibliography: p.
  Includes index.
  1. Cherokee Indians—Antiquities. 2. Appalachian
Mountains, Southern—Antiquities. I. Title.
E99.C5K37   970'.004'97   75-41444
ISBN 0-87049-189-X

Preface

The Appalachian Summit Area, which was the heartland of the Cherokee Nation in the 17th and 18th centuries, is the southernmost and highest part of the Appalachian mountain system (Kroeber 1963:95). The Cherokee Indians are certainly one of the best-known groups of native Americans, but the details of their archaeological remains and those of their antecedents in the Southern Highlands are virtually unknown except to a few American archaeologists. This monograph attempts to provide the reader with many of those details.

I was involved in archaeological investigations of this Cherokee region from May 1964 to March 1972, except for the period from September 1967 to October 1969. Most of my time was spent in the field conducting site surveys and excavations, examining private collections, or working in the laboratory with data collected from the fieldwork. I also studied historic documents and the archaeological literature of the area and visited other institutions which had information related to the prehistory and early history of the region. During this time I became especially interested in the Woodland cultures, which were beginning to be isolated. By 1966 it was evident that the Woodland manifestations of the area were different from what had been expected on the basis of knowledge about the areas adjacent to the Appalachian Highlands. At the same time, some striking similarities existed between these and other Woodland tradition phases in the eastern United States.

The present study is but a small part of a much larger program of research currently being carried out by the Research Laboratories of Anthropology of the University of North Carolina at Chapel Hill under the overall supervision of Joffre L. Coe. This program deals with both prehistoric and historic aspects of the Cherokee Indian culture, with the following objectives:

1. The identification of Cherokee material culture in both its prehistoric and historic forms. There are a number of studies on the Cherokees, but very little was known about the archaeology of this group when the current

investigation was inaugurated. Already this program has produced worth-while results (Dickens 1970; Egloff 1967; Holden 1966), and as more of the data are analyzed, additional detailed information will be forthcoming.

2. The identification of the ecological base which supported the aboriginal inhabitants of this area.

3. The recognition of prehistoric cultural phases within the area occupied by the Cherokees in order to understand the development of the Cherokee Nation in particular and culture in general.

4. The temporal ordering of the cultural phases isolated in the study area. Without chronological controls, the taxonomic segregation of cultural units would be largely meaningless in determining the trajectory of cultural growth in the area.

5. Analyzing the processual relationships between the various cultural units found in the study area and comparing them with those of similar ages in the neighboring regions.

Although this monograph approaches all of these aims, it deals primarily with the identification and definition of the Woodland phases within the Appalachian Summit Area. Three Woodland phases are defined and placed in chronological order, and their absolute chronological duration is estimated. As well, the relationships between these South Appalachian phases and the relationships they shared with phases in other areas of the eastern United States are discussed.

The problem of identifying or isolating distinct archaeological phases from the mass of specimens collected by the archaeologist is at best difficult. The rarity of single-component sites makes such identification virtually impossible. Furthermore, experience has shown that sites once considered single-component stations are actually composed of several components. It is dangerous to consider material collected from individual strata at a site as a single component. The stratum in question may be contaminated with material introduced, by whatever agency, from both earlier and later occupation. It is also dangerous to consider separate strata as representing different components because a site may have been occupied by the same cultural group after a very brief interval of time in which an intervening stratum such as a spring flood deposit or a layer of wind-blown sand was deposited.

I have considered the attributes of the specimens and the recurrence of the taxonomic groups based on the combinations of attributes in specific strata at individual sites to be paramount in identifying or establishing a cultural unit. Thus, if two taxonomic groups repeatedly occurred in contexts with demonstrably different stratigraphic or vertical separation, the two contrasting groups were considered different assemblages. As each of these assemblages was replicated at other sites, the individual assemblages were combined to form an archaeological phase.

As the phases were defined, some idea of their relative chronological position became apparent from the stratigraphic positions the assemblages occupied at the various sites. Unfortunately, only one carbon 14 date was available for any of the Woodland period phases at the time this study was written. By comparing the local Woodland phases with other cultural units which have been dated by radiocarbon determination, however, I have produced a fairly accurate estimate of the absolute time periods occupied by the local manifestations. This comprehensive comparison also led to the recognition of relationships between the local archaeological units and contemporary units in other areas. For example, specific trade items derived from the Midwest were found associated with the Middle Woodland Connestee phase. However, the local late Early Woodland manifestation (Pigeon phase) shows an unmistakable affinity to the Deptford phase of central Georgia, whereas the preceding phase (Swannanoa) in the local Woodland sequence shows attributes which tie it to a Northern tradition.

Excavations conducted by the Research Laboratories of Anthropology yielded most of the data used in this study. In addition, field notes and specimens from the Hiwassee Island, Candy Creek, Camp Creek, Lay, Bible, Westmoreland-Barber, Icehouse Bottom, and Chota sites in Tennessee were studied at the University of Tennessee, and specimens from the Mandeville and Tunacunnhee sites in Georgia were made available by the University of Georgia for study. A portion of Robert Wauchope's (1966) collection of pottery type sherds from northern Georgia, which was given to the Research Laboratories of Anthropology, offered a representative sample of the range of variation for the northern Georgia pottery types, and served as a cross-reference between the published type descriptions and the actual physical characteristics of the types. Aboriginal remains from the Fort Prince George, South Carolina, area also were studied, and the entire North Carolina collection in the Museum of the American Indian-Heye Foundation, New York City—especially the specimens collected by George G. Heye in 1915 from Garden Creek Mound No. 3 (Hw 3)—added much information (Heye 1919). The collection from the C and O Mounds, Kentucky, was examined at the University of Kentucky, as well as collections from several Ohio Hopewell sites at the Ohio State Museum.

From 1963 to 1970, the Research Laboratories of Anthropology conducted extensive site surveys and excavations in southwestern North Carolina, and surveys were conducted in the adjacent parts of Georgia, South Carolina, and Tennessee. In this eight-year period more than 1,400 archaeological sites were recorded in the Appalachian Summit Area. The amount of material recovered from the surface collections and excavations was enormous—by June 1970, about 1 million potsherds and more than 10,000 artifacts had been processed. Abundant animal bone and charred plant remains were collected at all of the excavated sites. To date, only a small sample of these biological remains has been analyzed (Wing 1970; Yarnell 1970), but as more of this material is studied, additional information concerning the patterns of human adaptation and utilization of the ecological resources in this region will be revealed.

This particular study is based primarily on data recovered from three multicomponent sites excavated between 1964 and 1970. The stratigraphy of these sites made it possible to construct a fairly comprehensive cultural sequence that covers a span of at least 6,000 years. Certain projectile point types, including fluted forms, found in surface collections and private collections or recovered from excavations suggest that human occupation of the area began some 12,000 years ago.

The first site described (Chapter 2), Tuckasegee (Jk 12), is located in Jackson County, North Carolina. Here remnants of a circular structure of the historic period overlay the remains of earlier occupations. These earlier remains could not be divided into Mississippian (Pisgah phase), Woodland (Connestee, Pigeon, and Swannanoa phases), and Archaic period units except on typological grounds.

In Chapter 3 the investigations conducted at Garden Creek Mound No. 2, which is situated on the Pigeon River just west of Canton, Haywood County, North Carolina, are described. This low mound produced the first evidence of contact between local Middle Woodland peoples and the famous Hopewell culture of Ohio. Stratigraphic information recovered here allowed me to demonstrate that the Connestee phase preceded the Qualla and Pisgah and further that it had been preceded by the Pigeon and Swannanoa phases. The mound and the upper portion of the premound midden compose the Connestee type site. As part of the analysis of this site, the excavations conducted by the Valentine Museum in 1880 were studied from manuscript sources. The collection from this exploration was added to our own resources. I have also chosen to include a short description of our excavations at Garden Creek Mound No. 1 (Dickens 1970) and George G. Heye's 1915 exploration of Garden Creek Mound No. 3 (Heye 1919) in order to indicate the place this locality occupies in the archaeological research of the region.

The Warren Wilson site, or Fawcette site (Bn 29) as it is sometimes called, is the only site of the three discussed in detail in this monograph where we were fortunate enough to find deeply stratified deposits. Although the evidence obtained at Garden Creek Mound No. 2 amply demonstrated that the Pigeon and Swannanoa phases preceded the Connestee and subsequent phases, it failed to indicate clearly which was earlier. Conclusive evidence for the priority of the Swannanoa phase in the form of a Swannanoa midden found stratigraphically below deposits of Pisgah, Connestee, and Pigeon materials and above preceramic Archaic horizons was recovered. The Warren Wilson site is located on the north bank of the Swannanoa River about 10 miles east of Asheville, Buncombe County, North Carolina.

In the concluding chapter the data presented in the descriptive portions of this work are used to describe and define the Woodland phases and to summarize briefly the Archaic, Mississippian, and Historic phases which have been recognized at the Tuckasegee, Garden Creek, and Warren Wilson sites so as to offer a general picture of the archaeology of the Appalachian Summit Area.

At a time when many of the basic ideas concerning the goals of archaeological research are undergoing change, I feel it necessary to comment on the rationale adopted for this study. While agreeing with the fraternity of "New Archaeology" about goals set for archaeology (cf. Deetz 1965; Binford and Binford 1968; Chang 1967, 1968; Clarke 1968; Longacre 1970), I must argue that there are other goals equally worthy. The blending of humanistic leanings and scientific methodology is, to me, a most valuable aspect of anthropology. A well-documented culture history has more value than a poorly conceived processual interpretation, for a bad culture history can lead to faulty processual reconstructions. Therefore I am presently concerned with an accurate historical interpretation. Future researchers may wish to use the phases defined herein as the basis for processual studies; if so, then I shall consider my labor well spent.

Many of the terms used in American archaeology have a wide
range of meanings. So that the reader will be aware of my concepts
and use of some of these terms, I feel it necessary to define those
which might cause some confusion. An *assemblage* is "an associated
set of artifacts from the same synchronic unit" (Leonhardy 1970:2-
3). A *component* represents not only the associated set of artifacts
(assemblage) but the behavioral relationships, as abstracted by their
context, as well. In my use of the term *phase,* I have followed David
G. Clarke's definition:

> PHASE.   an archaeological unit constituting the smallest taxomically homo-
> geneous set of entity states having a higher mutual affinity within the unit
> than across its borders, which may be distinguished within a minimal time
> slice of that entity's system continuum [Clarke 1968:667] .

The concept of *type* used here also closely follows that of Clarke
(1968:191), who considers a type as "an homogeneous population
of artefacts which share a consistently recurrent range of attribute
states within a given polythetic state." Clarke (1968:198) has
further stated that artifacts belong to two other groups at the same
time: the *type group,* which is characterized by a common component subset of attributes that define a complex, and the *subtype,*
which is the "homogeneous population of artefacts which share a
given sub-set within an artefact type's polythetic set attributes."
These concepts are quite useful when applied with a bit of care and
foresight.

In ceramic analysis, for example, I have used Clarke's definition
for *subtype* to group together variations within a ceramic type; i.e.,
all of the variations in Pigeon Check Stamped were considered to be
subtypes of the Pigeon Check Stamped. I have further considered
that the *type* Pigeon Check Stamped belongs to the *type group*
Pigeon series.

"The *Woodland cultural tradition* may be defined, minimally, by
the presence of Woodland pottery" (Willey 1966:267), which in its
earliest forms is characterized by cord and fabric impressed surfaces.
Other elements which characterize this tradition are mound building,
almost universally dome-shaped burial mounds, the tubular tobacco
pipe, and the introduction of agriculture. Despite its "decreasing
usefulness," Woodland is a term that is understood by all American
archaeologists to refer to a general period of time when a number
of archaeologically recognizable cultural traits were present over a
wide area of the eastern United States (Jennings 1968:184).

In this study I have made the following assumptions:

1. Recognizable attributes useful for analytical purposes usually occur on cultural remains.
2. Attributes have a range of states or modes.
3. Certain states (modes) of the attributes will cluster, i.e., occur together to form a more or less homogeneous group.
4. These clusters, which I refer to as types or type groups, have meaning, generally culture-historical in nature.

The procedure of analysis followed throughout this study can best be illustrated by outlining the steps used on the surface collections made during 1964. The large surface collection from the Garden Creek locality was spread out on a table. Sherds were separated from other classes of specimens. Sherds that looked alike were grouped together in piles. The initial segregation was based on physical characteristics including temper, color, and general appearance rather than surface finish, decoration, or form. Next the piles were broken down according to surface finish, decoration, and appendages. These characteristics were listed on a 5 × 8 inch card divided into 10 columns of 18 rows. The physical characteristics were listed across the columns and the surface finish characteristics along the rows. A sample representing the range of modes expressed in each collection was removed and placed in a small box for future reference. As each additional collection was studied, the preliminary piles were compared with the samples of segregated material. If the piles matched the samples, they were recorded in the appropriate blanks; if they did not conform, then new spaces were allocated on the cards to record the characteristics these specimens exhibited. The initial method of classifying led to the recognition of 53 clusters of modes. At this time, the chronological position of these groups could not be demonstrated. However, typological similarities to other ceramics in the Southeast suggested placement for some of them. Subsequent analysis of ceramics has increased the number of clusters of modes to well over a hundred. For example, Egloff's (1967) study of Qualla ceramics from certain Cherokee towns isolated 37 clusters. Dickens' (1970) study of ceramics at the Warren Wilson site (Bn 29) utilized 34 clusters; no Qualla series sherd occurred in that collection. To be sure, many of these clusters represent subtypes, but my analytical procedure allowed these to be recognized. Consolidation of subtypes into types took place following analysis, not during analysis. The close agreement of types recognized by four investigators, working independently on materials from the same areas, tends to give authenticity to the defined types.

Collections from excavated sites were classified in the same manner. Excavation units were combined at the sites according to their stratigraphic position; e.g., all squares of plowed soil were combined and treated as one unit at any given site. This procedure validated the occurrence of different congeries of types at demonstrably sequential time levels. The distinctiveness of the types coupled with demonstrable temporal placement led me to consider these types as being historical types.

Initially, I thought that the projectile points in the collections could be relegated to types already described in the literature. Operationally, as I have noted, all projectile points were sorted and grouped together without reference to previously defined types, but rather in terms of the attributes they shared. The resulting clusters of attributes of each group were compared to the type descriptions and, where possible, to type collections. If a group of points conformed to the published description or was identical to type collections, the group was referred to the particular preexisting type; if not, a new type was defined. Artifacts other than pottery and projectile points were divided into categories based on material, method of manufacture, form, or function. These categories are comparable to categories described from other sites and areas.

ACKNOWLEDGMENTS

This publication is a substantial revision of my doctoral dissertation submitted to Washington State University in 1972.

I am indebted to the faculties of Florida State University (1957-1960) and Washington State University (1967-1969) for my formal training in anthropology. I am especially beholden to my dissertation committee, Dr. Richard D. Daughtery (chairman), Dr. Robert E. Ackerman, and Dr. Allan H. Smith. Their sound advice and clearly stated criticisms eased many of the problems that arose during the preparation of this study. Among my co-workers and fellow students, who have had no little role in the formation of my understanding of anthropology, I must acknowledge Roy S. Dickens, Jr., Leland G. Ferguson, David L. Dibble, Tom E. Roll, and Frank C. Leonhardy.

For access to collections and documents used in this study I am indebted to the following institutions and individuals: Frank H. McClung Museum, University of Tennessee, Dr. Alfred K. Guthe, director; Institute of Archaeology, University of South Carolina, Mr. John D. Combes, assistant director; Laboratory of Archaeology, University of Georgia, Dr. Arthur R. Kelly, director emeritus; Museum of the American Indian-Heye Foundation, Dr. Frederick J. Dockstader, director; Ohio State Museum, Dr. Raymond S. Baby, archaeologist; and the Department of Anthropology, University of Kentucky, Dr. Lathel Duffield, chairman. I also wish to express my indebtedness to a number of individuals, who are now, or were at one time, associated with some of these institutions, for sharing unpublished information. Among these are the late Dr. Joseph R. Caldwell, Dr. James Kellar, Mr. Stuart Neitzel, Mr. Richard W. Jefferies, and Mrs. Betty A. Smith, who have been involved in the University of Georgia archaeological work; and Dr. Charles H. Faulkner, Mr. Paul F. Gleeson, and Mr. Jefferson Chapman, who conducted research in the Tellico Reservoir in eastern Tennessee. I am also especially grateful to Dr. James B. Griffin of the University of Michigan for advice and information based on his long experience with the archaeology of the eastern United States.

All photographs and drawings are the work of the author or former members of the Research Laboratories of Anthropology staff. To those responsible I am most thankful. I must express my sincere appreciation to Madge and Paul Gleeson, who read and edited the final draft of my dissertation. I also wish to thank Mrs. Lucille Leonhardy, who typed the dissertation, and Ms. Joy L. Medford, who typed the present manuscript, helped with the illustrations, and performed a multitude of chores related to the final version.

The "Cherokee Project" has been financed by the Research Laboratories of Anthropology from its budgeted funds and by the National Science Foundation through Grant No. GS-717, Joffre L. Coe, principal investigator. Grants for preparation of the dissertation were made by the Department of Anthropology, Washington State University, and the Louisiana Research Foundation. The revision of the dissertation for publication was made possible by a grant from the College of Liberal Arts, Wright State University.

My greatest debt in this undertaking is to Joffre Lanning Coe. I cannot adequately enumerate all that he has done for me during the years of our association; neither can I adequately express my appreciation.

Finally, to my wife, Alice, I offer my sincerest gratitude for her support throughout my academic career. Only her willingness to work and her tolerance and affection have made this study possible.

Contents

Illustrations

PLATES

FIGURES

TABLES

Cherokee Archaeology

1. Introduction

The Appalachian Summit Area, the locale of this study, is the highest part of the Appalachian mountain system that extends from Maine to Georgia (Fig. 1). It is a land of steep high ridges separated by narrow fertile valleys, blessed with a moderate climate and the heaviest rainfall in the temperate eastern United States. Its natural wealth provided the existence of the Cherokees and countless generations of their predecessors.

In these wooded mountains and narrow valleys Europeans found, in the 17th century, the Cherokee heartland. Although from the earliest colonial times the Cherokees claimed much territory beyond the mountains—as much as 40,000 square miles (Mooney 1900:14), covering areas in Kentucky, Virginia, North Carolina, South Carolina, Georgia, Alabama, and Tennessee—they considered this rugged highland area their home. Throughout much of the 18th and 19th centuries soldiers, merchants, statesmen, scientists, and a few theologians described the people, their customs—especially their wars—and their lands, and pondered the origin of this proud people. Often these writers fabricated explanations when none, or at least none which suited their purposes, could be elicited from Indian informants. Among the most observant and competent writers about the Cherokee country was William Bartram, the Philadelphia naturalist, who in 1776 begins his description of the Cherokee country from the summit of Oconee Mountain near present-day Walhalla, South Carolina:

> I enjoyed a view inexpressibly magnificent and comprehensive. The mountainous wilderness which I had lately traversed, down to the region of Augusta, appearing regularly undulated as the great ocean after a tempest; undulations gradually depressing, yet perfectly regular, as the squama of fish, or imbrications of tile on a roof: the nearest ground to me of a perfect full green; next more glaucous; and lastly almost blue as the other with which the most distant curve of the horizon seemed to blend.
>
> After being recovered of the fatigue and labour in ascending the mountain, I began . . . to descend the other side; the winding rough road carrying

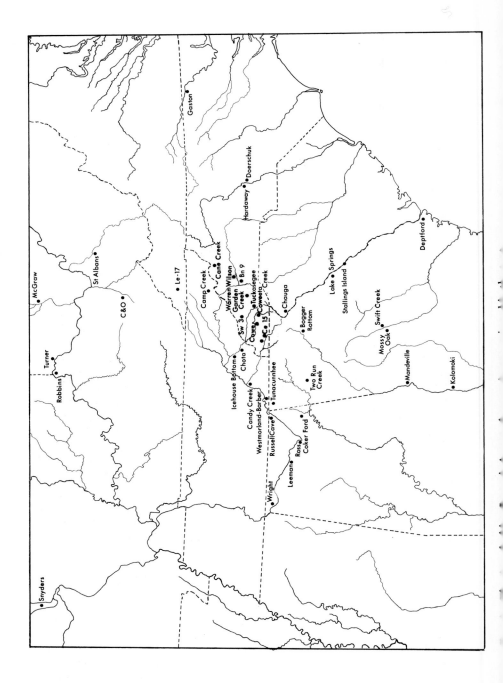

Snyders

McGraw

St Albans

C&O

Turner

Robbins

Le-17

Gaston

Camp Creek

Cane Creek

Warren Wilson
Garden Creek
Sw 3a
Bn 9
Tuckasigee
Coweeta
Coweeta Creek
Ce 15
Cowe
Chota

Icehouse Bottom

Candy Creek

Westmorland-Barber
Russell Cave
Tunacunnhee

Wright

Leemans
Ross
Coker Ford

Two Run
Creek

Bogger
Bottom

Hardaway
Doerschuk

Chauga

Lake Springs

Stallings Island

Mossy
Oak

Swift Creek

Mandeville

Kolomoki

Deptford

me over rocky hills and levels, shaded by incomparable forests, the soil exceedingly rich, and of an excellent quality for the production of every vegetable suited to the climate. . . . Passed through magnificent high forest, and then came upon the borders of an ample meadow on the left, embroidered by the shade of a high circular amphitheater of hills, the circular ridges rising magnificently one over the other. . . . The upper end of this spacious green plain is divided by a promontory or spur of ridges before me, which projects into it: my road led me up into an opening of the ascents through which the glittering brook which watered the meadows ran rapidly down, dashing and roaring over high rocky steps. . . .

The surface of the land now for three or four miles is level, yet uneven, occasioned by natural mounds or rocky knobs, but covered with a good staple of rich earth which affords forest of timber trees and shrubs. . . .

On my arrival at this town [Cowe] I waited on the gentleman to who I was recommended by leter. . . .

Next day after my arrival I crossed the river in a canoe, on a visit to a trader who resided amongst the habitations on the other shore . . . on his mentioning some curious scenes amongst the hills, some miles distant from the river, we agreed to spend the afternoon in observations on the mountains.

After riding near two miles through the Indian plantations of Corn, which was well cultivated, kept clean of weeds, and was well advanced, being near eighteen inches in height, and the beans planted at the Cornhills were above ground . . . began to ascend the hills of a ridge which we were under the necessity of crossing; and having gained its summit; enjoyed a most enchanting view; a vast expanse of green meadows and strawberry fields; a meandering silver gliding through, saluting in its various turnings the swelling, green, tufy knolls, embellished with parterres of flowers and fruitful strawberry beds, flocks of turkies [sic] strolling about them; herds of deer prancing in the meads or bounding over the hills; companies of young innocent Cherokee virgins, some busily gathering the rich fragrant fruit . . . [Bartram 1940:274-289].

The scene, a picture of the Appalachian Summit Area when it was still entirely occupied by the Cherokees, was painted by Bartram nearly 200 years ago. Although much of the beauty of the mountains has been destroyed by civilization, views equal to those he described can still be seen in some areas.

GEOLOGY

The Southern Blue Ridge Province (Fenneman 1938) includes all of Kroeber's (1963:95) Appalachian Summit Area. The bulk of the Appalachian mountain system in the study area is composed of pre-Cambrian rocks, although intrusive plutonic rocks of Permian age are present (Stuckey 1965:26). The principal geologic process of the Tertiary and Quaternary periods has been erosion.

Physiographically, the southern portion of the Blue Ridge Province is characterized by high mountains, among them Mount Mitchell (6,684 feet), the highest peak in eastern North America. Over 80 peaks south of the Roanoke River reach above 5,000 feet, and half of these attain elevations of more than 6,000 feet. The province is also characterized by a sharp eastern frontal scarp, with outliers as far as 50 miles away. Most drainage is to the Gulf of Mexico via the Tennessee-Ohio-Mississippi river system (Thornbury 1965:103).

Viewed from a high altitude, the area is characterized by southwest-northeast trending mountain chains with transverse ridges at approximately right angles to the trend of the range. Mountain slopes are steep, but only in the southern part of the area are vertical faces common.

The mountain peaks are generally rounded, but vertical rock faces and rugged summits do occur. These are most commonly found in the southern part of the area, e.g., Whiteside Mountain, Looking Glass Mountain, the Horseshoe, and the Pinnacle. Coves are common throughout the area. A cove "is a smooth-floored, somewhat oval-shaped valley that rarely exceeds 10 square miles in area" (Thornbury 1965:103-104). The local inhabitants, however, refer to all minor drainage valleys as coves regardless of shape or size. The largest and best known coves—Cades Cove, Wears Cove, and Millers Cove—are in the Great Smoky Mountains.

Two major chains are recognized in the province: the Blue Ridge, which forms the eastern scarp, and the Unakas, which form the western boundary of the province (Fenneman 1938:173-174). The local inhabitants make much finer distinctions. These smaller divisions generally reflect major stream divides; hence the Balsams separate the waters of the Tuckasegee and the Pigeon, and the Cowee Mountains divide the waters of the Little Tennessee and Tuckasegee.

Streams are formed both at the divides of the major chains and along the transverse ridges. Their gradients are fairly gentle west of the Eastern Continental Divide except in their headwater sections, where falls and cascades commonly occur. The flood plains of the major rivers are narrow, never exceeding about 3 miles in width. The streams were for the most part well fitted, but the development of TVA projects, which have locked up tremendous stores of water on the stream heads, have tended to produce underfit streams in those drainage basins affected. The upper French Broad River seems to be underfit without the benefit of man. Several explanations have been offered for this circumstance: stream piracy, reducing discharge, climatic change, increased loss of volume by underflow through the alluvium. Wright (1942:160) has concluded that climatic change has probably not been a contributing factor.

The area between the edge of the flood plain and the mountain slope—the intermountain land (Lee 1955:87)—is characteristically hilly and rolling.

The local mineral resources utilized during the prehistoric period included quartz, quartzite, diorite, various schists and gneisses, mica, steatite, and talc. It is noteworthy that no flint, chert, or chalcedony occurs in the area, and yet many of the chipped stone artifacts were made of these materials. The nearest place these materials are abundantly available is the Ridge and Valley Province of eastern Tennessee (Kellenberg 1963:1-7).

The prehistoric populations of the area utilized all parts of the province. During the 1965 survey and subsequently, camp and village sites were found on the flood plains, on the terraces or intermountain lands, in the coves, on the peaks, and in saddles along the ridges. Materials dating from the earliest to the latest periods were recovered from all topographical situations.

Geological studies of the area have principally dealt with periods of time well beyond the range of possible human occupation. These studies have been concerned with reconstructing the geologic history of the area or have centered on problems related to the economic exploitation of mineral resources. William M. Davis' (1889) ideas concerning the geomorphic history still remain the most common interpretation of landscape development in the Appalachian Highlands, even though some workers have questioned Davis' hypothesis (cf. Richards and Judson 1965:129-136). The paucity of Quaternary studies in the area is best illustrated by Judson's (Richards and Judson 1965:133-135) use of a few short paragraphs to summarize what is known about the Appalachian Highlands during this period.

The lack of knowledge about the late Pleistocene has been somewhat filled by D. D. Michalek's (1969) study. His hypothesized periglacial climate for the area during the terminal Wisconsin should be considered by anyone working on Paleo-Indian problems in the area.

CLIMATE

The mountains of western North Carolina form a partial barrier to the extreme cold of the central United States. The area is still severely chilled, but only for short periods of time. Snowfall is quite variable, ranging from 8 inches in the warmer valleys of the southern part of the area to more than 30 inches on the mountain peaks (Carney, Hardy, and van Bavel 1963:21). All other aspects of climate show similar divergences. For example, temperatures are quite variable; the mean annual temperature atop Mount Mitchell is 43.3°, but at Asheville, some 34 miles southwest and 4,400 feet lower, the mean annual temperature is 56.5° (Carney, Hardy, and van Bavel 1963:Table 1). In general, summer temperatures are controlled primarily by elevation, while winter temperatures are controlled by latitude (Lee 1955:Figure 2). The number of frost-free days averages between 170 and 180 days in the valleys, where most agriculture is practiced. The growing season, however, may be shortened by three weeks at higher elevations. Marked thermal belts are outstanding features on the mountain slopes. Temperature inversions of as much as 20° have frequently been noted (Kichline 1941:1044; Carney, Hardy, and van Bavel 1963:17-18).

Perhaps rainfall reflects the climatic variation best: both the lowest and highest mean annual precipitations in North Carolina are reported from monitoring stations located in the mountains, and in fact the heaviest rainfall in the eastern United States is recorded in the area. Rockhouse, Macon County, had a 25-year average of 82.96 inches, while Asheville averaged only 38.47 inches per year during the same period. These differences are largely the result of geographic location and elevation. Asheville, located in the French Broad Basin, is surrounded by mountains, while Rockhouse, located near the Georgia-South Carolina line, receives the warm moist air from the south as it rises over the mountains. Torrential rainstorms occur occasionally, usually in the summer or early fall, as a result of tropical storms moving into the area. At such times local flooding and consequent damage are often severe (Lee 1955:13).

SOILS

William D. Lee (1955) has presented a key for the identification of mountain soil series. This key is based on the topographic position and the parent material of the soil as the beginning point for identification. The "high mountain" soils occur at elevations from about 2,000 to 3,500 feet. Parent material suites consist of acid crystalline rocks (dark gneisses, granite, and low mica schists), basic crystalline rocks (diorite, hornblende), very micaceous rocks (light gneisses and schists, talcose schists, and similar rocks), shales, slates, quartzites, fine-grained sandstone, and very localized limestone deposits (Lee 1955:87-96).

The soils of the mountains represent several stages of maturity. The Clifton, Fannin, Halewood, Hayesville, Perkinsville, and Watauga series represent mature soils associated with the upland areas. These soils are classified as good to poor for the production of corn. They probably had little use as agricultural soils in aboriginal times due to the difficulty in working them by primitive methods. The soils associated with the alluvial valleys are young soils, for sufficient time has not passed for the climate and organisms to produce well-defined soil horizons. Alluvial soils include the Buncombe, Chewacla, Congaree, Pope, Toxaway, Tusquitee, Transylvania, and Wehadkee series. All of these except the Buncombe soil, which is classified as a poor type because of its low fertility, are ranked as very good soils for corn production. Their ease of cultivation and high yields made these soils especially sought during and after the Mississippian period.

Soils which occur on mountainsides and steep terrace slopes such as the Chandler, Fletcher, Ramsey, and Talladega series are also young soils since erosion continuously exposes new parent material. These soils are rated as poor or very poor corn producers. It is very unlikely that these soil types were ever used by the Indians for crop lands (Lee 1955:21 and Table 9).

FLORA

The Appalachian Summit Area is covered primarily by a deciduous forest type related to the northern hardwood complex, although at higher elevations more northerly trees such as spruce and balsam fir occur. The Southern Blue Ridge Province of the biologists is considered part of the Northern and Upland Forest Region (Shelford 1963:17-50). In the Southern Blue Ridge Province several forest types are found, but these seem to reflect differences in elevations rather than other ecological limitations. In the lower valleys, for example, a mixed mesic oak-chestnut forest was once present. However, the chestnut blight which entered this area during the second or third decade of the 1900s has eliminated the American chestnut. Today this forest type is composed of red oak, chestnut-oak, and white oak, with increased numbers of red maple, sourwood, and similar trees. Because pines have recently been introduced by man, they still form part of the initial sere of natural plant succession. Their use in the lumber and paper industries will probably preclude the return of the mature forest type since as they are harvested, they will be replaced by seedlings of similar types.

The oak-chestnut forest of the valleys is replaced by the maple-beech-basswood forest at an elevation of about 2,700 feet. American chestnut is also present in this assemblage as a minor species. At the upper end of its range, the maple-beech-basswood forest merges with the hemlock, spruce, and balsam fir forest which occurs above 4,200 feet. Before the land was extensively lumbered, the oak-chestnut forest was an open wood on ridges and intermountain soils.

A great variety of herbs and shrubs grows in the area. The following is only a small number of them. Evergreen shrubs include the rhododendrons, dog hobble, mountain magnolia, and laurel. The non-evergreen shrub group is composed of witch hazel, strawberry shrub, wild hydrangea, sweet pepperbush, spicewood, azalea, old-man's-beard, horse sugar, dogwood, chinquapin, dwarf locust, and clammy locust. Floor covering plants such as jack-in-the-pulpit, Clintonia, mayapple, lady's slipper, trillium, Solomon's seal, black cohosh, cardinal flower, umbrella leaf, devil's bit, fly poison, baneberry, hepatica, blueberry, huckleberry, and ginseng are but a few of the flowering plants. Ferns, including cinnamon royal, Christmas, woodfern, lady fern, and hayscented fern, are common.

James Mooney (1891:324-327) selected 20 plants used by the Cherokee for medicinal purposes. In this list he included snakeroot which was used in the treatment of fevers, toothache, and snake bite; life everlasting was employed in the treatment of a wide variety of ills and was considered a most valuable plant by native practitioners, although it has little real healing properties; milkweed was used in the treatment of several illnesses including gonorrhea; kidney ailments were treated with a concoction made from the beggar-lice plant; a poultice of Solomon's seal was applied to sores, boils, and carbuncles. The use of these and other plants for medicinal purposes probably has considerable antiquity.

The uses that other forest products were put to are almost infinite. To mention only a few: logs were used in house construction and for canoes, bowls and mortars; white oak was used for trays, baskets, and matting; cane was split and used in baskets, trays, and mats, as well as blowguns and arrow shafts; and naturally acorns, nuts, berries, leaves, roots, and fruits were eaten.

FAUNA

The animal population of the temperate deciduous forest is a varied one. Prior to white settlement the important animals were deer, wolf, puma, black bear, bobcat, gray fox, raccoon, fox and gray squirrels, eastern chipmunk, white-footed mouse, pine vole, short-tailed shrew (Shelford 1963:23), bat, bison, groundhog, beaver, opossum, otter, skunk, and weasel (Holden 1966:14). Many of the larger animals, especially the large carnivores, are rare or locally extinct. Among these mammals deer, bear, raccoon, and beaver were the most important sources of food, hides, and furs for the Indians. Their bones were often made into tools such as awls, needles, pins, fishhooks, and projectile points.

Year-round avian residents included the turkey; blue jay; tufted titmouse; red-bellied, hairy, and downy woodpeckers; white-breasted nuthatch; owl; hawk; quail; and eagle. Migrants include warm-season wood pewee, wood thrush, Acadian flycatcher, red-eyed vireo, yellow-throated vireo, cerulean warbler, ovenbird, scarlet tanager, yellow-billed cuckoo, and great crested flycatcher. Winter residents were coots, ducks, and geese (Shelford 1963:23; Holden 1966:14). For food the most important birds were turkeys, ducks, and geese; but their feathers and skins and those of other species were used for a variety of goods, e.g., feather cloaks, headdresses, dance wands, and medicine bags.

The copperhead and the timber rattlesnake are the only poisonous reptiles in the area. Other snakes include the common garter snake, black racer, spreading adder, milk snake, and water snake (*Natrix* sp.). Box turtles are very common. Toads, frogs, salamanders, and lizards make up the amphibians found locally (Shelford 1963:23; Holden 1966:14). The shells of turtles were used for rattles, and their flesh was eaten. Henry Timberlake (1927:72) reports developing a taste for rattlesnake during his sojourn in the Cherokee country. The skins of snakes were used as adornments, and rattlesnake fangs were used as scratchers in ceremonies.

Game fish such as trout, perch, bass, pike, sturgeon, and catfish were once common in the unpolluted streams. Shellfish seem never to have been abundant in the area although some were present (Holden 1966:15). The Cherokee obtained fish by constructing a weir, driving the fish into its mouth, and dipping them out in baskets (Timberlake 1927:69). They were also obtained by hook and line, spearing, bow and arrow, and possibly nets.

ECOLOGICAL CONSIDERATIONS

In the preceding parts of this section the various aspects of the natural setting have been described in some detail. Acknowledging that the undisturbed conditions of the deciduous forest can be but crudely approximated, Victor E. Shelford (1963:26-29) has made an effort to present a picture of the situation as it was during the 16th century. He detailed the ecology in terms of areas of 10 square miles.

In appraising the applicability of such a model of the deciduous forest for the present study, circles to the scale of 3.57 miles in diameter were drawn on topographic and soil maps around the sites which are discussed here in detail. There was no evidence that any of the sites were situated in areas where Shelford's reconstruction might be inappropriate. The highest elevation noted in any of the circles was 3,000 feet, well within the margin of the deciduous forest types and fully 1,200 feet below the spruce-balsam fir forest type.

According to Shelford (1963:26-29), a circle containing an area of 10 square miles would have 750,000 trees 3 inches or more in diameter and at least 4 feet tall. About two dozen species are significant, the more important ones being the American chestnut, oak, hickory, maple, basswood, and walnut. At any given time about 786,000 tree seedlings would be found beneath the canopy along with almost 3 million shrubs. The herbaceous constituents of the forest floor would range from 230 to 460 million plants.

During the first two months of summer about 26,880 million invertebrates provided nesting birds with food and at the same time caused serious damage to their plant hosts. Throughout this interval, the 7,680 pairs of nesting birds (approximately 1 pair per 90 to

95 trees) would consume daily about 250 invertebrates each. However, rapid breeding of the insects and the maturation of early-stage individuals would keep the population fairly constant.

Such an area could be expected to contain between 20 and 50 predatory birds, preying largely on mice, but including other small vertebrates as well as invertebrates in their diet. There would be from 160,000 to 320,000 mice, predominantly white-footed mice, in the circle. The mice would consume seeds, nuts, and snails.

The gray squirrel was important for its root-digging and nut-burying habits. In the absence of the gray squirrel, or even low population density of this species, the fox squirrel was usually present. A 10-square-mile area could reasonably contain up to 20,000 of the larger squirrels and a similar number of Southern flying squirrels. Man might find himself competing with upwards of 40,000 arboreal rodents for nuts and acorns.

The turkeys fed on acorns, dogwood seeds, and beechnuts. Under favorable conditions upwards of 200 individuals might inhabit a 10-square-mile area. It should be noted that the turkey does not seem to have been uniformly distributed in the forest; nonetheless, it is reasonable to assume many more were present three or four hundred years ago than today.

The major dominant animal prior to the arrival of the white man was the Virginia white-tailed deer. The deer herd size varied between 100 and 800 individuals per 10 square miles. The optimum number of deer on the Pisgah National Wildlife Refuge, which is located in the study area, is estimated to be about 400. Elk, or wapiti, were important as far south as northern Georgia, particularly in the more open forest zones. Bison were present, but only in small numbers. Approximately 5 of the large predators (3 wolves, 2 pumas) could be expected to reside in a 10-square-mile area. These predators would consume about 100 large animals per year.

Red and gray foxes were prime omnivores which consumed everything from berries to snakes and grasshoppers to birds. Estimates of 30 individuals per 10 square miles have been given for the gray fox. Another important omnivore, found even today in the Great Smoky Mountains, was the black bear. Population density for this animal is thought to have been about 5 per 10 square miles.

The preceding ecological reconstruction can be summarized by noting that in any given 10 square miles of the deciduous forest we could reasonably expect to find 750,000 trees, mostly acorn and nut bearers; 786,000 tree seedlings; abundant herbs and shrubs;

literally millions upon millions of invertebrates; 16,000 nesting
birds; 20 to 50 predatory owls and hawks; 160,000 to 320,000
mice; upwards of 40,000 squirrels; 200 turkeys; 400 deer; some elk
and bison; 3 wolves; 2 pumas; 5 bears; and 30 foxes. Additionally,
rabbits, opossums, raccoons, otters, groundhogs, bobcats, Eastern
chipmunks, pine voles, short-tailed shrews, bats, beavers, skunks,
and weasels would be present in varying numbers.

Although floral and faunal analyses have yet to be completed on
all of the sites used in this study, summaries of Yarnell's (1970:283-
293) discussion of flora and Wing's (1970:294-299) treatment of the
fauna from the Warren Wilson site are given in Chapter 4.

Joseph R. Caldwell (1958:6) has presented the idea that the economic basis for the cultures of eastern North America prior to the
establishment of agriculture was the development of a "primary
forest efficiency" system or adaptation. He cognizantly argues that
cultures of the East reached rather complex levels of development
because they developed specialized exploitation techniques and patterns which allowed them to efficiently exploit the rich forest en-
vironments in which they existed. In view of the natural resources
described and quantified above, one cannot argue otherwise. Even
though local cultigens may have added to the diet of Woodland
period peoples, these plants never seemed to have been as important
as domesticated plants introduced from Middle America used by
later folk.

A HISTORY OF APPALACHIAN SUMMIT AREA ARCHAEOLOGY

The area between the Blue Ridge escarpment and the western
slope of the Unaka Mountains (Figure 1) has received the attention
of archaeologists for almost a century. In fact, the first report dealing with prehistoric problems of the area is almost two hundred
years old. In 1776 William Bartram, the Philadelphia naturalist, regarding the mounds he saw in the area, said: "The Cherokees themselves are as ignorant as we are, by what people or for what purpose
these artificial hills were raised . . ." (Bartram 1940:297). In the
1880s the Valentine family of Richmond, Virginia, assisted by local
workers, opened several mounds in the area. No adequate publication of this work has appeared to date, but since 1969 most of the
specimens and copies of field notes, journals, and letter books have

been under study at the Research Laboratories of Anthropology in Chapel Hill.

Expeditions by the Division of Mound Exploration of the Bureau of American Ethnology under Cyrus Thomas were contemporary with the Valentine work. Most of the BAE fieldwork was conducted by John Emmert and John Rogan; the results were, for the time, adequately treated by Thomas (1887, 1891, 1894). Contrary to the theory then current, that a vanished race much superior to the Indians of eastern North America was responsible for the thousands of earthworks found in the area, Thomas (1894) reviewed his evidence and concluded that these monuments were the handiwork of Indians, specifically the Cherokees. Thomas' study of the distribution of the mounds indicated that the prehistoric movements of this tribe were in the not too distant past. In the light of present knowledge, we know Thomas was incorrect in many of his conclusions largely due to his lack of temporal insight (Keel 1970).

No further work seems to have been carried out in the Southern mountains until 1915 when George G. Heye began his research in Haywood County, North Carolina. Mr. Heye published "Certain Mounds in Haywood County, North Carolina" in 1919. This short paper provides an account of his excavation of the Garden Creek Mound No. 3. Heye's interest in the general area continued for several years, and his foundation sent workers into the Cherokee area of northern Georgia and eastern Tennessee (Heye, Hodge, and Pepper 1918; Harrington 1922). Heye and his associates were not out to prove any thesis, but rather to add to the collection of Heye's Museum of the American Indian. Their reports, therefore, were mostly descriptions of the sites, the work accomplished, and the artifacts recovered. The exception, peripheral to my study area, was Mark R. Harrington's (1922) work in the upper Tennessee River Valley. From the information he gathered, Harrington was convinced that at least three periods of time, each associated with a different ethnic group, could be identified. He correctly pointed out that the Euro-American trade goods found with aboriginal remains belonged to the Cherokee occupation, but like others who were to follow, he assigned similar aboriginal material not associated with trade goods to other groups ("Siouans"), and earlier remains to Algonquian peoples.

Fourteen years later, Jesse D. Jennings, working for the Smithsonian Institution, excavated the Peachtree Mound and Village (Setzler and Jennings 1941). The site was selected for excavation, not only because John R. Swanton (1932) had identified it as Guasili, one of the towns visited by DeSoto in 1540, but also because it was situated in an area in need of public relief work. Jennings, who wrote most of the report, concluded "that the Peachtree site is a component in which both Woodland and Mississippi traits occur simultaneously, blended or fused to make a culturally homogeneous site" (Setzler and Jennings 1941:57); he failed to realize that the broad range of material culture items obtained at Peachtree was due to the locality having been occupied over many centuries by distinct archaeological phases. In light of our research we can show that this site was occupied during the Archaic, Early Woodland, Middle Woodland, Mississippian, and historic periods.

At about the same time Jennings was digging at Peachtree, Major William S. Webb inaugurated the TVA program of salvage archaeology in the Wheeler Basin of western Alabama and the Norris Basin in the Overhill Cherokee area of northeastern Tennessee. This work was continued by Thomas M. N. Lewis and his associates at the University of Tennessee, and in fact continues even today as the rivers flowing into existing lakes are further impeded by new dams. Although work on the Tennessee River lies outside the study area, the conclusions reached by these investigators regarding Cherokee prehistory extend to the Appalachian Summit Area and so form part of the larger picture. Webb (1938:370-382), who followed Harrington's lead, considered certain cave and village occupations to be those of Algonquian peoples. He divided the later remains into those belonging to the "small-log town-house people," i.e., the Yuchis, and those belonging to the "large-log town-house people," i.e., the Creeks. The Cherokees were dismissed as latecomers who left rather unimportant remains. Later, Lewis and Kneberg (1941) followed Webb's ideas but pointed out that Webb's model of tribal displacement was not tenable since data from the Chickamauga Basin suggested the contemporary existence of Woodland and Mississippian peoples on the lower Hiwassee River. Although this position was somewhat modified in 1946 with the publication of *Hiwassee Island*, they still insisted that some Woodland peoples were contemporary with the Dallas and Hiwassee Island populations.

The Research Laboratories of Anthropology have had a continuing interest in the Appalachian Summit Area through the leadership of Joffre L. Coe. Even before the Laboratories were organized, Coe in 1935 excavated at the Connestee, or Puette, site (Tr 1).

During the WPA-University of North Carolina statewide archaeological survey Harold T. Johnson recorded more than 130 sites in Buncombe County. Plans to excavate several sites in western North
Carolina were frustrated by the outbreak of World War II (Coe
1961). Finally a program of extensive research was begun in 1963
with Edward M. Dolan's survey of Macon County. At that time
only 165 sites had been recorded west of the Blue Ridge (130-odd
of them were the result of Johnson's work as noted above). Dolan's
work in Macon County, and his limited reconnaissance in the adjacent counties, adds 133 new sites to this inventory. In the summer
of 1964 under Coe's direction, I inaugurated a comprehensive survey; it was continued through 1965, 1966, and 1967 by Brian J.
Egloff, who had assisted me in 1964. Patricia P. Holden under Coe's
direction carried out an extensive survey of Transylvania County in
1964 and 1965 (Holden 1966). She also worked in adjacent Henderson County and in northwestern South Carolina during those
years. By the early 1970s these surveys plus incidental site discoveries pushed the total number of sites to over 1,500 recorded in the
study area. Data recovered from these surveys were used for Hold-
en's "An Archaeological Survey of Transylvania County, North
Carolina" and Brian J. Egloff's "An Analysis of Ceramics from
Cherokee Towns"; both are master's theses submitted to the University of North Carolina (Holden 1966; Egloff 1967).

During the 1964 season, the writer conducted excavations at five
sites: Tuckasegee, Jk 12; Nununyi, Sw 3; the Townson site, Ce 15;
Cy 42; and Jk 150. The Townson and Tuckasegee site excavations
were limited to the exposure of single structures, and the work at
the other sites was even more restricted.

Subsequent undertakings on the part of the Research Laboratories of Anthropology were greatly implemented by National Science Foundation Research Grant No. GS-717, Joffre L. Coe, principal investigator. In 1965, excavations were initiated at Garden
Creek Mound No. 1 under the direction of Joffre L. Coe and the
writer. Three seasons (1965-1967), lasting from early spring until
Thanksgiving of each year, were required to excavate this 7-foot-tall
mound and parts of the associated village. In 1966, the work was
supervised by Coe and James J. Reid, while I excavated what remained of Garden Creek Mound No. 2. In 1967, the Garden Creek
Mound No. 1 excavations were supervised by Coe and Reid assisted
by Leland G. Ferguson, while I continued the excavations at the
Coweeta Creek Mound, which had been directed by Brian J. Egloff

in 1965 and 1966. During 1966-1968, Roy S. Dickens conducted excavations at the Warren Wilson site, where they have been continued each year by various research assistants. Several more years of work will be needed to explore this site fully.

In 1968 and 1969 work was continued at Coweeta Creek and was not terminated there until September 1971. Some results of the work mentioned above have been presented in theses, in dissertations, and in papers read at professional meetings (see Coe 1968, 1969; Coe and Keel 1965; Dickens 1969, 1970; B. J. Egloff 1967; K. T. Egloff 1971; Ferguson 1971; Holden 1966; Keel 1964, 1967, 1968; Keel and Chapman 1972). The extensive investigations carried out by the Research Laboratories of Anthropology during the last decade have added much needed information. This volume will present some of the results of these efforts.

Recent work performed by other institutions in adjacent areas has been important to my understanding of the prehistory of this area. Among these are the University of Tennessee's work in Nickajack Reservoir (Faulkner and Graham 1965, 1966a, and 1966b) and in the Tellico Reservoir, which still continues in 1975 (Salo 1969; Gleeson 1970, 1971), and the University of Georgia's efforts in the Lower Cherokee Towns area (Wauchope 1966; Kelly and Neitzel 1961; Kelly and de Baillou 1960). The work of the South Carolina Institute of Archaeology in the Keowee-Toxaway Basin will no doubt furnish much needed information when published if my personal observations of the field data are correct.

INTRODUCTION TO THE CULTURAL SEQUENCE

During the last decade, emphasis in Southern Appalachian archaeology has shifted from the collection of cabinet specimens (Valentine Ms. A, B, and C; Heye 1919) and the almost impossible problem of tribal identification (Webb 1938; Setzler and Jennings 1941; Lewis and Kneberg 1946) to the more rigorous and clear definition of units of study, i.e., assemblage, component, and phase (Coe 1961, 1968; Dickens 1970; Egloff 1967; Faulkner and Graham 1965, 1966a, 1966b; Gleeson 1970; Holden 1966; Keel 1964, 1967; Salo 1969), to ecological considerations (Guthe 1965; Keel 1965; Faulkner and Graham 1967), and to prehistoric culture systems (Ferguson 1971). Before hypotheses concerning cultural processes as reflected by archaeological remains can be explored, however, these resources must be placed in a reliable chronological framework.

In defining three phases of the Woodland cultural tradition this study also takes into account archaeological culture phases which preceded and succeeded them, in order to place the Woodland phases chronologically (Fig. 2).

The earliest evidence of human occupation found in the Appalachian Summit Area consists of fluted projectile points. Before 1965, Stephen Williams and James B. Stoltman (1965:669-683) noted that only four fluted points had been found in the area. Since 1965, I have examined seven more Clovis-like points, all from North Carolina, with the following distribution: Henderson County 1, Jackson County 5, and Macon County 1. Also, Patricia Holden (1966:81) indicated that she saw fluted points in private collections that had been made in Transylvania County. Interestingly, all of the fluted points for which I have provenience data occur south of the hypothetical line drawn by D. D. Michalek from east to west through Asheville, North Carolina. This line, according to Michalek (1969), would separate a periglacial climate north of the line from a milder climatic regime south of the line during the final Wisconsin glacial periods.

The occurrence of points belonging to the Hardaway, Palmer, Kirk, Stanly, and Guilford complexes suggests an Early Archaic sequence identical to that described by Coe (1964) for the Carolina Piedmont. None of the types diagnostic of these complexes has been found in the proper stratigraphic context yet.

The earliest *in situ* artifacts yet discovered are a number of Morrow Mountain I points found below Savannah River Stemmed type points at the Warren Wilson site (Bn 29). The Savannah River phase is estimated to have occurred between 3000 B.C. and 600 or 700 B.C. in the study area. The Morrow Mountain phase is considered to date a thousand to fifteen hundred years earlier.

The earliest archaeological culture in the study area which manufactured ceramics has been termed the Swannanoa phase. The ceramics of this phase were quite dissimilar from most of those of the later phases. But I might also add that some of the ceramics occurring in the later phases had attributes which were initially expressed by Swannanoa potters. I have suggested an initial date for the Swannanoa phase of about 600-700 B.C. This phase is considered to have developed into the Pigeon phase by 200 B.C.

Date	Phase	Ceramic Tradition
1800	Qualla	South Appalachian
1500	Pisgah	South Appalachian
1000		
600	Connestee	South Appalachian and Northern Woodland
A.D. 200		
0		
200 B.C.	Swannanoa	Northern Woodland
800	Otarre Savannah River	
2000	Guilford Morrow Mountain	
6000	Stanly Kirk Palmer Hardaway	
10,000	Fluted Point occupation	

FIG. 2.   Cultural phase chronology from the Appalachian Summit Area.

The Pigeon phase shows strong connections to the initial spread of carved paddle stamping that occurred across the southeast about 500 B.C. The ceramics of the Pigeon phase owe their style to what could be termed the Deptford Check Stamped horizon. This phase, as a definite archaeological unit, was not formed until about 200 B.C. It lasted from that time until about A.D. 200.

The next phase, Connestee, is characterized by pottery of an entirely different sort. Here simple stamped, brushed, cord marked, and smoothed plain were the predominant surface finishes. The phase seems to have stronger ties with northern Georgia and eastern Tennessee than with central Georgia. The Connestee phase seems to have developed as a recognizable entity about A.D. 200 and by A.D. 600 had developed into a hypothesized transitional phase which would eventually transform to the Pisgah phase which became recognizable by the 11th century A.D.

The Pisgah phase (Dickens 1970) is entirely prehistoric in time, beginning about A.D. 1000 or 1100 and lasting until the Qualla phase became an identifiable entity. It is not until the Pisgah phase that complicated carved paddles used to finish ceramics became popular. This is the trait which led Holmes (1903:131) to include the ceramics of "Georgia and contiguous portions of all the adjoining states" into a group which later became known as South Appalachian pottery.

The Qualla phase, although it has not been formally defined to date, represents the material culture of the Cherokees from about the middle of the 16th century until the removal of most of the tribe to the West in the second quarter of the 19th century. This phase will be of great difficulty to define in rigorous form without extremely refined dating because of the greatly accelerated acculturation that occurred during the 18th century. While many aboriginal items were being replaced by Euro-American goods, it is noteworthy to observe that Qualla types of pottery made in the last quarter of the 19th century were collected by Valentine, and even as late as the first decade of the 20th century M. R. Harrington (1922) collected pottery made by a Cherokee woman that is for all practical purposes identical to 18th-century materials.

In the following three chapters I will describe the sites and materials collected therefrom which form the basis of present knowledge concerning the prehistory of the Appalachian Summit Area and in the final chapter evaluate the relations of this area with other eastern United States regions.

2. The Tuckasegee Site

INTRODUCTION

The Cherokee town of Tuckasegee first appeared on the George Hunter map of 1730 (Salley 1917) located at the forks of the Tuckasegee River in southern Jackson County, North Carolina (Plate 1). This town may have been burned by Captain William Moore in the fall of 1776 (Dickens 1967:6). James Mooney (1900:537) listed the town as *Tsiksitsi,* stating that the meaning was unknown; the archaeological site of Tuckasegee was recorded but was not excavated by Edward M. Dolan in 1963. During the winter of 1964 the landowner's son discovered a burned structure at the edge of a river-cut bank just below the forks of the Tuckasegee. Upon learning of this discovery, the Research Laboratories of Anthropology gained permission to explore the remains from the landowner, O. D. Moses, Sr., who also allowed the field party to take up residence in the abandoned Tuckasegee Elementary School.

The site (Fig. 3) of this structure was cleared, a grid system was established, and a contour map of the area was made preparatory to excavation. The grid system had a base line, designated 80, which ran parallel to the cut bank from east to west; a north-south base line, designated L100, was placed well beyond the eastern margin of the structure. The intersection of the base lines, Station 80L100, served as the point of origin for a series of nine squares measuring 10 feet on a side which were placed over the area of the structure. The coordinates at the southeast corner of each square were used to denote the square. Vertical control was established by assigning the lower rail of the NC 107 bridge over the east fork of the river an arbitrary elevation of 100 feet. All disturbances visible on the surface were recorded on the site plan before excavation began. A total of 1,075 square feet of surface area was explored, including the nine 10 × 10 feet squares, a 5 × 20 foot step trench down the face of the cut bank, and three 5 × 5 feet test squares.

PLATE 1. The Tuckasegee site (Jk 12). The view is the northwest; the forks of the river are in the foreground. The excavated profile in the center is the 80 line from L100 to L130.

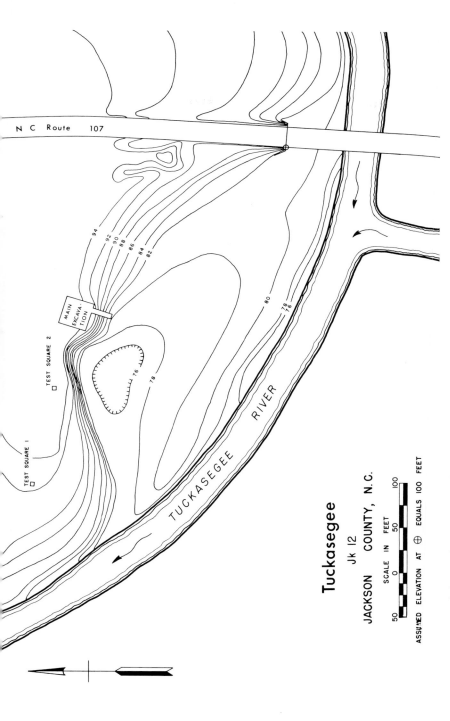

FIG. 3. Map of the Tuckasegee site (Jk 12), Jackson County, North Carolina.

Most of the data recovered from this site—more than 15,000 cultural specimens, architectural remains, and contextual information—were associated with the historic period occupation and were used to define that portion of the cultural sequence of the Appalachian Summit Area. The stratigraphic position of this occupation was important because it served as the capstone of the cultural sequence.

GEOLOGY

The geologic character of the locality was best seen in the 18-foot-high cut bank along the southern margin of the excavation. The sediments exposed indicated that the archaeological site was situated on alluvium. Most geologists familiar with the Blue Ridge Province consider the alluvial valley fills to be of Recent age, and although D. D. Michalek (1969:36, 149) is convinced that at least some fill units date to the late Pleistocene, there is no evidence to indicate an exceptionally early age for any of the sediments exposed in this location.

The stratigraphic column (Fig. 4), which is described in Table 1, was based on two profiles exposed during excavation: the profile along the 90 line and the profile along the L110 line. Slumpage along the 80 line at the margin of the cut bank prohibited the use of a single exposure. Nonetheless, the two exposures were connected and no breaks in the stratigraphy were detected. The 14 stratigraphic units were distinguished in the field on the basis of color and texture.

The upper two strata were composed of sediments deposited by the 1940 flood. The present plowed soil (Stratum 1) was distinguished from Stratum 2 on the basis of color and evidence of cultivation.

The 1940 flood was the most severe flood on record in the upper Tuckasegee River (U. S. Geological Survey 1949:7). Several landslides were reported in the area along the steeper valley walls, but the localized scouring of topsoil and alluviation in the broader portions of the valley seem to have been the major effects of the flood. No definite correlation of a similar flood in 1916 with any stratigraphic unit recognized at the site was possible. However, Stratum 3, the pre-1940 plowed soil, may have been affected by that inundation. The 1940 flood, like the 1916 flood, was

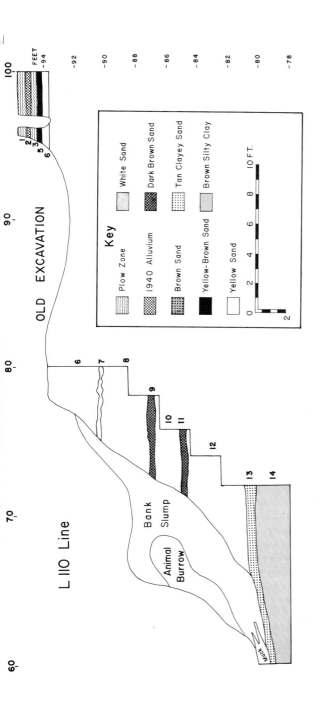

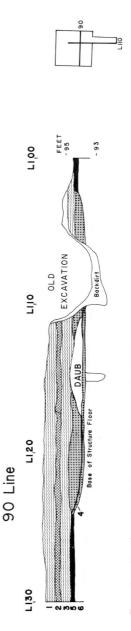

Fig. 4. Stratigraphy of the L110 line and the 90 line, Tuckasegee site (Jk 12). Boldface numbers refer to strata. L110 line view is to the west; 90 line view is to the north.

TABLE 1. Description of stratification of the Tuckasegee site (Jk 12).

Stratum Number	Elevation (Datum=100.0)	Thickness (Feet)	Description	Analytical Unit
1	96.30 - 95.70	0.60	This unit was the modern plow zone. It was composed of dark gray to black sand and contained well rounded pebbles of quartzite and schist. Cultural debris was abundant in this layer. It had an abrupt smooth boundary with Stratum 2.	Post-Structure Unit
2	95.70 - 95.40	0.30	This layer was composed of dark tan sand that contained well rounded quartz and schist pebbles and abundant cultural material. It shared a clear wavy boundary with Stratum 3. This layer was deposited by the 1940 flood.	Post-Structure Unit
3	95.40 - 94.70	0.70	This layer was identical to Stratum 1. It represented the pre-1940 furrow slice.	Post-Structure Unit
4	94.70 - 94.20	0.50	This stratum was composed of brown sand containing charred wood, bark, daub, and cultural debris. This layer was the remains of a burned structure. The bottom of the layer (the structure floor) truncated Stratum 5 but the boundary between them was clear and smooth.	Structure Unit
5	94.70 - 94.10	0.60	This unit was a dark yellow-brown sand that contained well rounded pebbles, fire-cracked cobbles and cultural material. In the area where it was covered by Stratum 4 it varied in thickness from 0.4 to 0.15 feet. This unit was an old midden. It had a clear wavey boundary with Stratum 6. This is the earliest stratum to contain cultural remains.	Pre-Structure Unit
6	94.10 - 90.40	3.70	This layer was composed of yellow flood sand. A smooth gradual boundary separated it from Stratum 7.	
7	90.40 - 90.15	0.25	This unit was made up of lensed, coarse, white sand. It was not continuous over the site and is thought to represent micro-episodes of erosion and deposition. It shared a clear boundary with Stratum 8.	
8	90.15 - 87.10	3.05	This stratum was composed of yellow flood deposited sand. It was separated from Stratum 9 by a clear smooth boundary.	
9	87.10 - 86.85	0.25	This layer was composed of dark brown sand which contained numerous flecks and pieces of charcoal. A clear smooth boundary separated it from Stratum 10. This unit may be a weakly developed A1 soil horizon.	
10	86.85 - 85.10	0.75	A yellow sand, identical to Strata 6 and 8, made up this layer. It was separated from Stratum 11 by a clear smooth boundary.	
11	85.10 - 84.70	0.40	Other than being twice as thick, this stratum was identical in appearance to Stratum 9. It is considered to represent a weakly developed A1 soil horizon. A gradual smooth boundary separated it from Stratum 12.	
12	84.70 - 81.00	3.70	Yellow sand similar to that which composed Strata 6, 8, and 10 made up this layer. It was separated from Stratum 13 by a smooth clear boundary.	
13	81.00 - 79.30	0.70	This stratum was composed of tan colored clayey sand and silt. A gradual boundary divided this layer from Stratum 14.	
14	79.30 - 77.5+	1.80	This layer was excavated to a point 18.8 feet below the surface of the site. It was composed of brown silty clay. It was much darker in color, more sticky, plastic and formed a wire much easier than Stratum 13.	

produced by a tropical depression. The hurricane system responsible for the 1940 storm produced torrential rainfalls over a period of several days. During one 24-hour period between 8 and 13 inches of rain fell on western North Carolina. The severity of this storm was increased because the ground had been thoroughly saturated by heavy rains the previous week. Elsewhere, on the Roanoke River in Virginia, for example, the worst flood since 1607 occurred at this time (Hoyt and Langbein 1955:393).

The 1940 flood was well remembered by the landowner. His store and home were lost, and the corn and tobacco he had planted on the site were swept away. Although floods in the area are not annual phenomena, they certainly have caused periodic distress to the flood plain farmers, both Indian and white.

Stratum 3 was the pre-1940 plowed soil. Stratum 4 was the remains of the structure. Stratum 5 was a dark-colored sand and was the deepest layer that contained any cultural remains. If Strata 5, 9, and 11 represent stable land surfaces, as suggested by the development of weak A1 soil horizons, there were at least three periods in the geological history of the site when flooding was relatively infrequent. The physical characteristics of Strata 5, 9, and 11 do not indicate the phenomenon of charcoal migration as described by Brown and Gould (1964:387); nor are they representative of percolation lines that are often present in alluvial sediments.

Strata 6, 7, 8, 10, and 12 were composed of yellow or white sand deposited by floods. Stratum 13 was a tan clayey sand and silt, and the lowest stratum, Stratum 14, was a brown sandy clay. These lowermost strata may represent the weathering products of coarser materials.

The profiles of the test pits indicated that Stratum 1 was continuous over the site, but Strata 2, 3, 4, and 5 were absent in the areas tested. Because the test pits were all located downslope from the main excavation, it is probable that the earlier cultural levels have been eroded from this area of the site.

EXCAVATION

The several small holes dug into the structure by the landowner's son were recorded on the site plan so that when these disturbances were encountered in later excavations they would be recognized. The information gained from inspecting the holes dug by the younger Moses indicated that the most practical method for excavating the site would be to strip off the overlying soil to the level of the burned structure. Unfortunately, the true nature of the upper three strata was not appreciated until much of the area had been stripped. Ideally, the post-1940 plowed soil, the unplowed portion of the 1940 deposit, and the pre-1940 furrow slice should have been removed as natural layers. If such a procedure had been followed throughout the excavations, perhaps more information would have been gained concerning the nature of secondary mixing which the archaeologist so frequently encounters. The unplowed portion of the 1940 deposit and the pre-1940 plow zone were most frequently excavated as combined units. Strata 4 and 5, on the other hand, were so distinctive that very little of either unit was included in the removal of Stratum 3 (the pre-1940 plow zone).

All units excavated by shovel were sifted through ½-inch mesh hardware cloth. Sediments from special features, the structure debris (Stratum 4), the postholes, and selected portions of Stratum 5 were excavated by trowels and were water-screened through standard-gauge windowscreen (about 1 × 1.5 mm mesh). Elevations were recorded by telescopic alidade; plans and profiles were documented by drawings and photographs.

As the area was cleared of overburden (Strata 1, 2, and 3), the outline of the structure (Plate 2) became apparent at the base of Stratum 3. The structure was marked by a circular area of dark brown sand mixed with charcoal, daub, burned roof timbers, pieces of pottery, and slabs of charred bark (Fig. 5). Beyond the margin of the structure, the top of Stratum 5 was exposed and several pre-structure features were visible.

After the upper surface of the structure had been cleaned, photographed, and recorded, the roof timbers were cleared by troweling out the debris between them. The exposed roof beams were recorded, photographed, and removed. The floor of the structure was next exposed by careful troweling. Finally, the holes which held wall posts and roof supports and Feature 4, the hearth (Plates 3, 4; Fig. 5), were excavated.

THE STRUCTURE

The structure encountered at Tuckasegee was approximately 23 feet in diameter. In the center of the floor (Feature 4) was a

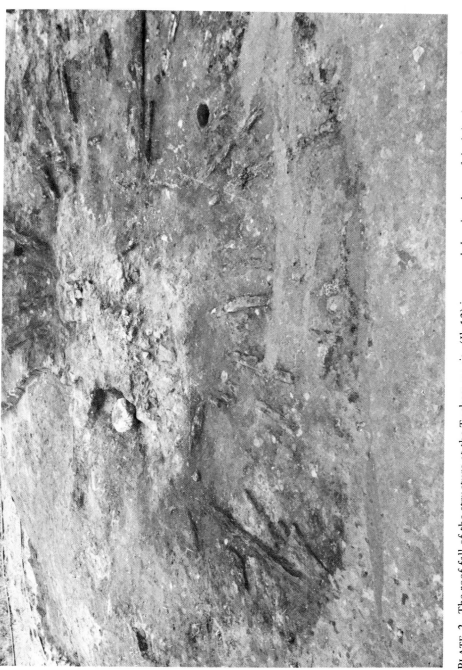

PLATE 2. The roof fall of the structure at the Tuckasegee site (Jk 12) is exposed showing the roof daub in the center of the radiating rafters. The disturbed area in the upper left of the photograph was dug by O. D. Moses, Jr., in 1963. The view is to the south.

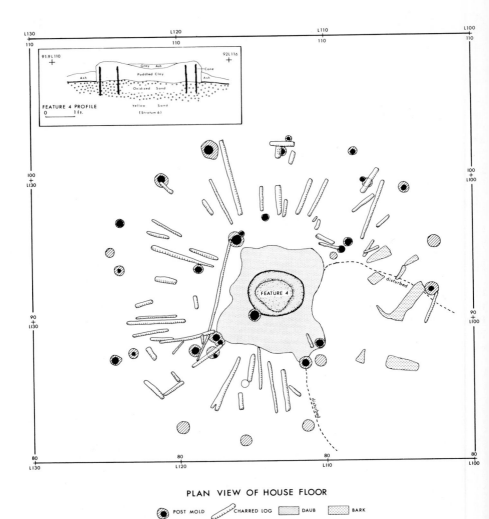

PLAN VIEW OF HOUSE FLOOR

⬤ POST MOLD   〰 CHARRED LOG   ▦ DAUB   ▦ BARK

FIG. 5. Plan view of structure and Feature 4 profile, Tuckasegee site (Jk 12).
Top of page is north. Inset view is to the southwest.

PLATE 3 (*above*). The floor of the structure at the Tuckasegee site (Jk 12) after the final cleaning. The central raised basin is Feature 4. The view is to the south.
PLATE 4 (*below*). A cross section of Feature 4 at the Tuckasegee site (Jk 12). Note the ends of the charred cane sections used to define the limits of the rim of the basin. The view is to the west.

puddled-clay fire basin raised approximately 0.45 foot above the level of the floor and covered by 0.40 foot of roof daub (Plate 3; Fig. 5). The outer wall of the building was composed of at least 15 posts, varying from 0.5 to 0.9 foot in diameter, set in holes which had an average depth of about 1 foot and were spaced, on the average, 4.0 feet apart. The interior roof supports consisted of four sets of paired posts placed about 5 feet out from the center of the house. Four beams placed across the main roof supports carried a minimum of 29 rafters. The outer ends of the rafters rested on stringers spanning the space between the wall posts. The center of the roof was left open for smoke exhaust. The underside of the roof around the smoke hole had been plastered with clay. When the building burned, this clay was baked and fell directly on top of the central fire basin (Feature 4). Thomas Lewis and Madeline Kneberg (1946:48) have suggested that the interior roof plaster, commonly found in the structures uncovered in the Chicamauga Basin, served as a fire retardant.

The walls and roof may have been covered with bark since several large slabs were found in the southeastern quadrant and near the center of the house. If not bark, then some other type of flammable material must have been used because no daub was found except that associated with the roof. The sand mixed with the burned roof elements suggested that the roof covering was held down by a thin layer of soil. The entrance to the structure was not definitely located. A large gap in the wall post alignment on the west side of the building, however, may have served as a doorway.

Abundant cultural material was found on the floor of the structure. Most was located along the interior of the walls, but two Qualla vessels were found near the center of the house.

The construction of Feature 4 (Plate 4; Fig. 4), the central fire basin, warrants description. This raised fire basin was nearly a perfect circle in plan, measuring 3.6 × 3.5 feet in diameter from rim to rim. The surface of the rim was well smoothed, was 0.5 foot wide, and 0.75 foot high. The central depression was 2.5 feet in diameter and 0.25 foot deep at the center. This basin was constructed by modeling clay over at least 92 pieces of cane (*Arundinaria gigantea*) about 1 foot long which had been stuck into the sand floor for about one-half their length. Some of the pieces had been sharpened to facilitate insertion into the soil. These pieces of cane were arranged in two circles; the outer ring was 3.3 feet in diameter, the inner ring 3.0 feet. After the clay had been modeled and smoothed, it was fired almost to brick hardness.

A. R. Kelly and R. S. Neitzel (1961:24) described a hearth found at the Chauga site, Oconee County, South Carolina, as a "circular bowl, fashioned by placing small canes and at least one corncob upright in the ground." This feature belonged to the historic Cherokee component. A. R. Kelly (1972:personal communication) considers this hearth to have ceremonial implications. Paul Gleeson (1970:125) indicated that the central hearth of the great rotunda at Chota was of similar construction. This hearth certainly had ceremonial functions. In the fall of 1970, a similar fire basin was excavated by the author at the Coweeta Creek Mound site, Ma 34, in an early historic Cherokee context. This particular hearth was approximately 3.0 feet in diameter and 0.33 foot high at the rim and had a central depression 1.5 feet in diameter and a depth of 0.3 foot. The clay, in this case, had been modeled over a single circle of 15 hardwood stakes which were about 0.06 foot in diameter and 0.75 foot long. This hearth was in a structure associated with the mound and plaza area of the site and is considered to have ceremonial significance.

In a preliminary paper Coe and Keel (1965) suggested that the structure at Tuckasegee may have served as a ceremonial building. The lines of evidence for such an interpretation were as follows:

1. The circular floor plan is comparable to town houses observed by many early travelers such as Adair, Bartram, and Timberlake.
2. A peculiar type of fire basin is present. Previous (and subsequent) discoveries hint that fire basins of this type are associated with Cherokee ceremonial structures.
3. Large quantities of domestic debris commonly associated with dwellings are absent.
4. Debris concentrated along the interior of the wall, similar to the midden deposits encountered on the six town house floors at the Coweeta Creek Mound, is present.

Although this evidence suggests the Tuckasegee building may have been used as a town house, it must be pointed out that the Cherokees also built rectangular ceremonial structures. If the Cherokees built circular town houses exclusively, as W. S. Webb (1938:379) argued, then no doubt would exist about the function of the structure at Tuckasegee. However, the opinion expressed by Joffre L. Coe (1961) that the Cherokees probably used rectangular town houses has been demonstrated as a true appraisal of the situation by the excavations at Garden Creek Mound No. 1, where a series of rectangular ceremonial structures including two semisubterranean lodges were uncovered (Dickens 1970), and by the explorations of the Coweeta Creek Mound, where a series of rectangular town houses were discovered (Egloff 1972).

FEATURES

Seven rock-filled pit hearths and three basin-shaped clay-lined hearths were the only archaeological remains uncovered which warrant the designation of features. The former type of hearth was characterized by a cluster of fire-cracked cobble-sized stones deposited in a shallow pit (Features 7 and 8), or if disturbed by cultivation or aboriginal digging (Plate 5; Fig. 6), by a scattered group of fire-cracked stones (Features 1, 2, 3, 9, and 10).

The second category, prepared clay fire basins, was represented by Features 4, 5, and 6. Feature 4, associated with the structure, was the best-preserved example and has been described in detail. Descriptions and other data relative to the features are presented in Table 2. The ceramics and artifacts associated with the features are tabulated in Tables 3 and 4.

The two categories of features had mutually exclusive temporal and cultural distributions. The prepared clay fire basins occurred only in Stratum 4 and were associated exclusively with Qualla phase materials. The rock-filled pit hearths occurred deeper, only in Stratum 5, and were associated with materials of earlier phases.

ARTIFACTS

The amount of material recovered from our small excavation at Tuckasegee was surprisingly large. Although potsherds constituted the bulk of the collection, lithic, botanical and zoological specimens were plentiful. The presence of Late Archaic period material *in situ* with such close physical proximity to a historic period structure was somewhat surprising. Fortunately, we recognized the difference between Strata 4 and 5 at the time of excavation and kept the mixing of specimens from these two strata to a minimum. We were also fortunate to recover the small glass trade beads, for without

PLATE 5.   Feature 1, a scattered group of fire-cracked stones, was typical of the surface-hearth-type features unearthed at the Tuckasegee site (Jk 12).   The steatite elbow pipe is indicated by the arrow.   The view is to the south.

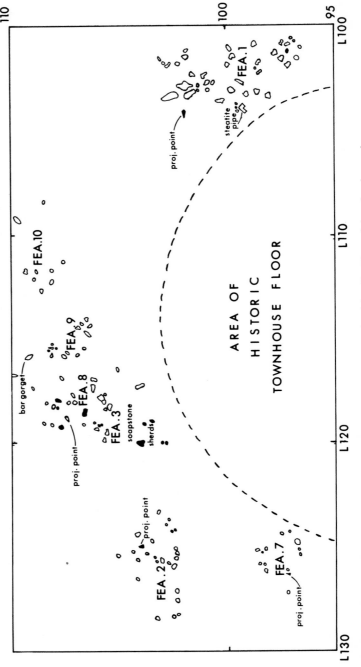

FIG. 6. Plan view of features outside of structure, Tuckasegee site (Jk 12). Top of drawing is north.

TABLE 2. Feature data, Tuckasegee site (Jk 12).

Feature Number	Description	Dimensions (feet)	Location of Center	Stratigraphic unit	Culture Phase
1	Scattered mass of fire-cracked rocks	6.7x4.3	100L102	Stratum 5	Connestee
2	Scattered mass of fire-cracked rocks	7.8x2.3	103L125.3	Stratum 5	Swannanoa
3	Scattered mass of fire-cracked rocks	5.4x2.5	106L118.8	Stratum 5	Savannah River
4	Circular prepared clay fire basin	3.6x3.5 max. dia.; central depression,2.5 dia.; depth 0.25	91.7L113.5	Stratum 4	Qualla
5	Circular prepared clay fire basin	3.3x3.2, max. dia.; central depression,2.0 dia.; depth 0.3	97.5L108.5	Stratum 4	Qualla
6	Circular prepared clay fire basin	4.0x3.5 max. dia.; central depression, 1.7x1.5; depth 0.3	117.3L122.5	Stratum 4	Qualla
7	Cluster of fire-cracked rocks	3.0x2.5	97.4L126	Stratum 5	Swannanoa
8	Cluster of fire-cracked rocks	2.8x2.5	107L128	Stratum 5	Savannah River
9	Scattered mass of fire-cracked rocks	3.5x3.0	107.5L125	Stratum 5	Unknown
10	Scattered mass of fire-cracked rocks	3.5x2.0	108.5L112	Stratum 5	Unknown

TABLE 3. Distribution of pottery types recovered from features at the Tuckasegee site (Jk 12).

Type	Feature Number						TOTAL
	1	2	3	4	5	8	
Qualla Burnished					2		2
Qualla Incised				2			2
Connestee Simple Stamped		1					1
Connestee Plain	1						1
Connestee unclassified	1						1
Connestee Brushed	2	1					3
Pigeon Complicated Stamped		3					3
Pigeon Check Stamped		1					1
Pigeon Plain	2	1					3
Swannanoa Cord Marked	5	6			2		13
Swannanoa Fabric Impressed	6	2					8
Swannanoa Plain		2					2
Swannanoa unclassified	2	8					10
Steatite vessel fragments			1			8	9
TOTALS	19	25	1	2	4	8	59

TABLE 4. Distribution of artifact types recovered from features at the Tuckasegee site (Jk 12).

Category	Feature Number					TOTAL
	1	2	3	7	9	
Projectile points:						
Savannah River Stemmed			1			1
Coosa Notched		1				1
Garden Creek Triangular	1			1		2
Polished stone:						
Gorget					1	1
Pipe	1					1
TOTALS	2	1	1	1	1	6

these it would have been difficult to demonstrate that the structure
was occupied during the early 18th century.

The analytical procedures used in establishing the local ceramic
types, as well as the typology used for other artifact classes, were
discussed in the Introduction. The natural stratigraphy of the site
has been discussed in a preceding section of this chapter. In the
subsequent analysis Strata 1, 2, and 3 have been combined to form
the entity referred to as the Post-Structure Unit. Because these
layers represent strata that postdated the final occupation of the
site and consisted of plowed soils (Strata 1 and 3) or flood deposits
(Stratum 2) occurring between periods of plowing, combining them
seems reasonable. Stratum 4, the debris resulting from the house, is
referred to as the Structure Unit. Finally, Stratum 5 is referred to
as the Pre-Structure Unit.

All excavation units were analyzed and compared with one another before they were combined into the gross units presented
here as the Post-Structure, Structure, and Pre-Structure units. Ceramics and steatite vessels are tabulated in Table 5. All other artifacts are tabulated in Table 6. More exact provenience data of
important specimens are given in the artifact descriptions.

CERAMIC AND STONE VESSELS

The ceramic collection included representative sherds of all five
ceramic series manufactured in western North Carolina and a few
sherds that represented trade with peoples to the south. No complete vessels were recovered, but two large Qualla series vessels
found on the structure floor were complete enough for restoration.
Major portions and distinctive parts of several other vessels which
were recovered have served to identify the various forms of pots
present in the collection. This analysis is based on the study of
13,907 of the total 15,136 potsherds recovered; sherds collected in
the excavation of the test pits and those found on the surface of the
site have been omitted from this presentation because they added
no additional information. The various ceramic series present at
Tuckasegee will be discussed beginning with the latest series, Qualla,
followed by the earlier series: Pisgah, Connestee, Pigeon, and
Swannanoa.

Qualla Ceramic Series (Plate 6a-e)

Qualla ceramics, the product of the late prehistoric and historic
Cherokees throughout North Carolina, constituted 81 percent of

TABLE 5. Distribution of pottery types by analysis units, Tuckasegee site (Jk 12).

Type	Post Structure Unit		Structure Unit		Pre-Structure Unit		TOTALS	
	N	%	N	%	N	%	N	%
Qualla Series								
Complicated Stamped	3868	36.576	1082	41.551	42	6.185	4992	36.022
Check Stamped	103	.973	74	2.841			177	1.277
Cob Impressed	5	.047					5	.036
Cord Marked	187	1.768	31	1.190	2	.294	220	1.587
Brushed	3	.028	29	1.113	2	.294	34	.254
Smoothed	1865	17.635	508	19.508	46	6.774	2419	17.455
Plain	103	.973	22	.844	3	.441	128	.923
Burnished	33	.312	17	.652	2	.294	52	.375
Incised	26	.245	7	.268	1	.147	34	.254
Simple Stamped	25	.236	25	.960	1	.147	51	.368
Rims	415	3.924	98	3.763	6	.883	519	3.745
Unclassified	2119	20.037	455	17.473	23	3.387	2597	18.740
Total Qualla Series	8752	82.761	2348	90.168	128	18.851	11228	81.021
Pisgah Series								
Complicated Stamped	44	.416	1	.038	3	.441	48	.346
Brushed	1	.009			2	.294	1	.007
Rims	7	.066					9	.064
Unclassified	9	.085	1	.038	1	.147	11	.079
Total Pisgah Series	61	.576	2	.076	6	.883	69	.496
Connestee Series								
Complicated Stamped	4	.037					4	.028
Check Stamped	4	.037	4	.153	1	.147	9	.064
Simple Stamped	91	.860	7	.268	58	8.541	156	1.125
Brushed	207	1.957	23	.883	28	4.123	258	1.861
Cord Marked	284	2.685	15	.576	42	6.185	341	2.460
Fabric Impressed	60	.567	4	.153	2	.294	66	.476
Plain	249	2.354	22	.844	48	7.069	319	2.301
Rims	14	.132	11	.422	4	.589	29	.201
Unclassified	79	.747	5	.192	32	4.712	116	.837
Total Connestee Series	992	9.380	91	3.494	215	31.664	1298	9.366
Pigeon Series								
Complicated Stamped	51	.482	2	.076	11	1.620	64	.461
Check Stamped	68	.643	8	.307	19	2.798	95	.685
Simple Stamped	20	.189	6	.230	4	.589	30	.216
Plain	67	.633	14	.537	19	2.798	100	.721
Rims	6	.056	1	.038	1	.147	8	.057
Total Pigeon Series	212	2.004	31	1.190	54	7.952	297	2.143
Swannanoa Series								
Check Stamped	6	.056	3	.115	3	.441	12	.086
Cord Marked	215	2.033	65	2.496	149	21.944	429	3.095
Fabric Impressed	151	1.427	30	1.152	44	6.480	225	1.624
Brushed	29	.274	6	.230	19	2.798	54	.389
Plain	123	1.163	18	.691	39	5.743	180	1.299
Rims	9	.085			3	.441	12	.086
Unclassified	23	.217	10	.381	17	2.503	50	.360
Total Swannanoa Series	556	5.257	132	5.069	274	40.353	962	6.941
Steatite Vessel Fragments	2	.018			2	.294	4	.028
TOTALS	10575	99.996	2604	99.997	679	99.997	13858	99.996

TABLE 6. Distribution of artifact types by analysis units at the Tuckasegee site (Jk 12).

Category	Post-Structure Unit	Structure Unit	Pre-Structure Unit	TOTAL
Projectile points				
Palmer Side Notched	1			1
Kirk Corner Notched	1			1
Savannah River Stemmed	1		1	2
Coosa Notched			1	1
Pigeon Side Notched			2	2
Swannanoa Stemmed			1	1
Garden Creek Triangular	2		1	3
Madison	6	16		22
Unclassifiable	3		2	5
Micro-tool, perforator		1		1
Flake scrapers	4	2		6
Gunflint		1		1
Cut Mica		2		2
Discoidal		2		2
Gorget			1	1
Pipes	2	2	1	5
Polishing pebbles		2		2
Hammerstones		1	1	2
Net weight			1	1
Antler drift		1		1
Pottery scraper, mussel		1		1
Ceramic bead	1			1
Ceramic discoidal		1		1
Ceramic pipes	3	2		5
Euro-American trade goods				
Glass beads		26		26
Wine bottle	1			1
Iron object		1		1
TOTALS	25	61	12	98

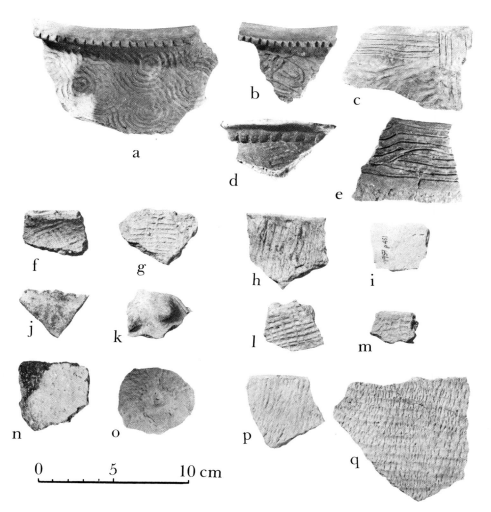

PLATE 6.   Ceramics from the Tuckasegee site (Jk 12). a-e, Qualla Complicated
Stamped; c and e have incised necks; f and g, Pisgah Rectilinear Stamped;
h-k, Connestee series; h, Cord Marked; i, rim interior; j, Plain with notched
rim; k, Simple Stamped with podal supports; l-n, Pigeon series; l and m, Check
Stamped; n, Plain; o-q, Swannanoa series; o and p, Cord Marked; Q, Fabric
Impressed.

the ceramics recovered from Tuckasegee. The most homogeneous
sample of this series came from the Structure Unit, where 90.1 percent of the pottery belonged to this group. The presence of earlier
ceramics in this unit can be accounted for in a variety of ways: aboriginal disturbances such as posthole and pit digging; natural agents
including tree growth and animal burrowing; and our inability to de-
tect and isolate all of the disturbances resulting from these activities.
Still, only 9.9 percent of the material recovered from Stratum 4 is
considered to be earlier than the Qualla phase. The Pre-Structure
Unit (Stratum 5) contained Qualla ceramics, but more than 95 percent of the Qualla ceramics recovered from this layer were found in
squares covered by the structure. This fact suggests that most of
the Qualla sherds found in Stratum 5 were trampled into that layer
by the people utilizing the structure.

   Brian J. Egloff (1967), in his study of pottery collected from
documented Cherokee towns, demonstrated that the ceramics made
during the historic period in the Appalachian Summit Area were
similar, but not identical, to Lamar ceramics of central Georgia, as
assumed by Kelly and de Baillou (1960) and Kelly and Neitzel
(1961). Egloff described the differences between the two series as:

> The [Qualla] series possesses the basic attributes of the Lamar style horizon:
> folded finger impressed rim fillets, large sloppy carved stamps, and bold in-
> cising. The complicated stamp motifs illustrating Lamar Complicated
> Stamped exhibit a greater degree of regularity and symmetrical design than
> is found on Qualla Complicated Stamped. The same holds true for the in-
> cised cazuela bowls, though to a lesser degree. Incising accompanied by
> reed punctations, which is common upon Lamar Bold-Incised vessels, was
> absent in the material analyzed. . . . The distinctive qualities of the Qualla
> paste . . . moderate to abundant quantities of grit coupled with partial bur-
> nishing of the vessel's interior make Qualla sherds distinctive even when the
> exterior surface finish is obliterated [Egloff 1967:34-35].

In the main, sherds referred to the Qualla type categories at Tuckasegee conformed to Egloff's descriptions. There were minor differences, but these were probably due to the nature and size of the
collections studied. Egloff's sample was composed of sherds collected from 13 different Cherokee sites. These sites were not
strictly contemporary in every instance, and consequently a longer
period of time was represented in his sample as well as greater geographical distance than the Tuckasegee sample, which represented a
relatively short period of time and came from a 900 square foot
area of one site. The Tuckasegee sample (15,136 sherds) was also

approximately 40 percent larger than Egloff's collection of 9,990 sherds.

Egloff identified six surface finishes as the major types of the series: complicated stamped, burnished, plain, check stamped, cord marked and corncob impressed. Specimens recovered from Tuckasegee indicate that the series should be expanded to include a brushed surface finish.

Vessel forms found at Tuckasegee included simple bowls, carinated bowls, globular jars with short necks, and large jars with constricted mouths. Appendages are rare on Qualla vessels, and none were found in the Tuckasegee sample.

The rim sherds confirm the rim profile categories given by Egloff (1967:Table 6) as reliable characteristics of the series (Fig. 7). The 15 rim profile classes attributed to the Qualla series were all present except one, No. 18. This particular class constituted only 1 percent of Egloff's rim sample and, therefore, may not be important as a definitive form. Qualla rim sherds conforming to Egloff's classes 13, 14, 19, and 20 were present in the Tuckasegee sample and have been included by this writer as members of the series.

A comparison of the Tuckasegee sample of Qualla ceramics with Brian J. Egloff's (1967) study of historic period ceramics from 13 Cherokee towns suggests, as it should, that the Tuckasegee potters were producing vessels similar in form and finish to their neighbors in other Out Towns. The Tuckasegee sample tends to support Egloff's (1967:68-75) argument that there is marked variation in the ceramics produced in the Georgia and South Carolina Cherokee settlements (Lower Towns), the North Carolina Villages (Middle, Valley, and Out Towns), and the Tennessee Overhill towns (Egloff 1967:68-75).

Pisgah Ceramic Series (Plate 6f, g)

The Pisgah Culture (phase), defined by Roy S. Dickens, Jr., is the immediate predecessor of the Qualla phase and represents the climax of Mississippian influence in the Appalachian Summit Area (Dickens 1970). Western North Carolina, particularly the French Broad River drainage where the best and most recent data have been obtained, seems to have been the geographical center of this phase. Prior to Dickens' study Pisgah pottery had been recovered at a number of sites, but its significance had not been perceived. Joffre L. Coe had recovered Pisgah ceramics in his limited digging in 1935 at the Puette site (Tr 1) in Transylvania County, North Carolina. He initially thought

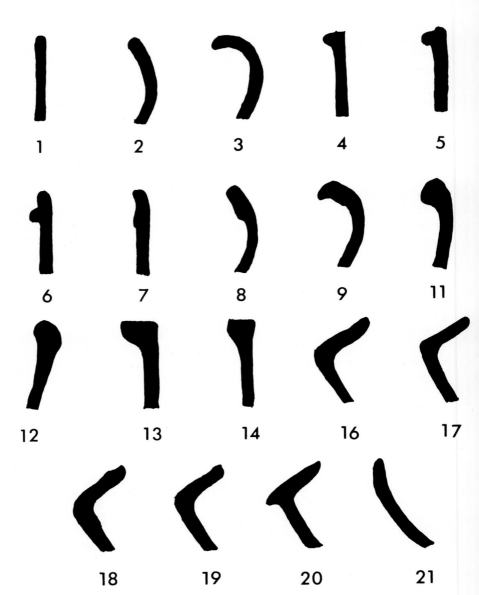

FIG. 7. Qualla Series rim profiles (after Egloff 1967).

that the characteristic Pisgah rims could be fitted to Connestee tetrapodal supports (Coe, personal communication). Thomas M. N. Lewis (n.d.) recovered Pisgah ceramics in his excavations in the Douglass Reservoir at Fain's and Zimmerman's islands, but did not suggest that the Pisgah occupation was responsible for the mounds (Dickens 1970:223-224). A. R. Kelly and R. S. Neitzel (1961:36-37) recognized the unique character of Pisgah pottery, which they recovered at the Chauga site, Oconee County, South Carolina. They referred to it as "pseudo-Iroquoian" pottery, perhaps because of the presence of castellated rims somewhat reminiscent of Castle Creek pottery of New York. Recent discoveries of Pisgah pottery in northeastern Tennessee and southwestern Virginia have also added to the terminological confusion surrounding this series; Polhemus and Polhemus (1966:13-24) have called it the Cobb Island series in the former instance, while in the latter instance it has been called the Lee series (Holland 1970:58-61).

At Tuckasegee 61 sherds of this series were recovered from the plowed soil, 2 from the Structure Unit, and the remaining 6 from the Pre-Structure Unit. The majority (78.1 percent) were classed as Pisgah Complicated Stamped; 1.6 percent were classed as Pisgah Brushed; the remainder was unclassifiable. The general appearance of the sherds, particularly the thickened rim form, suggests that the Pisgah component at Tuckasegee might belong to the early part of the phase (Dickens, personal communication).

The outstanding characteristics of Pisgah ceramics were summarized by Dickens:

> Ceramics of the Pisgah Series can be grouped, on the basis of surface finish, into four types—Pisgah Rectilinear Complicated Stamped, Pisgah Curvalinear Complicated Stamped, Pisgah Check Stamped and Pisgah Plain. There are a few sherds with woven reed (or quill), corncob, cord, fabric or net impressions. Within the rectilinear category there are three designs. The most common form is composed of groups of parallel lines set perpendicular to each other in a series of ladder-like patterns. Less frequent variations have slanted lines either on the central or the flanking portions of the design element. There are two curvilinear designs, one consisting of two pairs of concentric circles separated by a single line, and the other composed of interlocking scrolls flanked by sets of parallel lines. The plain category contains both smooth and rough finishes. In most collections, rectilinear stamping is dominant, followed by check stamping, plain and curvilinear stamping.
>
> The basic vessel form is a globular jar with an everted rim, on the top of which has been attached an additional clay strip to form a collar. There are

also unmodified and thickened everted rims, straight rims, and inslanted rims. Rim decoration consists of bands of punctations or incised patterns. There are rim appendages in the forms of handles, nodes, vertical lugs, and appliqued strips. Shallow bowls are frequently decorated with a thin, pinched, or notched strip around the outer edge of the lip. Temper is fine to coarse river sand, occasionally crushed quartz, and rarely shell (seen only in Tennessee). The color is light gray to buff on the exterior of the vessel and dark gray to black on the interior. There is frequently a high percentage of mica in the clay [Dickens 1970:273-274].

Surveys and excavations at the Ward site, Watauga County, by Drs. Harvard Ayers and Burton Purrington in 1972 and 1973 indicate that in northwestern North Carolina Pisgah ceramics are commonly tempered with crushed steatite.

Connestee Ceramic Series (Plate 6h-k)

Only 9.36 percent of the pottery (1,298 sherds) recovered is referable to the Connestee series. This series was initially recognized by Joffre L. Coe and the writer from surface collections made by the 1964 survey. Formal definitions were made by Holden (1966). An extensively revised description based on a much larger sample is presented in the Appendix. She placed the Connestee series in the Middle Woodland period.

The majority (992 sherds, or 76 percent) of Connestee pottery was recovered from the Post-Structure Unit and few (91) from the Structure Unit. But 215 sherds from the Pre-Structure Unit are important because they demonstrate that the Connestee phase is earlier than the Qualla phase.

Connestee Simple Stamped and Connestee Brushed were the most common types in the Pre-Structure Unit. Plain, cord marked, fabric impressed, check stamped, and complicated stamped types were less frequently encountered. It is difficult to distinguish Connestee Simple Stamped from Connestee Brushed sherds when dealing with small specimens. The ability to sort these types from one another comes with considerable practice and familiarity with the materials. The differences are subtle, and they seem clearer in description than they actually are in practice.

Motifs that appeared on four sherds, classified as Connestee Complicated Stamped, were similar to some Swift Creek and Woodstock stamped designs (Wauchope 1966:Fig. 3). Some, if not all, of these sherds likely represent vessels imported from the south.

Rim forms on the Connestee series vessels were vertical or flaring. Lips were rounded, chamfered, flat, or (rarely) folded. Decoration composed of an incised line placed below the lip was exceedingly rare; however, lips were frequently embellished by oblique incised lines or round punctates. Deep notching of the lip occurred less often. Three small tetrapodal supports, hemispherical or conical in form, attached to flat-bottomed basal sherds were classified as Connestee series appendages. Vessel forms present in the Tuckasegee sample included shouldered jars, straight-sided jars (some with tetrapodal supports and slightly flaring rims), globular jars with flaring rims, and simple open bowls. The distribution and type frequencies are given in Table 5.

Pigeon Ceramic Series (Plate 6l-n)

The Pigeon series was established as a taxonomic group from sherds collected by the 1964 survey. Holden (1966:64-67) formally defined the major types in the series. This pottery was characterized by fairly abundant amounts of crushed quartz temper. Generally, Pigeon sherds are thinner than the later Connestee or earlier Swannanoa sherds. The most distinctive single characteristic of this series is the iridescent sheen on the interior surface of the vessel. This type of polish occurs only on Pigeon series in the Southern Appalachians.

Pigeon rims are usually straight or only slightly flaring. Lips are rounded or flattened, and they are folded even more rarely than in the Connestee series. The occurrence of tetrapodal supports is an attribute shared with the Connestee series. However, the Pigeon feet are large, often over 40 mm long, and conical or wedge-shaped in form, whereas the Connestee tetrapods are small, seldom exceeding 25 mm in length, and knobby or rounded. Vessel forms include simple open bowls, rather straight sided jars, subconical jars, and necked jars. All except the simple-bowl form have tetrapods.

Only 297 Pigeon series sherds were recovered from Tuckasegee. The type distribution is shown in Table 5. The predominant types were Pigeon Check Stamped and Pigeon Plain, which constitute 32.6 and 33.8 percent of the series, respectively. Pigeon Checked Stamped is usually the major type in similar assemblages from the Appalachian Summit Area. Pigeon Simple Stamped and Pigeon Complicated Stamped were present in the collection, but Pigeon Cord Marked and Pigeon Fabric Impressed were absent.

Pigeon Check Stamped is one of the many ceramic types that represent the pan-Southeastern early check stamped horizon style which is recognized by a plethora of local names across the region. Bettye J. Broyles (1967:7), in a recent bibliography of pottery types, has listed about 50 check stamped types in the eastern United States. At least half of these types are but local varieties of the early check stamped horizon style.

Swannanoa Ceramic Series (Plate 6o-q)

Patricia Holden (1966:61-64) correctly referred to Swannanoa ware as the "Early Series," as subsequent research has demonstrated. This series was characterized by abundant coarse crushed quartz or abundant coarse sand temper. Wicker fabric impressions and cord marking were the predominant surface finishes. Simple stamped and large, shallow check stamped finishes, as well as plain surfaces, also were present. Rims were straight and vertical; lips were rounded or, infrequently, flattened; bases were conoidal, often with a single nipple-like projection. The common vessel form was a large amphora, but simple open bowls were also present. The closest equivalents to the Swannanoa series are the Watts Bar ceramics of eastern Tennessee, Dunlap Fabric Marked and Mossy Oak Cord Marked of Georgia, Benson Fabric Marked of northern Alabama, and the Badin series of the Carolina Piedmont.

As with the other early pottery recovered at Tuckasegee, most specimens of this series were found in the plowed soil. However, about 40 percent of the ceramics found in Stratum 5 is referable to this series.

Steatite Vessel Fragments

Only four fragments of soapstone vessels were recovered. Two came from the plowed soil and the others from Stratum 5. These sherds represented the typical Late Archaic or Early Woodland thick, heavy-bodied bowls. None were well finished.

OTHER CERAMIC ARTIFACTS

A single well-made bead, 30 mm long, was recovered from the plowed soil. This specimen was cylindrical, 16 mm in diameter. It was slightly constricted at the midpoint to 15 mm in diameter. Single rows of punctates decorated each end and the constricted center of the bead. The perforation (punched through the long axis prior to firing) was 4 mm in diameter. The paste of this specimen resembles that of Pisgah ceramics. A discoidal made from a

Qualla Complicated Stamped sherd, 40 mm in diameter, was found mixed into the daub used to plaster the interior of the structure roof at the smoke hole. Five fragments of clay pipes were recovered, none large enough to warrant detailed description. All were evidently parts of small elbow pipes typical of Qualla phase forms known from other sites.

CHIPPED STONE ARTIFACTS

The sample of chipped stone artifacts consists of 36 projectile points, a microtool, 6 flake scrapers, and a gunflint of aboriginal manufacture. The distribution of chipped stone artifacts is presented in Tables 4 and 6. A few of the projectile points are referable to types firmly placed in the North Carolina Piedmont cultural sequence.

Projectile Points

Palmer Corner Notched (Plate 7a). The Palmer type projectile point defined by Coe (1964:67-68) from specimens recovered at the stratified Hardaway site is characteristic of the Early Archaic period. The specimen found at Tuckasegee was incomplete, measuring only 21 mm long, 22 mm wide, and 7 mm thick. The notches and edges were finished by pressure flaking, and the base was well ground.

Kirk Corner Notched (Plate 7b). The base of a point referable to the Kirk type was found in the plowed soil. It measured 30 mm wide at the shoulder, 26 mm wide at the base, and 5 mm thick. The chipping, including the fine pressure retouch and basal grinding, is characteristic of the type as defined by Coe (1964:70).

Savannah River Stemmed (Plate 7f). Two fragmentary Savannah River Stemmed points (Coe 1964:45) were recovered. This widespread type is synonymous with several other local names such as Appalachian Stemmed (Harwood 1959), Benton Stemmed (Kneberg 1956), and Kays Stemmed (Kneberg 1956). This type of point is perhaps the diagnostic implement of the Late Archaic period in the Southeast.

Coosa Notched (Plate 7c). Coosa Notched, an Early Woodland type, was defined by the writer and associates on the basis of specimens from the Weiss Reservoir in northeastern Alabama (DeJarnette,

PLATE 7. Chipped stone artifacts from the Tuckasegee site (Jk 12). a, Palmer
Corner Notched; b, Kirk Corner Notched; c, Coosa Notched; d, Swannanoa
Stemmed; e, Pigeon Side Notched; f, Savannah River Stemmed; g, Garden
Creek Triangular; h, Madison; i, perforator; j, flake scrapers; k, gunflint.

Kurjack, and Keel 1973). A single specimen was found in Feature 2. It was 40 mm long, 17.5 mm wide, and 10 mm thick. Cambron and Hulse (1969:24) consider this form as Middle Woodland and suggested that a carbon 14 date of 2050 ± 250 B.P. (Faulkner 1967:19) from the Camp Creek site, Tennessee, was applicable. This date may be correct, but it was used to date a 5-foot-thick midden containing a wide range of materials now known to belong to various assemblages of widely different ages.

Swannanoa Stemmed (Plate 7d). A single Swannanoa Stemmed point was recovered from the old midden, Stratum 5. This type is defined on page 196. The specimen, although fragmentary, was complete enough to justify its inclusion in this category. The stem was 9 mm wide, 8 mm long, and 9 mm thick. This type was abundant in Zone B associated with Swannanoa ceramics at the Warren Wilson site. Points identical in all respects to this type occur in eastern Tennessee (Faulkner and Graham 1966a:73, Plate 19c) where they are regarded as Early Woodland period points.

Pigeon Side Notched (Plate 7e). Two Pigeon Side Notched points made of chert were associated with features: the larger specimen with Feature 1 and the smaller with Feature 7. The metric attributes of these specimens were: length, 37 mm and 24 mm; width, 22 mm and 19 mm; and thickness, 7 mm.

Garden Creek Triangular (Plate 7g). Basal fragments of three Garden Creek Triangular points were recovered. This type, which is defined on page 130, was evidently associated with the Pigeon phase at Garden Creek Mound No. 2.

Madison (Plate 7h). A total of 22 specimens referable to the Madison type (Scully 1951; Perino 1968) was found on the structure floor, and 6 were found in the plowed soil. This type was clearly associated with the Cherokee occupation. Since the sample was fairly large, a detailed description is warranted.

Summary Description: This is a small, thin, straight-bladed, flat or slightly concave based, triangular arrowpoint.

Form:
   (1) Blade: Sides straight, rarely concave or convex.
   (2) Base: Straight or slightly concave. Width-to-length ratio averaged 1:1.3.

Size:
    (1) Length: Range, 20-27 mm; mean, 22 mm.
    (2) Width: Range, 14-19 mm; mean, 17 mm.
    (3) Thickness: Range, 2.5-5 mm; mean, 3 mm.

Material:
    Approximately 94 percent of the sample was made of chert. The precise
    source of this material is unknown, but eastern Tennessee is the most
    likely locality. Six percent of the specimens was made of locally available
    quartzite.

Technique of Manufacture:
    These points were made from flakes struck from rather small chert nodules
    or quartzite cobbles. The primary flake was shaped by percussion flaking
    and finished by pressure retouch.

Comment:
    The recovery of this type point on the floor of the structure and in similar
    contexts at the Townson site (Coe and Keel 1965) makes it impossible to
    consider this type as anything other than the arrowpoint used by the his-
    toric Cherokee, at least in western North Carolina. This appraisal is rein-
    forced by its occurrence in the 18th-century Cherokee sites in the Tellico
    Reservoir (Salo 1969; Gleeson 1970). C. G. Holland (1955, 1970) places
    this type in the latest period of Virginia prehistory and notes that it oc-
    curs with European trade goods.

Unclassified Projectile Point Fragments. Five bifacially chipped
fragments were recovered. One, a thin corner notched basal section,
was found in the plowed soil. Two tip sections suggesting Archaic
period types also were recovered from the plow zone, as well as two
similar specimens found in Stratum 5.

OTHER CHIPPED STONE ARTIFACTS

Gunflint (Plate 7k)

A small (16 × 15 × 5 mm) black chert gunflint of aboriginal
manufacture was found on the structure floor. The size and form
of this artifact are comparable to flints used in pistols.

Miscellaneous

Six small scrapers made of chert (Plate 7j), showing retouch along
only one edge, were recovered from the following proveniences:
Plow Zone, four; Structure Floor, two. The mean dimensions of
these artifacts were: length, 23 mm; width, 14 mm; and thickness,

8 mm. A gray-colored chert sliver (Plate 7i) 17 mm long, 9 mm wide, and 2 mm thick was found in the house depression fill (Stratum 4). One end of this object, like those reported at the Westmoreland-Barber site (Faulkner and Graham 1966a:83-84), showed abrasion and secondary chipping.

CUT AND GROUND STONE ARTIFACTS

Cut Mica

Two pieces of worked mica were recovered from the structure floor. One was circular, measuring 12 mm in diameter, and the other, a rectangular fragment, measured 38 × 26 × 4 mm.

Discoidal

Approximately one-half of a finely polished quartzite chunkey stone, 36 mm thick, was found on the structure floor. The restored fragment is composed of three pieces which were found at points on the floor at least 10 feet apart. Complete, it would have measured approximately 90 mm in diameter.

Pipes

Five pipes were recovered. One found in Feature 1 was complete, but the others were fragmentary. One fragment was comparable to the thin-walled Qualla phase pipes. The others were large, thick-walled pipes similar to the pipe found in Feature 1 (Plate 8a). The large square-stemmed, square-bowled, equal-armed elbow pipe recovered from Feature 1 had a maximum length of 122 mm. The bowl portion measured 57 × 55 mm with a conical-shaped cavity 41 mm in diameter and 58 mm deep. The stem portion measured 57 × 45 mm with a conical cavity 35 mm in diameter and 92 mm deep. Pipes of this form are generally regarded as Late Archaic or Early Woodland period artifacts.

Gorget (Plate 8b)

An unfinished bar gorget, 96 mm long, 32 mm wide, and 12 mm thick, was recovered from Feature 9 in Stratum 5.

Polishing Pebbles (Plate 8c)

Two extremely smooth pebbles were found in the postholes which formed the wall of the structure. Such specimens are

a

b

c

d

e

0 ━━━━━━━━ 5 cm

PLATE 8.   Stone artifacts from the Tuckasegee site (Jk 12). a, steatite pipe;
b, unfinished gorget; c, polishing pebbles; d, pitted hammerstone; e, net
weight.

generally regarded as pottery smoothing or polishing stones. This functional classification seems accurate according to my research. In 1963 I examined pebbles used to polish pottery by a Catawba potter (Mrs. Arzeda Sanders), and in 1970 I also examined polishing stones in the Museum of American Indians collected by M. R. Harrington from a Cherokee potter (Harrington 1922:Plate 63b). In both instances the pebbles known to have been used for smoothing pottery were identical to the specimens from Tuckasegee.

OTHER STONE ARTIFACTS

Hammerstones

Two hammerstones were found; one was on the structure floor, and the other in Stratum 5. The latter specimen, 100 mm long, 69 mm wide, and 26 mm thick, was a pitted hammerstone (Plate 8d) of quartzite. The oval depression was 16 mm long, 9 mm wide, and 2 mm deep. The second specimen, a fist-sized quartzite hammer, measuring 57 × 52 × 27 mm, showed abrasion along one edge.

Net Weight (Plate 8e)

The term "net weight," as it is loosely used in the Southeast, refers to any notched stone. The specimen recovered from Stratum 5 was 105 mm long, 68 mm wide, and 21 mm thick. One notch was made by a single blow from one side. It is comparable to Early Woodland net weights found in eastern Tennessee (Faulkner and Graham 1966a:Plate 23g; Gleeson 1970:39).

SHELL AND ANTLER ARTIFACTS

Pottery Scraper

An edge-abraded freshwater mussel valve (*Cardium*) was found on the structure floor. This implement may have served as a pottery scraper like those in use on the Cherokee reservation at the turn of this century as described by Mark R. Harrington (1922:202).

Antler Drift

The brow tine of a deer (*Odocoileus virginianus*) found in the structure had been used as a drift or punch, as evidenced by its blunted and splintered distal end. The tine had been removed from the rack by scoring at the base and then snapping the piece away.

EURO-AMERICAN TRADE OBJECTS

Twenty-seven items indicating contact with European settlements to the east or south were recovered from the sediments screened from the structure floor or were found *in situ* on the structure floor during our investigation. A wine bottle fragment was found in the pre-1940 plow zone.

Trade Beads

Twenty-six glass beads comprised this category of trade goods. This assemblage was composed of the following types of beads: one black, one red with green glass core, five blue, eight turquois, and eight white seed beads; one turquois barrel bead; and two lemon colored, lobed spherical beads. Except for the lobed specimens which seem to be unique and undatable all of the other types were long used during the Indian trade. Chronologically speaking, the most that can be stated about this assemblage of beads is that they represent 17th or 18th century trade.

Wine Bottle

A basal sherd of a dark green glass wine bottle was found in the pre-1940 plowed soil. This fragment was too incomplete to measure the depth of the "kick," or basal depression, and consequently no date can be arrived at for the artifact.

Metal Object

A single piece of iron was found on the structure floor just inside of the south wall. Stanley South (personal communication) has examined this specimen and suggested that it was probably a piece of strap iron and not a finished artifact.

SUMMARY

The cultural remains recovered at Tuckasegee have been placed into three time units on the basis of stratigraphy. The Post-Structure Unit consists of Stratum 1, the modern plowed soil; Stratum 2, unplowed deposits of the 1940 flood; and Stratum 3, the 1940 plowed soil. Stratum 4, consisting of the remains of a burned structure and containing the remains of the Cherokee occupation, comprised the Structure Unit. The earliest layer containing cultural material, Stratum 5, is termed the Pre-Structure Unit and represents a prehistoric occupation.

The presence of Euro-American trade goods on the floor of the structure and the absence of these items in the Pre-Structure Unit made it possible to assign the cultural assemblage associated with the structure to the historic period and the cultural material found in the Pre-Structure Unit to the prehistoric period.

Typological differences between artifact groups present in these units strengthen the interpretation that temporal differences between the Structure Unit and the Pre-Structure Unit were of some magnitude. For example, Figure 8a indicates the dichotomous distribution of ceramics of the two units. This marked difference in the ceramics of the two units is even more pronounced when the Qualla series sherds found in squares covered by the town house floor are removed from the counts (Fig. 8b). The trampling of Qualla series ceramics into the floor of the structure is considered to be the main source of contamination in the Pre-Structure Unit (Stratum 5).

THE ARCHAIC PERIOD

The Archaic tradition was represented by diagnostic projectile points except for its terminal phase, Savannah River.

The Palmer phase, like the subsequent Kirk phase, was scarcely represented, each being indicated by a single projectile point. Joffre L. Coe's (1964) long sequence from the Uwharrie area of the Carolina Piedmont places the Early Archaic Palmer phase at about 8000 B.C. The Kirk phase, which is the immediate successor of the Palmer phase, is placed at about 7000 B.C. Other than noting the presence of a Palmer Corner Notched point and a Kirk Corner Notched point, little can be stated concerning the Early Archaic period cultures in the Tuckasegee area.

The Late Archaic period Savannah River phase was more adequately represented than the Early Archaic phases just described. The Savannah River component consisted of Features 3 and 8, and possibly Feature 9. Artifacts associated with Feature 3, a scattered fire-cracked-rock hearth area, were a Savannah River Stemmed point and a steatite vessel fragment; with Feature 8, a shallow pit filled with fire-cracked rocks, eight steatite sherds were found; and Feature 9, another scattered mass of fire-cracked stones, contained an unperforated steatite gorget. The steatite elbow pipe from

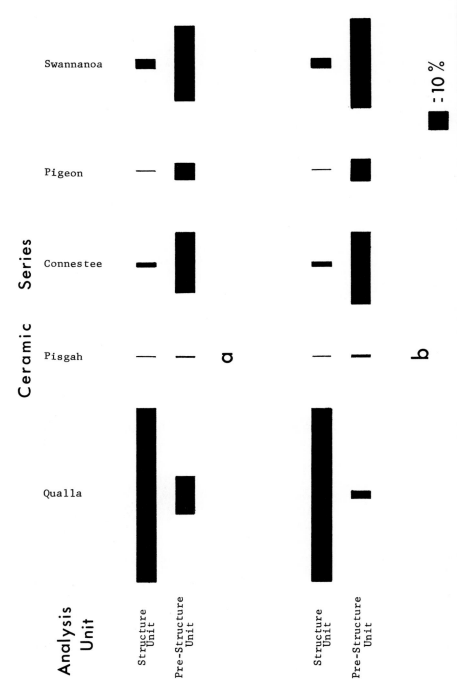

FIG. 8. Distribution of ceramic series, Tuckasegee site (Jk 12): a, all sherds from general excavations; b, Qualla series sherds

Feature 1 and the net weight from Stratum 5 could be considered with equal justification as belonging to the Savannah River component or the subsequent Early Woodland Swannanoa component. The proximity of Features 3, 8, and 9 suggests that the site was used on three separate occasions by Savannah River phase peoples.

THE WOODLAND PERIOD

The Swannanoa Component

The Early Woodland period Swannanoa phase was represented by a component characterized by thick, abundantly tempered, predominantly cord marked and/or fabric impressed pottery, but plain, simple stamped, and check stamped types are also present. Vessel forms include conoidal jars with straight sides and open bowls. Rims are vertical; lips are rounded or flat and are not decorated. Both crushed quartzite and coarse sand were used as tempering material. Major C. R. McCollough and Charles H. Faulkner (1973:92) and Lawr Salo (1969:135) have suggested that the eastern Tennessee Watts Bar focus ceramics (which are comparable to the Swannanoa series) can be divided into an early group characterized by sand temper and cord marking and a later group characterized by crushed quartzite temper and fabric impressing. The Swannanoa Stemmed point in Stratum 5 can definitely be assigned to this phase. Features 2 and 7 were attributed to the Swannanoa component; both were hearths composed of fire-cracked river cobbles resting on the truncated surface of Stratum 5.

The Pigeon Component

The Pigeon phase component was represented primarily by ceramics. The Pigeon series has as a predominant type, Pigeon Check Stamped, which is the local expression of the early pan-Southeastern carved paddle horizon. Minor types included in this series were plain, simple stamped, and complicated stamped. Vessels of this group were conoidal jars or open bowls. A new form—characterized by a restricted neck, an outflaring rim, a definite shoulder, and a flat bottom supported by four conical or wedge-shaped feet—was introduced by Pigeon potters. Lips on all types in the series were usually rounded or flattened, but some were thickened and others appeared to have been the result of paddling of the rim, rather than of actual design.

Few other artifacts in the Tuckasegee collection could be assigned with certainty to the Pigeon phase. The Garden Creek Triangular and Pigeon Side Notched projectile points are the only lithic artifacts which can be considered representative of this phase. No features were assigned to this component.

The Connestee Component

The Connestee phase component was recognized at Tuckasegee on the basis of ceramics. Surface finishes and vessel forms present in the Pigeon phase continued to be used by Connestee potters. To be sure, there were marked shifts in frequencies of the surfaces finishes popular in the Pigeon phase. For example, check stamped sherds, which made up 32 percent of the Pigeon series, accounted for only 0.7 percent of the Connestee sample. Cord marking, the most common surface finish in the Connestee series sample (26 percent), was altogether absent in the Pigeon ceramics series at Tuckasegee. The addition of brushing as a technique for surface finish was also a Connestee phase innovation.

Vessel forms remained basically unchanged from those present in the earlier phases. The large conoidal jar and the open bowl are similar to their Swannanoa antecedents. The footed jar which appeared initially in the Pigeon phase became more refined in the Connestee phase. This form was made smaller, the feet were reduced in size, and the shoulder was more pronounced. Rims were artistically elaborated. They were notched, punctated, or transversely incised. Manufacture of Pigeon Side Notched and Garden Creek projectile points may have been carried over from the Pigeon phase. Like the preceding Pigeon component and succeeding Pisgah component, remains of the Connestee occupation occurred in Stratum 5 and later sedimentary units; no features can be attributed to this occupation of the Tuckasegee site.

THE MISSISSIPPIAN PERIOD

The Pisgah phase is the Appalachian Summit Area expression of the Mississippian pattern. At Tuckasegee a component representing this phase consisted of a few sherds and, perhaps, one clay bead.

THE HISTORIC PERIOD

The delineation of the material culture of the early historic period Cherokee has been given as one of the aims of the University of North Carolina Cherokee project. The evidence recovered from the Tuckasegee site is but one body of data that will be used in reconstructing this aspect of Cherokee tribal history. The identification of site Jk 12 as the 18th-century town of Tuckasegee is beyond reasonable doubt. The archaeological manifestation representing the historic Cherokee occupation of the Appalachian Summit Area has been termed the Qualla phase. The name for this phase was taken from the main reservation of the Eastern Band of the Cherokees. Most of the cultural material recovered from Tuckasegee belonged to this phase and was largely found in the Structure and Post-Structure Units. Since these data were obtained from a single structure, the reader must be mindful that the following description of the Qualla phase was based on very limited information.

Cherokee ceramics have been treated in detail by Egloff (1967), and the Qualla ceramics from Jk 12 add nothing new. Ceramics of this series, like other series made throughout the area, were produced by the coiling technique. Vessel walls were thinned with mussel shell scrapers. Interiors, as well as some exteriors, were highly polished with small river pebbles. Surface finishes were produced by being paddle stamped (complicated, simple, and checked types), cord marked, fabric impressed, smoothed-over-stamped, plain, burnished or polished, corncob marked, and brushed. Decoration of vessels consisted of incised rectilinear or curvilinear patterns on the upper parts of casuela bowls; however, the decoration of rims occurs on all types of the series. Simple rim forms are uncommon; they compose only 14.6 percent of the total rims in the sample. Flanges, at or just below the lip, are quite common (33.6 percent); but the most popular (49.0 percent) was the everted rim with an added fillet usually embellished with fingernail punctations, notches, or short oblique incisions.

The Madison point, a few flake scrapers, a microtool perforator, and a gunflint constituted the chipped stone industry associated with the Qualla occupation at Tuckasegee. The gunflint, of native manufacture, indirectly indicates European contacts. But it also suggests some measure of self-reliance. The Indian provided for himself some necessities for the newly acquired weapons. Pebble hammers and antler drifts or flakers seem to have been used in the production of chipped stone artifacts. Thin-walled elbow forms of smoking pipes were produced in pottery and carved stone. Recreation was suggested by the pottery disc and the stone discoidal. The stone disc may have been used in the chunkey game (Swanton 1946:547, 682). Trade with whites or with other Indians who had access to the Europeans' goods is indicated by glass beads, a wine bottle fragment, and a piece of iron.

The structure excavated at Tuckasegee, whether or not it was a ceremonial structure, gives some idea of early historic period aboriginal architecture. This structure, as the plan shows (Fig. 5), was 23 feet in diameter. Wall posts were set in individual postholes spaced about 4 feet apart. Stringers from one post to another supported the outer ends of the rafters. The interior of the roof was supported by stringers tied to four sets of paired posts which had been placed about 5 feet from the center of the building. In the center of the floor was a specially designed, raised fire basin made of puddled clay. The walls and roof were apparently some perishable material, possibly bark, rather than wattle and daub, and it is clear that the smoke hole in the center of the roof was protected by clay plaster.

Precise dating of the Qualla component is not possible on the basis of the trade materials recovered. We do know that the site was destroyed by Captain Moore in the fall of 1776 (Dickens 1967:3-24). It is remarkable that the radiocarbon date (GX593) obtained from organic material on the structure floor was A.D. 1775 ± 55 (175 ± 55 B.P.).

3. The Garden Creek Sites

INTRODUCTION

The Garden Creek locality (Fig. 9) is situated along the east bank of the Pigeon River approximately 2 miles upstream from Canton, North Carolina. The eastern boundary of the locality is formed by Garden Creek, the southern boundary by a ridge that runs from Garden Creek to the river, which, in turn, marks the western boundary. This triangle contains about 100 acres, but only some 12 to 15 acres indicate aboriginal use. The locality is divided into five site units:

1. Hw 1—Garden Creek Mound No. 1. This mound was referred to in the Valentine manuscripts as the "mound on Plott's land." Heye (1919) called it the Richard Plott Mound and the "conical mound."
2. Hw 2—Garden Creek Mound No. 2. Valentine referred to it as the Smather's Mound, and Heye denoted it as the "Second James Plott mound" or the "previously worked mound."
3. Hw 3—Garden Creek Mound No. 3. This was the mound that George G. Heye excavated in 1915 (Heye 1919). Valentine referred to it as the "mound on Plott's land also." Today only a gentle rise supporting a small home marks its former location.
4. Hw 7—the village associated with Hw 1.
5. Hw 8—the village associated with Hw 2.

Heye (1919) published the first report on this locality. He divided the locality into the farm of Richard Plott, which contained the conical mound (Hw 1), and the farm of James Plott, where the previously worked mound (Hw 2) and the "Heye Expedition Mound" (Hw 3) were situated. The Richard Plott Mound (Hw 1) was described as "conical in form and averages eighty feet in diameter by eighteen feet high" (Heye 1919:37). Heye made a superficial examination of this mound but was unable to open it because of unharvested crops. The second mound (Hw 2) was a low elongated ridge when Heye worked at Hw 3 in 1915. Older residents of

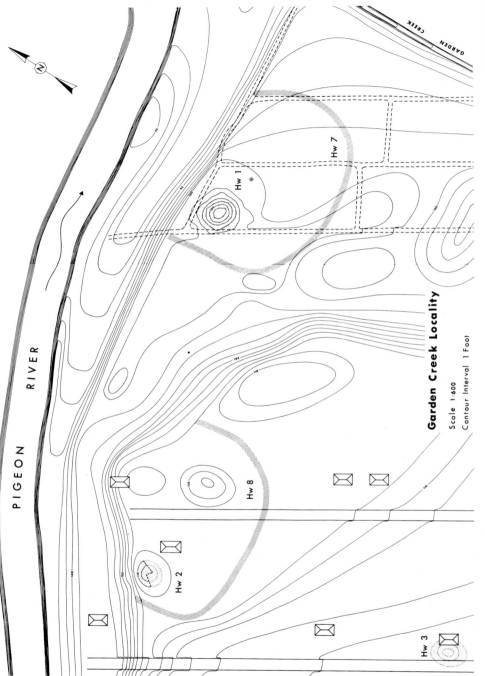

FIG. 9. Map of the Garden Creek locality, Haywood County, North Carolina.

the area assured him that it was comparable in size and shape to the other mounds, but somewhat more level at the top. The third mound (Hw 3) was dug by Heye in the spring of 1915 (Heye 1919).

Two mounds (Hw 1 and Hw 2) and one (Hw 7) of the associated villages were extensively investigated at the Garden Creek locality, Haywood County, North Carolina, by the Research Laboratories of Anthropology during extended field seasons in 1965, 1966, and 1967. The significance of our investigation of these sites to the overall understanding of the prehistory of the Cherokee area is that it produced stratigraphic evidence for establishing the sequence of several of the phases identified in this study. Although we had been able to demonstrate that the Qualla phase was the latest of the archaeological units in the mountains from our investigations at Tuckasegee, the reader may recall that we could only suggest what we thought to be the correct sequence of phases because of the lack of stratigraphic separation of the various components found at that site. The analysis of materials at Garden Creek Mound No. 2 showed that the Connestee phase was preceded by the Pigeon and Swannanoa phases and was succeeded by the Pisgah phase. Stratigraphic information at Garden Creek Mound No. 1 clearly documented that the Pisgah phase preceded the Qualla phase. Perhaps the most surprising discovery in our work in the Garden Creek locality was the recovery of a number of artifacts which undeniably proved that some form of culture contact existed between the Middle Woodland Connestee phase and the Hopewell culture of Ohio. In retrospect everything that we encountered in these excavations was important and of greater interest, simply because we were investigating prehistoric cultures that we had not even known to exist, as we were eventually to define them, only two years earlier.

This chapter deals primarily with the excavation and analysis of materials from the 1965 and 1966 field seasons at Garden Creek Mound No. 2, but in order to present as much information as possible at this time about the Garden Creek locality and its role in Cherokee prehistory, we have included brief summaries of our work at Garden Creek Mound No. 1 (Hw 1) and its associated village (Hw 7), as well as summaries of the work conducted by the Valentine Museum at Hw 2 in 1880 and the 1915 exploration of the third mound (Hw 3) carried out by George G. Heye.

GARDEN CREEK MOUND NO. 1 (HW 1) AND
ASSOCIATED VILLAGE (HW 7)

The investigations at Hw 1 and Hw 7 have been the subject of a
number of preliminary reports (Coe 1968, 1969; Dickens 1969;
Keel 1968). Much of the data recovered from the 1965-1967 work
was incorporated into Dickens' (1970) study of the Pisgah Culture
and Ferguson's (1971) study of South Appalachian Mississippianism.

The mound and the associated village were primarily manifestations of the Pisgah phase, although a historic period Cherokee
(Qualla) component was represented by Euro-American trade goods
and Qualla series ceramics. Evidence for earlier occupation came
from diagnostic artifact types, from ceramics recovered from the
surface, and from various mound-fill units.

Roy S. Dickens, Jr., (1970:197-217) has described the excavation
of the mound and offered the following reconstruction of the
mound building sequence:

First, a semi-subterranean structure was erected on a portion of
the village. Shortly thereafter a second earth lodge was built and
the two were used simultaneously. Later a multi-corridored arrangement of posts was set up behind the lodges. This post arrangement may have been roofed with light branches or straw. When this
structure became delapidated or for some socio-religious reason was
abandoned a layer of cobbles and small boulders was placed on the
area occupied by the posts. On top of the layer of rocks, soil
scraped from the village was piled to the level of the earth lodge
roofs. This soil was placed against the walls of the lodges but did
not cover them. On top of this midden derived soil a layer of yellow clay, forming a cap, was laid. A building was begun on this
layer; however, before it could be completed the roofs of the earth
lodges collapsed creating two cavities in the front of the mound.
To fill these holes, more midden soil was scraped up and piled into
them and the yellow clay cap was extended over them. Before a
town house or temple could be finished the fill in the earth lodges
further settled. To correct this another cap of yellow clay was
added. This cap covered the entire mound.

Finally, on the western portion of this stage two buildings were
erected. Although the eastern portion of the mound continued to
sag, it became the location for seven burials. The entire perimeter
of the mound was enclosed with a vertical log fence. The mound

probably had additional constructions at later times. All of the construction described above occurred during the Pisgah period.

During the fall and winter of 1965 and 1966 excavations in the village area (Hw 7) located three houses. Two of these were not well defined due to severe plowing. Nonetheless, it could be determined that they were about 20 feet square and had wall trench entrance ways. The third house was recognized in the fall plowing of 1966 and subsequently excavated. This structure measured 18 × 20 feet. It contained abundant Pisgah phase remains including charred cane matting, pottery, and food refuse. In the center of the house, a raised clay fire basin was present, and on the floor several refuse pits and three burials were situated. This structure was virtually identical in all details to at least six Pisgah phase houses excavated at the Warren Wilson site (Dickens 1970:158).

Three radiocarbon dates have been obtained from Hw 1. The earliest of these, A.D. 1435 ± 85 years (GXO595), came from wood charcoal collected from Feature 10, a Pisgah phase refuse pit. Dates of A.D. 1730 ± 100 years (GXO596) and A.D. 1745 ± 65 years (GXO729) were obtained from wood charcoal associated with the Qualla phase occupation.

GARDEN CREEK MOUND NO. 3

George G. Heye's 1915 examination of this tumulus leaves much to be desired in terms of present-day field techniques (Heye 1919). In 1970 when I studied the collection from this site, I was dismayed by the lack of accurate provenience data for the specimens that were saved and available for inspection in the Museum of the American Indian-Heye Foundation. Only Heye's published account, a few unpublished photographs, and a collection of some 207 specimens record his work. Field notes, if any were made, could not be located.

The mound was excavated by trenching, beginning with a cut along the southwestern edge about 45 feet from the center. The stratigraphy at the edge of the mound was described as follows:

> Twelve inches below the surface a mass of stones was found, the uppermost of which were small river pebbles but among them and underneath were heavy slabs. In a stratum of earth beneath this layer of stones many potsherds were found. This stratum averaged a foot in thickness and

beneath this was undisturbed soil. Above the stones was a layer of black loam that evidently had been brought from the flats near the river [Heye 1919:37].

In subsequent trenches the layer of stones was found to dip near the center of the mound and then to rise again. The construction of the mound was summarized: "Yellow sand and earth from the surrounding fields were piled in a circle, then covered with stones, then in turn piled with black loam" (Heye 1919:38).

These elements parallel some features of construction at Hw 1 and at the Peachtree Mound (Setzler and Jennings 1941). It appears likely that, contrary to Heye's interpretation, the circle of earth represented the wall of an earth lodge, the layer of stone represented a ceremonial deposit, and the layer of earth was used to fill in the earth lodge cavity in order to create a substructure mound. The mound was apparently built on a Connestee phase midden (see Heye 1919:Plate IIb—a dark zone at the base of the mound is apparent). In my view, this mound can tentatively be assigned to the Pisgah phase on the basis of constructional details and materials present in the collection.

Seventeen pits were recorded by Heye. Some of these were found in the floor of the mound and others originated from the layer of stones. These pits contained charcoal, mica, potsherds, small pieces of flint, burned clay, and bone. Seven burials were encountered according to the published account. One was contained in a stone-lined pit, while the others seem to have been partially plowed out or otherwise disturbed. All bone was very poorly preserved and fragmented.

The collection from the site in the Museum of the American Indian-Heye Foundation consisted of 207 specimens. Of these, 145 were potsherds and 62 were other artifacts.

It was apparent from the kinds of material in the Heye collection that the original sample from the mound had been "high-graded"; i.e., common items were discarded whereas exotic or "pretty" specimens were saved. For example, only complete projectile points were present, and 39 percent of the pottery was either rim or tetrapod sherds. Heye (1919:41) reported finding at least 19 "arrowheads," but only 13 were present in the collection. These were classified into the following types: Savannah River Stemmed—6, Haywood Triangular—4, and Garden Creek Triangular—3. In addition to the specimens described in Heye's report, the following items were attributed to the mound by the catalog: expanded center bar gorgets—2, polished stone discoidal galena nodules—2, fragment of sheet copper, conch shell dipper or vessel fragments—2, and an additional polished stone celt.

The 145 sherds in the Heye collection had the following series distribution: Pisgah series, 6.90 percent (N = 10, 5 rim and 5 body sherds); Connestee series, 65.53 percent (N = 95, 18 rim, 19 tetrapod, and 58 body sherds); Pigeon series, 15.17 percent (N = 22, 5 rim, 2 tetrapod, and 15 body sherds); Swannanoa series, 6.21 percent (N = 9, 4 rim and 5 body sherds). Trade pottery types present in the collection consisted of Swift Creek Complicated Stamped, 2.07 percent (N = 3, 1 rim and 2 body sherds); Napier Stamped, 3.45 percent (N = 5, 1 rim and 4 body sherds); and Mulberry Creek Plain, 0.67 percent (N = 1, rim sherd).

GARDEN CREEK VILLAGE (HW 8)

Most of the area surrounding Hw 2 has, since 1960, become a residential section of Canton. The homes in this section are modest, but their lawns are well developed. Consequently, we were able to surface-collect from only a small area: the roadside ditches, a few garden plots, and flower beds. This surface collection consisted of 32 sherds of the following series: Pisgah (15), Connestee (4), Pigeon (6), Swannanoa (1), Woodstock Stamped (1), and unclassified (5). During the summer of 1966 the construction of a house directly west of Hw 2 led to the discovery of a large rock-filled pit hearth which contained only Swannanoa Cord Marked pottery.

GARDEN CREEK MOUND NO. 2 (HW 2)

Garden Creek Mound No. 2 was initially investigated by Mr. and Mrs. A. J. Osborne in January 1880 for the Valentine Museum of Richmond, Virginia. In early 1969 the Research Laboratories of Anthropology acquired the majority of the specimens from North Carolina in the Valentine collection. We were also able to transcribe or photocopy all of the notes pertaining to the Valentine family's North Carolina archaeological endeavors. The notes, for the most part, were in the handwriting of Mann S. Valentine and were contained in two large ledgers, although some were found on miscellaneous scraps of paper. Some notes were also recorded by other members of the family. The earliest published reference to Hw 2 is contained in the Valentine Museum (1898) "Catalogue of Collections." This single entry was brief:

> Smathers Mound
> On the property of George Smathers, on Pigeon
> River, Haywood County, North Carolina.

and referred to the contents of a single exhibit case in the museum.

An account of Osborne's excavation was interspersed throughout the ledgers and other papers. These entries were in the form of letters from the Osbornes to Valentine, his recollections of verbal reports made to him, and his own observations. The earliest reference was a copy of a postcard dated January 13, 1880, from Mr. Osborne. It stated:

> This evening I commenced opening a mound not far from here [.] We found the bones of the Indian with beads made of bone, some bone implements also some black and red paint as we think [.] will write again soon [Valentine Ms. B:10].

Nine days later, Valentine received a more detailed account of this work from Osborne:

> I send you by express two boxes of relics. The small box containing what was gotten from the mound on the 20th inst [.] All that I got was found on the 1st day [.] I was mistaken about finding paint [,] the beads had been painted a beautiful red color but being decayed it all slipped off when picked up. You wanted to know how the mound appeared inside.
> It was made of loose rich soil except where the corpse lay [;] that was made of clay and burned [.] It was 7 or 8 feet deep in the centre [.] [T] here were three buried one on top of another with about 1-1/2 feet of soil between. The bones were decayed [.] I could only tell where they lay by their clay beads. Opening cost $1.15 [Valentine Ms. B:10].

Two additional entries in the ledgers relating to the Garden Creek locality were based on Valentine's visit to western North Carolina in the summer of 1880:

> July 26/80 Mrs. Os. statement in regard to opening Smathers Mound.
> 'Smathers mound is one of three of these objects on 35 acres of river land 1½ miles from Os. On one of these mounds was found the bowl of Mr. Goodale, a number of large shells and some "weights." This induced us to open Smathers Mound.'

The skeletons, three in number found in this mound, Mrs. O. described the positions as doubled up (Mr. and Mrs. O. and Mr. and Mrs. Smathers with the hands, were at the opening of this mound) 'The head,' says Mr. O. 'was dropped down towards the knees' (as at the Wells mound) and all the large bones laid in a pile together. The skeleton appeared to have been enveloped in a basin of clay. The clay envelope unlike the loamy earth of the balance of the mound, was very hard—as if it had been baked, and the envelope of clay was about 3 inches thickness. (This looks like the clay burial cases) In this mound, which was dug 6 feet deep, there occurred three burials, one above the other, and each skeleton was incased in the same hard clay mould. The rest of the earth was well pulverized and of a dark colour. The teeth were in good condition, and so were some of the bones. the (?) was soft and flexible as is usual in those of the mounds.

It will be remembered that Mr. Osborne sent us as the contents of this mound about 150 small perforated shells, 30 or 40 large white beads, resembling ivory which had been painted red, but much decayed; 50 small shell beads, a bear's tusk, now falling to pieces from exposure to the atmosphere. Two bone ivory pins, a symmetrically shaped yellow quartz weight 1½ diameter and ½ in. thick, a broken tablet of bone or ivory 1/8 in. thick and 1¾ in. across, with incisive markings; some plates of mica, with outer edges cut into angular shapes, charcoal, and large stone weight with concave center.

The beads found in this mound Mr. Osborne says were about the necks of two of the bodies—which could readily have been the case—as in personally and with my fingers working the skull out and freeing it from the surrounding earth, it was apparent that the earth had been tightly packed around it, and no appendage/ornament remaining could have had the slightest movement from its position on the person [Valentine Ms. B:130] .

July 26th [1880] Monday—Os. & myself in the carriage hunting for Plott, to get his consent to open the mounds below Os.—These we saw on Sunday 25th and they are fine mounds—and situated in the fields thus: [Valentine presents a drawing which shows a linear arrangement of three mounds along the south bank of the Pigeon River. Mound B, on the west, is separated from Mound A by a fence line which is in turn separated by another fence line from Mound C to the east. Valentine notes that Mound A is on Smathers' land whereas Mounds B and C are situated on the property of Mr. Plott.] The line marks include about 35 acres of land. A is the Smather's mound opened by Os. from which we have the objects. C is the mound ploughed over and from which we got a handful & found these were of different styles of ornamentation [Valentine Ms. A:45-46]

This account is resumed later in the ledger and states he and Osborne had no success in their attempt to persuade Mr. Plott to let them open Hw 1. Denied this, Valentine referred to Plott as "simply incorrigible—because said he, 'Let the dead rest' " (Valentine Ms. A:133).

The extent of Osborne's work at the site cannot be measured from the accounts in the ledgers except in an indirect way. We know that everything he found was discovered on the first day. Additional efforts, which proved fruitless, could not have been extensive because he gave the total cost of opening the mound as $1.15, which included his labor and that of his wife, the Smather's couple, and several hands. Two large pits located in 1966 have tentatively been assigned to Osborne's digging; they are of sufficient size that they would have required several diggers to complete in the time given by Mr. Osborne.

THE 1965 AND 1966 EXCAVATIONS

During the summer of 1965 Mr. Clarence Cathey of Waynesville, North Carolina, erected a dwelling on the lot adjacent to Hw 2. In preparing this property for sale, he removed a large part of the mound as fill dirt. When the writer learned of this destruction, he requested permission, which Mr. Cathey kindly gave, to investigate the remaining portion of the mound.

A crew of five worked at the site for two weeks in October 1965, recording and salvaging as much information as possible from the area which had been destroyed and digging two test pits into the mound. The test pits and a partial profile of the mound showed that it was composed of two constructional stages resting on an old midden layer. The material we recovered was entirely different from what we were finding at Hw 1. This, and the announced plans of the owner to level the remainder of the mound, made it imperative to excavate the site. The remainder of the mound was completely excavated between May 23 and September 7, 1966.

In 1965 a base line designated R100 was established parallel to the longest profile created by fill-removal operations. This line had no relationship to compass bearing or to the orientation of the mound, but was the most convenient reference line to record the burials, features, and postholes in the disturbed area. A block 45 × 85 feet containing the remaining portion of the mound was staked off from the R100 line. In addition to our work in this area, which was excavated to subsoil, three narrow trenches were dug in an attempt to locate the eastern margin of the primary mound. Unfortunately, these trenches did not produce the desired data. We were prohibited from further trenching by the sale of the property.

The plan of excavation was to expose the mound in reverse order of its construction. To do this, the plowed soil was stripped to reveal the secondary mound (Plate 9). Once the features, burials, postholes, and other intrusions had been recorded and excavated, the fill of the secondary mound was removed. This exposed the primary mound (Plate 10). All features and postholes which appeared at this level were recorded and excavated before this yellow clay platform was cut down. Rather than expose the entire premound layer at once, smaller areas were excavated to subsoil as they were uncovered. This allowed us to partially backfill the site as we dug. Some of the premound midden squares were excavated as a single natural zone, others in two arbitrary levels, and others in three arbitrary levels.

The rectangle which enclosed the mound was divided into 5-foot squares which were designated by the corner coordinates nearest the 0 point. The square was the horizontal control, and the constructional stage or natural zone served as vertical controls. In areas along the slopes of the mound where it was impossible to identify the natural zones, arbitrary levels 0.2 foot thick were excavated. Burials and features were recorded sequentially, but postholes were recorded according to square and zone of origin.

The general digging was done by shovel and mattock. Burials, features, and postholes were excavated using smaller tools. Mound fill and the premound midden were sifted through ½-inch-mesh wire screen. Fill from the burials and features was washed through standard-gauge window screen. Profiles were drawn every 5 feet and, in situations of special interest or complexity, more often.

STRATIGRAPHY AND SUPERPOSITION

Six layers of stratification were observed and recorded during our exploration of the mound. These layers are described in detail in Table 7. Our initial understanding of the structure of the mound was received from the profile created by the leveling of the southwestern side of the structure by the landowner. The observations made in 1965 concerning the structure of the mound were proved to be correct by our extensive excavations in 1966. The distinctive appearance of each of the major construction stages of the mound made it quite easy to excavate the mound in the reverse order of its construction. The only difficulties we encountered in the

PLATE 9 (above). The remnant of secondary mound exposed at Garden Creek Mound No. 2 (Hw 2). The view is to the west. PLATE 10 (below). The remnant of primary mound exposed at Garden Creek Mound No. 2 (Hw 2). The view is to the west.

TABLE 7. Description of the stratification at Garden Creek Mound No. 2
(Hw 2).

Stratum	Thickness (ft)	Description
Plow zone	0.6-1.8	Dark brownish black soil. Disturbed by plowing. Erosion had deposited up to 1.8 feet of cultivated soil along the toe of the mound
Mound slump	0.1-0.4	Dark black soil. Distributed along toe of mounds feathered into plow zone or premound midden at its margins
Secondary mound fill	0.2-1.1	Mixed dark brownish and gray basket-loaded clayey loam
Primary mound fill	1.7 maximum	Yellow clay with little evidence of loading. Thin discontinuous lenses of dark soil present at the base
Premound midden	0.3-0.7	Dark brownish black clayey loam. Truncated by plowing within 10-15 feet of mound toe

stratigraphic peeling of the site were along the eroded and disturbed margins of the mound where plowing had caused a great amount of soil mixing (Plates 9, 10; Fig. 10).

THE PRIMARY MOUND

The first mound (Plate 10; Fig. 10) was raised by constructing a small platform of yellow clay. This flat-topped mound was approximately 40 × 60 feet and had a height of 1.7 feet. The bottom 0.5 feet of the mound was characterized by many streaks or thin lenses of dark soil. In a preliminary report the author (Keel 1967) suggested that these thin lenses of dark soil may have represented a collapsed earth-covered building. However, an alternative explanation seems more likely since no evidence such as walls or floor of an earth-covered structure was found. It is probable that when the clay was dug to erect the mound, the upper part of the clay bed would have been stained by the overlying topsoil. This stained clay would have been the first soil to be placed down in the raising of the mound. Thus, it seems reasonable to assume these dark bands were the result of reversed stratigraphy (Plate 11; Fig. 10).

A structure of some type was placed on the summit of the mound. Details of this building could not be worked out due to the amount of previous digging and borrowing of soil from the mound. Nonetheless, the abundant postholes which originated from the surface of the primary mound indicated that a building was situated there. Feature 41, a burned area, which had been partially destroyed by Osborne's digging (Feature 54) and the 1965 destruction, was apparently the floor of this structure. The red burned surface of the mound was covered by a thin layer of ash which may have originated from the combustion of the roof. Five Connestee series sherds were recovered from this feature; all were under the ash layer previously mentioned. The area covered by Feature 41 was estimated to be 16 × 20 feet minimum (Fig. 11).

Eleven special features were related to the earlier mound. These features and their contents have been tabulated in Tables 8, 9, and 10. They were divided into six categories: large postholes, refuse pits, mound patch, hearths, ceremonial deposit of stones, and structure floor.

Three features, ranging in diameter from 0.9 to 2.9 feet with depths ranging from 0.9 to 4.9 feet, were classified as large postholes. These were also characterized by slightly rounded bottoms

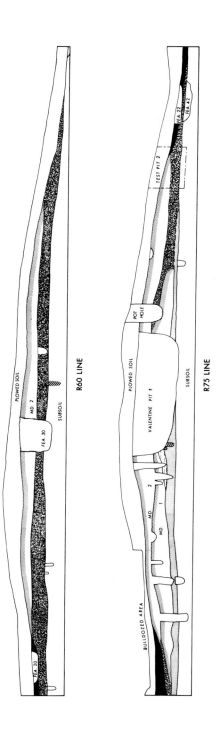

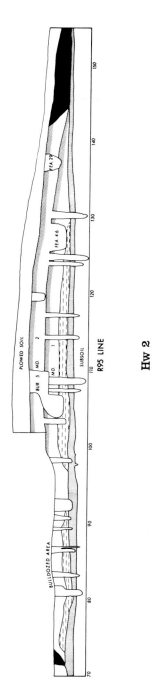

FIG. 10. Stratigraphy of the R60 line, R75 line, and R95 line; Garden Creek Mound No. 2 (Hw 2). The view is to the

PLATE 11 (above).   Stratification of Garden Creek Mound No. 2 (Hw 2) along the R100 line. The view is to the north.   PLATE 12 (below).   Feature 6, a rock-filled pit hearth. This feature was associated with the secondary mound at Garden Creek Mound No. 2 (Hw 2).

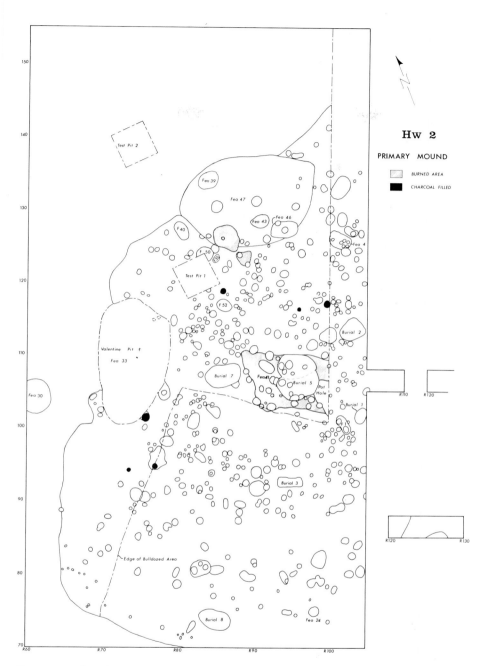

FIG. 11.   Plan view of primary mound, Garden Creek Mound No. 2 (Hw 2).

TABLE 8. Feature data, Garden Creek Mound No. 2 (Hw 2).

Feature Number	Category	Shape	Dimensions (Feet)	Stratigraphic Unit	Culture Phase	Comments
1	Rock-filled pit hearth	Rectangular	2.5x1.7x0.4	Primary Mound	Connestee	
2	Large Post hole	Circular	2.0 dia x 2.3	Secondary Mound	Connestee	
3	Refuse Pit	Oval	3.3x2.1x.5	Secondary Mound	Connestee	
4	Refuse Pit	Rectangular	3.1x2.1x1.9	Secondary Mound	Connestee	
5	Rock-filled pit hearth	Circular	3.0 dia x0.4	Pre-mound midden layer	Connestee	
6	Rock-filled pit hearth	Circular	3.8 dia x0.8	Secondary Mound	Connestee	
7	Rock-filled pit hearth	Circular	3.4 dia x0.7	Pre-mound midden layer	Connestee	
8	Scattered surface hearth	Oval	2.7x2.5x0.3	Pre-mound midden layer	Connestee	Feature 8-16 consisted of clusters of scattered fire-cracked rocks rest on the surface of the Pre-mound Midden in the northwest corner of the site. All of these should be considered Connestee Phase features even though earlier ceramics were found in Features 13 and 1...
9	Scattered surface hearth	Oval	4.0x2.4x0.3	Pre-mound midden layer	Connestee	
10	Scattered surface hearth	Circular	2.4 dia x 0.3	Pre-mound midden layer	Connestee	
11	Scattered surface hearth	Oval	2.0x2.4x0.3	Pre-mound midden layer	Connestee	
12	Scattered surface hearth	Circular	1.8 dia x 0.3	Pre-mound midden layer	Connestee	
13	Scattered surface hearth	Circular	2.2 dia x 0.3	Pre-mound midden layer	Pigeon	
14	Scattered surface hearth	Oval	2.4x2.0x0.3	Pre-mound midden layer	Swannanoa	
15	Scattered surface hearth	Oval	2.5x1.7x0.3	Pre-mound midden layer	Connestee	
16	Scattered surface hearth	Oval	3.3x2.0x0.3	Pre-mound midden layer	Connestee	
17	Rock-filled pit hearth	Circular	1.9 dia x 0.9	Pre-mound midden layer	Connestee	
18	Rock-filled pit hearth	Circular	3.7x3.4x0.3	Pre-mound midden layer	Connestee	
19	Stump	Irregular	3.7x3.4x2.9	Secondary Mound	Modern	
20	Rock-filled pit hearth	Circular	3.7x3.4x0.3	Pre-mound midden layer	Connestee	
21	Rock-filled pit hearth	Circular	2.3 dia x 0.3	Pre-mound midden layer	?	
22	Rock-filled pit hearth	Oval	5.4x3.6x0.4	Pre-mound midden layer	Connestee	
23	Surface hearth	Oval	2.0x1.0x0.1	Pre-mound midden layer	Connestee	
24	Large post hole	Oval	2.1x1.6x1.0	Primary Mound	Connestee	
25	Rock-filled pit hearth	Circular	2.5x2.3x0.2	Pre-mound midden layer	Swannanoa	
26	Rock-filled pit hearth	Circular	1.6x1.4x0.7	Pre-mound midden layer	Connestee	
27	Rock-filled pit hearth	Oval	3.0x2.0x0.6	Pre-mound midden layer	Connestee	
28	Refuse pit	Oval	1.0x0.6x0.2	Secondary Mound	Connestee (?)	Disturbed
29	Refuse pit	Circular	2.9x2.6x0.7	Secondary Mound	Connestee	
30	Rock-filled pit hearth	Circular	4.4 dia x 2.0	Secondary Mound	Connestee	C^{14} date: AD 805±85
31	Patch	Triangular	7.5x6.4x0.2	Secondary Mound	Connestee	
32	Rock-filled pit hearth	Oval	7.0x4.0x0.6	Secondary Mound	Connestee	
33	Valentine Museum Excavation	Oval	20x15x3.5	Secondary Mound	Modern	Osborne's 1880 excavation (?)
34	Basket load of Mound fill	Oval	2.5x2.0x0.3	Secondary Mound	Connestee	
35	Cache	Circular	0.8 dia x 0.2	Primary Mound	Connestee	
36	Rock-filled pit hearth	Circular	4.0x3.5x1.9	Pre-mound midden layer	Pigeon	
37	Refuse pit	Oval	2.0x1.8x0.5	Pre-mound midden layer	Swannanoa	
38	Refuse pit	Oval	1.6x1.0x1.9	Pre-mound midden layer	Connestee	
39	Rock-filled pit hearth	Oval	4.7x4.9x0.4	Primary Mound	Connestee	
40	Large post hole	Oval	2.9x2.0x0.4	Primary Mound	Connestee	
41	Floor	Rectangular	20x12x0.1	Primary Mound	Connestee	
42	Refuse pit	Oval	4.5x3.3x0.4	Pre-mound midden layer	Swannanoa	
43	Refuse pit	Oval	3.4x2.0x0.8	Primary Mound	Connestee	
44	Rock-filled pit hearth	Circular	5.9x5.7x1.5	Pre-mound midden layer	Pigeon	
45	Refuse pit	Circular	1.8x1.7x0.3	Pre-mound midden layer	Pigeon	
46	Refuse pit	Oval	4.3x3.1x1.0	Primary Mound	Connestee	
47	Patch	Oval	8.0x4.6x0.6	Primary Mound	Connestee	
48	Rock-filled pit hearth	Circular	2.1 dia x 0.4	Pre-mound midden layer	Connestee	
49	Refuse pit	Circular	2.5 dia x 0.2	Pre-mound midden layer	Connestee	
50	Rock-filled pit hearth	Circular	2.3 dia x 0.4	Primary Mound	Connestee	
51	Rock-filled pit hearth	Circular	2.5x2.3x0.4	Pre-mound midden layer	Connestee	
52	Large post hole	Circular	1.8 dia x 1.7	Primary Mound	Connestee	
53	Rock-filled pit hearth	Oval	4.1x3.3x0.4	Pre-mound midden layer	Connestee	
54	Valentine Museum Excavation	?	4.5x3.8x1.2	Secondary Mound	Modern	Osborne's 1880 excavation (?)

TABLE 9. Distribution of pottery types, primary mound, Garden Creek Mound No. 2 (Hw 2).

Ceramic Series or Type	Feature Number											
	39		40		41		43		47		52	
	No.	%	No.	%	No.	%	No.	%	No.	%	No.	%
Connestee Series												
Cord Marked	12	66.66	24	18.75	2	40.00	10	28.57	107	20.08	2	8.33
Brushed	1	5.55	21	16.40			11	31.42	179	33.58	4	16.66
Simple Stamped			14	10.93	1	20.00			10	1.78	3	12.50
Fabric Impressed												
Plain	1	5.55	20	15.62	2	40.00	12	34.28	77	14.45	8	33.33
Total Connestee	14	77.76	79	61.70	5	100.00	33	94.27	373	69.89	17	68.82
Pigeon Series												
Check Stamped			7	5.46					27	5.07	3	12.50
Simple Stamped									5	.93		
Cord Marked			2	1.56					1	.19		
Brushed												
Plain			5	3.90					2	.38		
Total Pigeon			14	10.93					35	6.57	3	12.50
Swannanoa Series												
Cord	1	5.55	6	4.68					20	3.75	1	4.16
Fabric									11	2.06	1	4.16
Simple Stamped									2	.38		
Check												
Plain			5	3.90					1	.19		
Unclassified									1	.19		
Total Swannanoa Series	1	5.55	11	8.58					34	6.57	2	8.33
Georgia Types												
Swift Creek Complicated Stamped												
Total Georgia Types												
Limestone Tempered Series												
Cord Marked			1	.78					17	3.18		
Plain	3	16.66	3	2.34								
Unclassified												
Total Limestone Tempered Series	3	16.66	4	3.12					17	3.18		
Unclassified Sherds			20	15.62			2	5.71	73	13.69	2	8.33
TOTALS	18	99.97	128	99.96	5	100.00	35	99.98	533	99.90	24	99.98

TABLE 10. Distribution of artifacts recovered from features at Garden Creek Mound No. 2 (Hw 2).

Category	Secondary Mound Features			Primary Mound Features			Premound Midden Features							TOTALS
	2	30	33	35	40	47	7	18	27	36	42	45	51	
Chipped Stone														
Projectile points:														
Savannah River Stemmed			2											2
Pigeon Side Notched													1	1
Garden Creek Triangular					1	1					1			3
Haywood Triangular												1		1
Unclassified						1	1	1			1			4
Flake scrapers					1					1				2
Hopewell blades						1			1					2
Polished stone														
Gorget fragment		2					1	1			1			5
Other stone														
Chlorite cobble				7										7
Abrading stone						2								2
Anvil hammerstone	1													1
Ceramics:														
Figurine fragments														
Anthropomorphic		5												5
Zoomorphic									1					1
TOTALS	1	7	2	7	2	5	2	2	2	1	3	1	1	36

and straight sides. They all contained Connestee series ceramics.
Features 43 and 46 were intrusive into Feature 47, a deposit of dark
midden soil which had been placed on the north side of the mound
to fill several erosional channels. These refuse pits contained large
amounts of refuse including burned animal bone, charcoal, and
stone chips. Feature 43 contained Connestee ceramics.

Features 1, 39, and 50 were rock-filled pit hearths that contained
large quantities of fire-cracked stones, food remains in the form of
charred animal bone and a few nutshell fragments, stone chips, and
some cultural material. Feature 35, located on the eastern side of
the mound, was a ceremonial cache of seven chlorite schist cobbles,
of which three were cut and pecked.

Feature 41 has been described in regard to the structure placed on
the summit of the mound; however, additional observations seem in
order here. First, Feature 54, a large intrusive pit originating from
the bottom of the plow zone, cut through the western edge of Feature 41. It may be recalled that Mrs. Osborne said that the burials
they encountered were enclosed in "a basin of clay . . . as if it had
been baked and the envelope of clay was about 3 inches thickness"
(Valentine Ms. B:130). This description could be applied to Burial 5,
which was intrusive into Feature 41. It is the writer's opinion that
the burials that the Osbornes found were located in Feature 54 and
that these graves were intrusive into Feature 41. Second, the evidence presented here for a building erected on this mound makes
this one of the earliest examples of a substructure mound in the
southeastern United States.

THE SECONDARY MOUND

After the latest structure atop the primary mound burned, the
secondary mound was constructed by placing basket loads of clayey
loam on its summit and along its sides (Plates 9, 11; Fig. 10). Since
half of the mound had been removed by machinery prior to our investigation, it was difficult to estimate accurately the size of this
mound. Nonetheless, a conservative estimate of 80 × 60 feet is offered. Its height must have been somewhat greater than we recorded
since plowing and erosion had certainly reduced this dimension. In
1965, the maximum height of the mound, including the plowed soil,
was 3.4 feet above the surface of the old village midden. The Osbornes reported that the lowest burial encountered in their digging
was between 6 to 8 feet below the surface. If the interpretation

offered below for the location of the burials found by the Osbornes is correct, the mound would have been between 7 to 9 feet tall. This height seems more likely than Heye's (1919:42) 13- to 18-foot estimate. It is impossible to state with certainty that additional mound construction occurred after the secondary mound was finished. But it is quite likely that additional stages were added. These postulated additions would have been most likely made during the Pisgah period. The burials we encountered as well as those found by Osborne all seem to belong to the Pisgah phase. If no other stages of mound construction occurred and the Osbornes' estimate of the mound height is correct, then these burials would have had depths of 6 to 9 feet. Such depths seem highly improbable for aboriginal graves.

Numerous postholes present on the summit of the secondary mound indicated that one or more structures were present (Fig. 12). No clear pattern could be discerned although the postholes clustered around the summit of the mound. An arc of seven postholes which averaged 1 foot in diameter and 0.9 foot deep was found on the west side of the secondary mound.

Thirteen features were found in conjunction with the final mound. They have been divided into six categories. Data on these features have been tabulated in Table 8. The artifacts and ceramics recovered from them have been listed in Tables 10 and 11, respectively. The areal distribution of these features is shown in Figure 12.

Feature 2, a large posthole measuring 2 feet in diameter and over 2.3 feet deep, was located in Square 110R100. This posthole contained several small pieces of mica, charred animal bone, and charcoal. Four refuse pits, Features 3, 4, 28, and 29, contained the usual matrix of dark earth mixed with debris. They varied in size from about 1 foot in diameter up to 3.3 × 2.1 feet and in depth from 0.2 to almost 2 feet. Feature 31, a triangular lens of yellow clay, was placed as a patch in an eroded area of the west side of the mound.

Three rock-filled pit hearths were found. Feature 30, located on the western side of the mound, was 4.5 feet in diameter and just over 2.0 feet deep. More than 100 rocks, many of which were fire-cracked and spalled, and abundant cultural remains were recovered from this feature. A radiocarbon date obtained from wood charcoal recovered from this pit was A.D. 805 ± 85 years (GXO593). This date is acceptable for some of the Connestee ceramics, but should not be construed to date accurately the earlier material included in

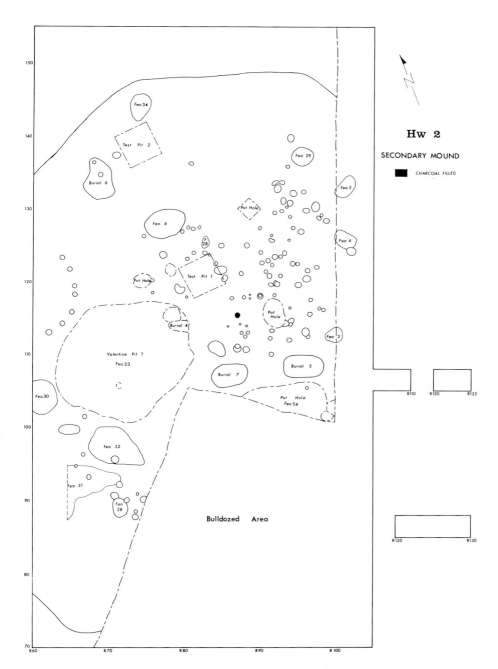

FIG. 12.   Plan view of secondary mound, Garden Creek Mound No. 2 (Hw 2).

TABLE 11. Distribution of pottery types, secondary mound, Garden Creek Mound No. 2 (Hw 2).

Ceramic Series or Type	Feature Number															
	1		3		4		6		30		32		33		34	
	No.	%	No.	%	No.	%	No.	%	No.	%	No.	%	No.	%	No.	%
Pisgah Series																
Complicated Stamped													8	8.89		
Total Pisgah													8	8.89		
Connestee Series																
Cord Marked	2	50.00	6	31.58	2	9.52	4	40.00	30	27.52	27	31.03	10	11.11	19	54.28
Brushed			1	5.26	8	38.12	1	10.00	18	16.50	18	20.68	27	30.00	4	11.43
Simple Stamped			1	5.26					7	6.42	6	6.90			2	5.71
Plain	2	50.00	5	26.31	1	4.76	1	10.00	4	3.70	9	10.34	15	16.66	3	8.57
Total Connestee Series	4		13	68.41	11	52.40	6	60.00	59	54.14	60	68.95	52	57.77	28	79.99
Pigeon Series																
Check Stamped			3	15.79	2	9.52			14	12.83	13	14.95	12	13.33		
Cord Marked					2	9.52										
Brushed																
Plain									2	1.84			3	3.33	2	5.71
Unclassified													1	1.11		
Total Pigeon Series			3	15.79	4	19.04			16	14.67	13	14.95	16	17.77	2	5.71
Swannanoa Series																
Cord					1	4.76	1(?)	10.00	1	.91			3	3.33		
Fabric					2	9.52	1	10.00					1	1.11		
Simple Stamped			1	5.26												
Plain			1	5.26	2	9.52			2	1.84			4	4.44		
Unclassified													2	2.22		
Total Swannanoa Series			2	10.52	5	23.80	2		3	2.75			10	11.11		
Georgia Types																
Swift Creek Complicated Stamped			1	5.26			1	10.00								
Napier Stamped											1	1.15				
Total Georgia Types			1	5.26			1	10.00			1	1.15				
Limestone Tempered Series																
Plain					1	4.76	1	10.00								
Unclassified																
Total Limestone Series					1	4.76	1	10.00								
Unclassified									31	28.44	13	14.95	4	4.44	5	14.29
TOTAL	4	100.00	19	99.98	21	100.00	10	100.00	109	100.00	87	100.00	90	99.98	35	99.99

the fill of the pit. Feature 6 (Plate 12), located on the north side of the mound, was circular in plan (3.8 feet in diameter) and 0.8 feet deep. The remaining hearth, Feature 32, was a large oval pit located on the north side of the mound that contained ceramics belonging to several series, the latest being Connestee. These ceramics included a large portion of a Connestee Brushed vessel.

A well-defined and carefully excavated single load of fill was designated Feature 32. This particular lens of soil had a volume of about 1.5 cubic feet. Seven intrusive pits of recent age were encountered in the excavations. Two of these, Features 33 and 54, were attributed to the Osbornes' 1880 investigation of the site for the Valentine Museum. The other five were evident on the surface of the mound as sunken or depressed spots. One of these was dug during the winter of 1965-1966. These five pothunter holes were not assigned feature numbers in the field.

Osborne unearthed at least three burials. The items found with the skeletons indicated that these were Pisgah phase graves. All of the burials encountered during the 1965-1966 work were most likely Pisgah phase interments. However, direct evidence was lacking for Burials 4 and 8. Burial 4 was a discarded pile of human bones found in the backfill of one of Osborne's pits (Feature 33). The pit that contained Burial 8 seemed to have been dug through the secondary mound in view of its shallow depth and the projected slope of the final mound at the location of this grave. It was recovered in an area where the topsoil and the secondary mound fill had been removed for fill material in 1965. All other burials were definitely Pisgah graves because they had distinctive artifacts of that culture or Pisgah ceramics in the burial pit fills.

Burials 1, 2, 3, 7, and 8 were pit-type graves, whereas Burials 5 and 6 were shaft-and-chamber affairs (Coe 1952:311; 1969). Burials 3 and 5 have been illustrated in Plates 13 and 14, and Fig. 13 for comparison. Additional information is contained in Tables 12, 13, and 14. Preservation was uniformly poor. None of the human skeletal remains will have much utility to physical anthropologists.

THE OLD VILLAGE MIDDEN

The midden layer under the mounds was present over the entire excavation. Where covered by the mounds, this layer was easily distinguished. However, in the northern part of the area where it had been plowed and mixed with soil eroding off the mound, it

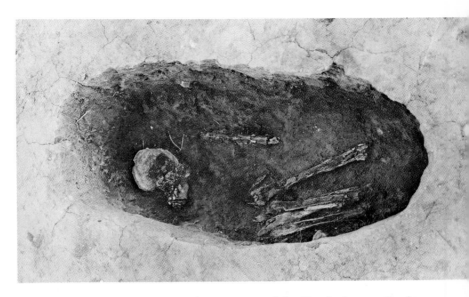

PLATE 13 (above). Burial 3, a pit-type grave of the Pisgah phase at Garden Creek Mound No. 2 (Hw 2). The view is to the east. PLATE 14 (below). Burial 5, a shaft-and-chamber-type grave of the Pisgah phase at Garden Creek Mound No. 2 (Hw 2). The view is to the west.

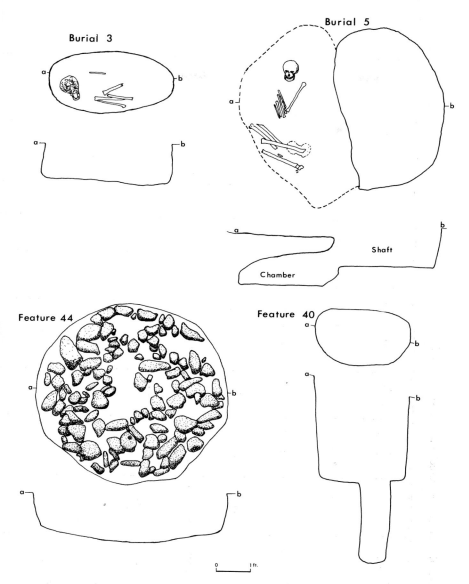

FIG. 13.   Burial and feature plans and sections, Garden Creek Mound No. 2
(Hw 2).

TABLE 12. Burial data, Garden Creek Mound No. 2 (Hw 2).

Burial Number	Origin of Pit	Pit Type	Size (Ft.)	Depth (Ft.)	Deposition	Orienta-tion	Age	Sex	Associated Objects	Cultural Phase
1	?	Oval	2.1x1.5	0.3	Flexed(?)	Nw(?)	Inf. ?	?	Shell bead	Pisgah
2	2^d Mound	Oval	3.2x1.9	0.9	Flexed(?)	Nw(?)	Inf. ?	?	Marginella & cut shell beads and shell gorget	Pisgah
3	?	Oval	3.5x1.9	1.2	Flexed on right side	N	Adl. ?	?		Pisgah
4	Fragments recovered from Feature 33 (Valentine Excavation)									
5	2^d Mound	Shaft and Chamber	4.8x2.9 / 4.9x3.5	1.2 / 0.9	Flexed on back	N	Adt.	F		Pisgah
6	2^d Mound	Shaft and Chamber	7.0x5.4 / 5.3x2.5	2.0 / 1.0	Flexed on back	Sw	Adt.	F	Shell beads	Pisgah
7	2^d Mound	Oval	4.5x3.3	3.3	Flexed on right side	Nw	Adt.	M		Pisgah
8	2^d Mound	Oval	4.2x2.1	0.7	Flexed on	S	Adl.	F(?)		Pisgah

TABLE 13. Distribution of pottery types recovered from burial pits at Garden Creek Mound No. 2 (Hw 2).

Type	Burial Number						
	1	2	3	5	6	7	8
Pisgah series:							
Rectilinear Complicated Stamped			2	18	17	14	
Check Stamped	1						
Plain				2	3	4	
Total Pisgah series	1		2	20	20	18	
Connestee series:							
Cord Marked			4	6	11	10	
Brushed			2		20	15	1
Simple Stamped	1			13	5	5	8
Check Stamped		1	1			3	
Fabric Impressed		1					
Plain	3			9	26	14	3
Total Connestee series	4	2	7	28	62	47	12
Pigeon series:							
Check Stamped		1	1	4	3		7
Cord Marked		1	1		1		
Fabric Impressed				1			
Plain				6	2	2	
Total Pigeon series		2	2	11	6	2	7
Swannanoa series:							
Cord Marked	1			2	8	3	
Fabric Impressed				2	2	1	
Check Stamped					1		
Simple Stamped					1		
Plain				6	1	3	
Total Swannanoa series	1			10	13	7	
Unclassified						17	3
TOTALS	6	4	11	69	101	91	22

TABLE 14. Distribution of artifact types recovered from burial pits at Garden Creek Mound No. 2 (Hw 2).

Category	Burial				TOTAL
	2	5	6	7	
Projectile points					
Pigeon Side Notched			1		1
Connestee Triangular				1	1
Haywood Triangular				1	1
Unclassified	1				1
Prismatic blade			2		2
Flake scraper		1			1
Hammerstone			1		1
Total	1	1	4	2	8

was more difficult to define. This layer varied in thickness from 0.7 foot under the mounds to about 0.2 foot in the plowed area (Figs. 10, 14).

Table 15, which represents about 50 percent of the ceramics recovered from the site, suggests that the occupation of the area was intense and relatively continuous. Although certain Archaic period projectile points were recovered from the midden, no specimens later than the Connestee period were found there.

The configuration of postholes (Fig. 15) which formed the structure pattern recognized at the base of the premound layer was identified by the distinctive fill in the postholes (Plate 15). The fill of these 29 postholes was composed of two types of soil; the upper one-third of the holes was filled with the dark colored midden soil, whereas the lower two-thirds of the hole was filled with a white coarse sand. The posthole pattern came to light when the sand-filled holes were denoted on the plot sheets. After the first few of these were plotted, it was possible to predict where the next posthole of this type would be situated. It appeared that this structure was removed and the holes filled with sand in one continuous operation, perhaps to clear the area for the construction of the primary mound. Some of the postholes contained Connestee phase ceramics and, therefore, place the removal of the house at least as late as that period. Sherd counts for the squares covered by this house were approximately 17 percent higher in Connestee ceramics than in squares outside of, but adjacent to, the structure. The posthole pattern measured 20 X 19.5 feet. An alignment of three postholes in the southeastern corner of the building may indicate a wind screen or portico. No hearth was located within the margin of the structure, but two features, Nos. 44 and 53, both Connestee phase rock-filled pit hearths, were found on the west side of the pattern.

More than 1,000 other postholes, shown on the plans of the premound midden and subsoil surfaces (Figs. 14, 15), undoubtedly represent a number of structures. Most of the postholes recorded at the subsoil level originated at the surface of the premound midden or within the accumulating midden but were undetected because they had been filled with midden soil.

The features were classified into two categories: refuse pits and hearths (Fig. 15). This latter category was subdivided into two subclasses: rock-filled pit hearths and surface hearths.

Five refuse pits (Features 37, 38, 42, 45, 49) were present. All were shallow, ranging in depth from 0.4 to 0.9 foot. Four of them were oval in plan, and one, rectangular in outline, was more than

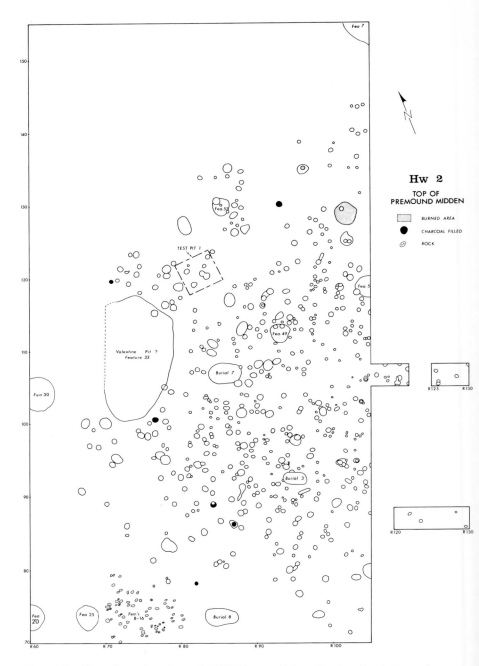

FIG. 14.   Plan view of surface of Old Village midden, Garden Creek Mound No. 2 (Hw 2).

TABLE 15. Distribution of pottery types, premound midden, Garden Creek Mound No. 2.

Ceramic Series or Type	25 No.	25 %	26 No.	26 %	27 No.	27 %	36 No.	36 %	37 No.	37 %	44 No.	44 %	45 No.	45 %	48 No.	48 %	49 No.	49 %	51 No.	51 %	53 No.	53 %
Connestee Series																						
Cord Marked					12	37.50									2	66.66	13	72.22				
Brushed			4	100.00	2	6.25											2	11.11				
Fabric Impressed																						
Plain					14	43.75											3	16.67				
Total Connestee Series			4	100.00	28	87.50									2	66.66	18	100.00				
Pigeon Series																						
Check Stamped					1	3.12	6	6.12			36	18.18	1	33.33	1	33.33			2	7.69	2	9.52
Simple Stamped							1	1.02														
Cord Marked																						
Plain					1	3.12	6	6.12			8	4.04							1	3.84		
Total Pigeon Series					2	6.25	13	13.26											3	11.53	5	23.80
Swannanoa Series																						
Cord Marked	3	100.00					65	66.33	5	41.67	28	14.14							9	34.61	3	14.28
Fabric Impressed											7	3.53							8	30.76	3	14.28
Simple Stamped							11	11.22			52	26.26									2	9.52
Check Stamped									1	8.33	1	.50									3	14.28
Plain							3	3.06	1	8.33	38	19.19							1	3.84		
Unclassified											10	5.05	2	66.66					1	3.84		
Total Swannanoa Series							79	80.61	7	58.33	136	68.67	2	66.66								
Georgia Types																						
Early Swift Creek Complicated Stamped					2	6.25																
Total Georgia Types					2	6.25																
Limestone Tempered Types (Tennessee Types)																						
Cord Marked											1	.50										
Brushed																			1	3.84		
Unclassified											1	.50										
Total Limestone Tempered																			1	3.84		
Unclassified							6	6.12	5	41.67	17	8.58							3	11.53	5	23.80
TOTAL	3	100.00	4	100.00	32	100.00	98	99.99	12	100.00	198	99.97	3	99.99	3	99.99	18	100.00	26	99.95	21	99.96

TABLE 15 (*cont.*). Distribution of pottery types, premound midden, Garden Creek Mound No. 2 (Hw 2).

Ceramic Series or Type	5 No.	5 %	7 No.	7 %	9 No.	9 %	12 No.	12 %	13 No.	13 %	14 No.	14 %	15 No.	15 %	17 No.	17 %	18 No.	18 %	20 No.	20 %	22 No.	22 %
Connestee Series																						
Cord Marked	4	33.33			1	25.00	1	33.33							1	3.70	10	10.63	2	2.40	18	18.00
Brushed	2	16.67	5	38.48	1	25.00	1	33.33							1	3.70	17	18.08	8	9.63	36	36.00
Fabric Impressed															1	3.70			3	3.61	13	13
Plain	2	16.67			2	50.00									3	11.10	4	4.25	10	12.04		
Total Connestee Series	8	66.67	5	38.48	4	100.00	2	66.66									31	32.96	23	27.68	67	67.00
Pigeon Series																						
Check Stamped	4	33.33							1	50.00					3	11.10	18	19.14	6	7.23	18	18.00
Simple Stamped			2	15.38											5	18.51						
Cord Marked			2	15.38					1	50.00							3	3.19	1	1.20	1	1.00
Plain															8	29.61	21	22.33			2	2.00
Total Pigeon Series	4	33.33	4	30.76					2	100.00									7	8.43	21	21.00
Swannanoa Series																						
Cord Marked											8	100.00			9	33.33	23	24.46	7	8.43	1	1.00
Fabric Impressed			1	7.69													1	1.06	11	13.25	2	2.00
Simple Stamped															3	11.10	5	5.31	30	36.14		
Check Stamped																						
Plain															1	3.70	8	8.51			5	5.00
Unclassified															2	7.40					3	3.00
Total Swannanoa Series			1	7.69											15	55.53	37	39.34	48	57.82	11	11.00
Limestone Tempered Types (Tennessee Types)																						
Cord Marked													2	100.00	1	3.70						
Brushed																						
Unclassified													1	3.70								
Total Limestone Tempered													2	100.00	1	3.70						
Unclassified			3	23.07			1	33.33									5	5.31	5	6.02		
TOTAL	12	99.99	13	100.00	4	100.00	3	99.90	2	100.00	8	100.00	2	100.00	27	99.94	94	94.94	83	99.95	100	100.00

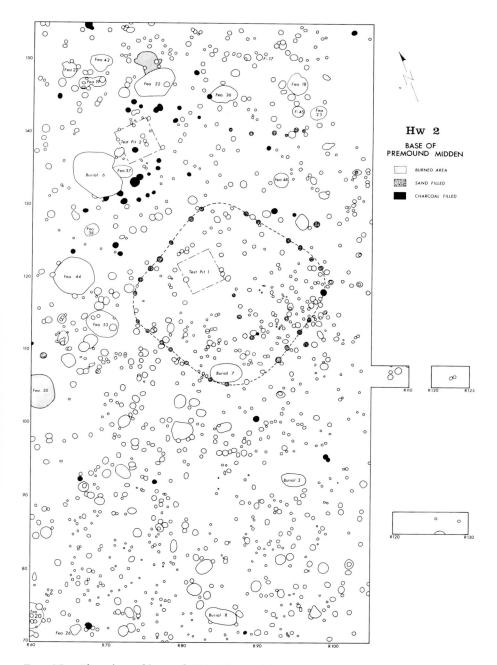

FIG. 15.   Plan view of base of Old Village midden, Garden Creek Mound
No. 2 (Hw 2).

PLATE 15. The house pattern at the base of the Old Village midden at Garden Creek Mound No. 2 (Hw 2). The white discs mark only postholes that were filled with white sand. The view is to the south.

twice the size of the largest oval pit. Feature 37 was of especial interest because it contained only Swannanoa series ceramics, which suggested that it was one of the oldest features encountered.

The rock-filled pit hearths (Features 5, 7, 17, 18, 21, 22, 25, 26, 27, 36, 44, 48, 51, 53) ranged in size from 5.9 to 2.1 feet in diameter with depths of 0.4 to 1.9 feet. These circular or oval pits were characterized by rather straight or slightly incurved sides and were filled with a matrix of dark soil containing ash, charcoal, charred animal bone, lithic chips, potsherds, occasional artifacts, and large amounts of fire-cracked or spalled cobbles.

Ten sets (Features 8, 9, 10, 11, 12, 13, 14, 15, 16, 23) of more or less clustered fire-cracked rocks were uncovered below the mound, resting on the surface of the premound midden. These rock clusters gave no indication of being placed in pits. Nine of them were located on the south side of the mound and one, Feature 23, on the north side of the mound. They ranged in size from 4.2 × 2.4 feet to 1.8 feet in diameter. There was abundant evidence of burning among and around the rocks in the form of charcoal, ash, burned animal bone, and discolored soil. On the basis of the ceramics associated with them they were assigned to various cultural phases, but in spite of the presence of Pigeon ceramics in Feature 13 and Swannanoa ceramics in Feature 14, their stratigraphic position suggests that these are Connestee phase features. Contents of the features are tabulated in Tables 10 and 15.

ARTIFACTS

More than 32,000 specimens were collected during the 1965 and 1966 investigations at the site. In addition to these specimens I was able to analyze the materials in the Valentine collection made in 1880. This collection contained 593 specimens, of which 512 were marginella beads. The provenience of the specimens obtained from the Valentine Museum was less than precise, but the specimens in themselves were quite informative. The 11 potsherds in this collection were classified as: Pisgah Complicated Stamped, 9; Pisgah Plain, 1; and Pigeon Plain, 1. The other artifacts present in this lot are discussed in subsequent paragraphs.

All of the artifacts and approximately one-half of the ceramics recovered in 1965 and 1966 have been analyzed. The total ceramic collection was examined in detail on two occasions before analysis

was initiated. Since one of the primary goals of this study was to
define time-specific cultural assemblages, only horizontal excavation units which contained all four superpositioned or stratigraphic
layers were included in the analysis (Table 16; Fig. 16). This procedure eliminated the slumped and plowed zones located beyond
the margins of the mounds. Ceramics and artifacts recovered from
the burials and the features were included in the analysis. These
have been presented in the appropriate tables. Ceramics recovered
from stratigraphic contexts have been tabulated in Table 16. Additionally, ceramic type frequencies have been calculated for eight
squares in which the premound midden was excavated in three arbitrary levels (Table 18), as well as series frequencies for these type
distributions (Fig. 19). Chipped stone artifact distributions have
been listed in Table 17 and the distribution of Hopewellian specimens listed in Table 21.

Unfortunately, the nature of the sediments, that is, the use of old
midden deposits as the source of fill for mound construction,
coupled with the generous amount of aboriginal digging and recent
disturbances, severely hampered the isolation of clear-cut and mutually exclusive assemblages. Yet, distributional data strongly suggest a transition through time from the Swannanoa phase to the
Pigeon phase and later to the Connestee phase. The presence of intrusive Pisgah phase was a later manifestation.

The presence of a Hopewellian assemblage at the site was unexpected. Until 1965 no direct evidence of contact at a Middle Woodland time level between the Midwest and the Appalachian Summit
Area existed.

CERAMICS

All of the ceramic series manufactured in the study area were
represented by specimens in the collection gathered in 1965 and
1966. Additionally, trade wares from Georgia, Tennessee, and the
Midwest also were recovered.

Qualla Series

A few Qualla sherds were found in the plowed soil and in plow
scars on the secondary mound. This material made up 0.2 percent
of the ceramics analyzed. It is likely that Valentine (Ms. B) was re-
ferring to the Qualla component at Hw 1 when he noted that the
material collected at "Mound C" was "of quite different styles of

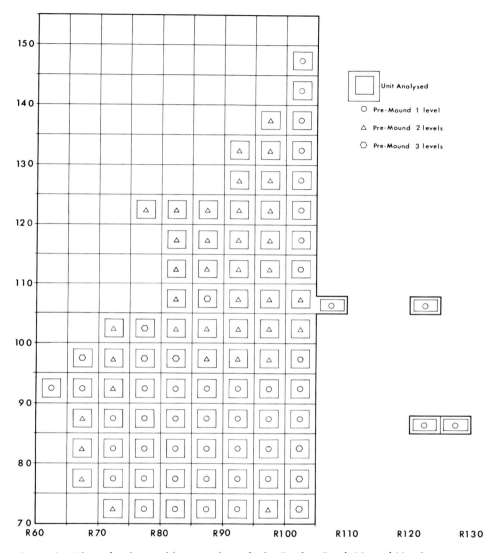

FIG. 16.   Plan of units used in ceramic analysis, Garden Creek Mound No. 2
(Hw 2).

TABLE 16. Distribution of pottery types, general excavation, Garden Creek Mound No. 2 (Hw 2).

Ceramic Type or Series	Plow Zone No.	%	Secondary Mound No.	%	Primary Mound No.	%	Pre-Mound Midden No.	%	TOTAL No.	%
Qualla Series	1	.18	21	3.01					22	
Pisgah Series	136	25.00	20	2.87					156	1
Connestee Series										
Cord Marked	33	6.07	45	6.46	327	24.08	595	7.20	1000	9
Brushed	90	16.55	158	22.67	316	23.27	1061	12.81	1625	14
Simple Stamped	8	1.47	27	3.87	47	3.46	354	4.28	436	4
Check Stamped	4	.74	37	5.31	1	.07	612	7.39	654	6
Fabric Impressed			45	6.46	1	.07	25	.30	71	
Plain	99	18.20	80	11.48	214	15.76	690	8.33	1083	9
unclassified	37	6.80	7	1.00	16	1.18	79	.95	139	1
Total Connestee Series	271	49.83	399	57.25	922	67.89	3416	41.26	5008	46
Pigeon Series										
Check Stamped	25	4.60	62	8.90	156	11.49	3271	39.51	3514	32
Simple Stamped	1	.18	2	.29	2	.15	183	2.21	188	1
Complicated Stamped					4	.29	5	.06	9	
Cord Marked	9	1.65	8	1.15	6	.44	171	2.07	194	1
Fabric Impressed	1	.18	5	.72			2	.02	8	
Brushed	4	.74	7	1.00	7	.52	58	.70	76	
Plain	13	2.39	10	1.43	16	1.18	228	2.75	267	2
unclassified	7	1.29	2	.29	10	.74	95	1.15	114	1
Total Pigeon Series	60	11.03	96	13.78	201	14.81	4013	48.47	4370	40
Swannanoa Series										
Cord Marked	4	.74	38	5.45	44	3.24	189	2.28	275	2
Fabric Impressed	5	.92	11	1.58	13	.96	38	.46	67	
Check Stamped	1	.18	5	.72	15	1.11	10	.12	31	
Simple Stamped	2	.37	25	3.58	36	2.65	64	.77	127	1.
Plain	6	1.10	27	3.87	26	1.91	69	.83	128	1.
unclassified	6	1.10	12	1.72	18	1.33	68	.82	104	
Total Swannanoa Series	24	4.41	118	16.92	152	11.20	438	5.28	732	6
Georgia Types										
Swift Creek Complicated Stamped	2	.37							2	
Napier Stamped			4	.57	1	.07	1	.01	6	
Total Georgia Types	2	.37	4	.57	1	.07	1	.01	8	
Hopewell Types										
Turner Simple-stamped			2	.29	1	.07	62	.75	65	
Chillicothe Rocker-stamped, plain-rocked	1	.18	4	.57			2	.02	7	
Chillicothe Rocker-stamped dentate-rocked			1	.14	6	.44	15	.18	22	
Rims							3	.04	3	
Total Hopewell Types	1	.18	7	1.00	7	.51	82	.99	97	
Limestone-tempered Types (Tennessee Types)										
Cord Marked					12	.88	5	.06	17	
Fabric Impressed							3	.04	3	
Brushed	1	.18					20	.24	21	
Check Stamped			3	.43			5	.06	8	
Plain					2	.15	15	.18	17	
Burnished			2	.29	12	.88	7	.08	21	
Zone Punctated							3	.04	3	
unclassified	1	.18					4	.05	5	
Total Limestone-tempered Types	2	.36	5	.72	26	1.91	62	.75	95	
Unclassified	47	8.64	27	3.87	49	3.61	268	3.24	391	3.
TOTALS	544	100.00	697	99.99	1358	100.00	8280	100.00	10,879	100.

TABLE 17. Distribution of pottery types from arbitrary levels excavated in the premound midden at Garden Creek Mound No. 2 (Hw 2).

Ceramic Type or Series	Level 1 No.	Level 1 %	Level 2 No.	Level 2 %	Level 3 No.	Level 3 %	TOTAL No.	TOTAL %
Connestee series								
Cord Marked	18	5.26	15	6.05	10	3.77	43	5.03
Brushed	61	17.83	34	13.71	15	5.66	110	12.87
Simple Stamped	3	.87	11	4.44	9	3.39	23	2.69
Check Stamped	4	1.16			1	.38	5	.58
Fabric Impressed	9	2.63			3	1.13	12	1.40
Plain	8	2.33	12	4.84	13	4.90	33	3.86
Unclassified	7	2.04	3	1.20	1	.38	11	1.29
Total Connestee series	110	32.12	75	30.24	52	19.61	237	27.72
Pigeon series								
Check Stamped	166	48.63	133	53.63	151	56.98	450	52.63
Simple Stamped	3	.87	2	.80	2	.76	7	.82
Complicated Stamped					1	.38	1	.12
Cord Marked	2	.58	7	2.82	13	4.90	22	2.57
Brushed	1	.29					1	.12
Plain	10	2.92	9	3.63	8	3.01	27	3.16
Unclassified	2	.58	1	.40	1	.38	4	.47
Total Pigeon series	184	53.87	152	61.28	176	66.41	512	59.89
Swannanoa series								
Cord Marked	7	2.04			3	1.13	10	1.17
Fabric Impressed	1	.29	1	.40	1	.38	3	.35
Brushed	3	.87	1	.40	14	5.28	18	2.10
Check Stamped	3	.87					3	.35
Plain			3	1.21	4	1.50	7	.82
Unclassified	11	3.21	4	1.62	6	2.26	21	2.46
Total Swannanoa series	25	7.28	9	3.63	28	10.55	62	7.25
Hopewell types								
Chillicothe Rocker Stamped, plain rocked	2	.58					2	.23
Chillicothe Rocker Stamped, dentate rocked	3	.87					3	.35
Hopewell Rim	1	.29					1	.12
Total Hopewell types	6	1.74					6	.70
Limestone Tempered types (Tennessee types)								
Burnished					2	.76	2	.23
Brushed	1	.29	3	1.21	2	.76	6	.70
Plain	3	.87	1	.40	2	.76	6	.70
Unclassified					1	.38	1	.12
Total Limestone Tempered types	4	1.16	4	1.61	7	2.66	15	1.75
Unclassified	13	3.81	8	3.22	2	.76	23	2.69
TOTALS	342	99.98	248	99.98	265	99.99	855	100.00

TABLE 18. Distribution of chipped stone artifacts, Garden Creek Mound No. 2 (Hw 2).

Ceramic Type or Series	Level						TOTAL	
	1		2		3			
	No.	%	No.	%	No.	%	No.	%
Connestee Series								
Cord Marked	18	5.26	15	6.05	10	3.77	43	5.0
Brushed	61	17.83	34	13.71	15	5.66	110	12.8
Simple Stamped	3	.87	11	4.44	9	3.39	23	2.6
Check Stamped	4	1.16			1	.37	5	.5
Fabric Impressed	9	2.63			3	1.13	12	1.4
Plain	8	2.33	12	4.84	13	4.90	33	3.8
Unclassified	7	2.04	3	1.20	1	.37	11	1.2
Total Connestee	110	32.12	75	30.24	52	19.59	228	27.6
Pigeon Series								
Check Stamped	166	48.63	133	53.63	151	56.97	450	52.7
Simple Stamped	3	.87	2	.80	2	.75	7	.8
Complicated Stamped					1	.37	1	.1
Cord Marked	2	.58	7	2.82	13	4.90	22	2.5
Brushed	1	.29					1	.1
Plain	10	2.92	9	3.63	8	3.01	27	3.1
Unclassified	2	.58	1	.40	1	.37	4	.4
Total Pigeon Series	184	53.87	152	61.28	176	66.41	512	59.9
Swannanoa Series								
Cord Marked	7	2.04			3	1.13	10	1.1
Fabric Impressed	1	.29	1	.40	1	.37	3	.3
Brushed	3	.87	1	.40	14	5.28	18	2.0
Check Stamped	3	.87					3	.3
Plain			3	1.21	4	1.50	7	.8
Unclassified	11	3.21	4	1.62	6	2.26	21	2.4
Total Swannanoa Series	25	7.28	9	3.63	28	10.56	62	7.2
Hopewell Types								
Chillicothe Rocker stamped, plain rocked	2	.58					2	.2
Chillicothe Rocker stamped, dentate rocked	3	.87					3	.3
Hopewell Rim	1	.29					1	.1
Total Hopewell Types	6	1.74					6	.6
Limestone Tempered Types (Tennessee Types)								
Burnished					2	.75	2	.2
Brushed	1	.29	3	1.21	2	.75	6	.7
Plain	3	.87	1	.40	2	.75	6	.7
Unclassified					1	.37	1	.1
Total Limestone Tempered Types	4	1.16	4	1.62	7	2.64	15	1.7
Unclassified	13	3.81	8	3.22	2	.75	23	2.6
TOTALS	342	99.98	248	99.99	265	99.95	855	99.9

ornamentation" from that found at "Mound A" (Hw 2). All the
22 sherds we recovered were Qualla Complicated Stamped.

Pisgah Series

   The majority of the Pisgah sherds came from the plowed soil.
Those listed in Table 16 in the secondary mound column were, like
the Qualla series discussed above, recovered from plow scars. Pisgah
sherds amount to less than 1½ percent of the sherds analyzed from
the general units. The presence of Pisgah sherds in grave fills made
it possible to attribute the majority of the graves to the Pisgah phase.

Connestee Series (Plate 16; see also Appendix)

   The chronological priority of Connestee ceramics over the Pisgah
series was suggested from information obtained at Tuckasegee
(Chapter 2). This suggestion was based on typological grounds and
the fact that many Connestee sherds were recovered in the old midden layer whereas Pisgah sherds were virtually absent in that layer.
The situation at Hw 2 clearly validated that interpretation since
Connestee series ceramics were found associated with both mounds
as well as the premound midden whereas Pisgah ceramics occurred
only in context which clearly postdated the construction of the
final mound. The distribution of Connestee ceramics by types is
given in Table 16 for general excavation units and in the tables pertaining to burials and features. The percentage relationships of this
series to other series are shown in Figure 19.

   The presence of small tetrapodal supports on some Connestee
vessels was one of the outstanding characteristics of the series.
However, other vessel forms, such as round-bottomed pots and
subconical jars, were also present in this pottery group. The general impression, from basal sherds of this series, was that footed vessels were usually smaller in size than the nonfooted forms. The
tetrapods were modeled from the base in most cases, although some
pods were added as separate appendages. Measurements made on
45 Connestee pods ranged in length from 8 to 29 mm and had a
mean of 13.9 mm. This figure was significantly different from the
mean length of Pigeon series podal supports, which was 26.7 mm.

   Connestee Brushed (Plate 16a-e). A detailed examination of 200
Connestee Brushed sherds that seemed representative of the range
of variation was made to prepare the following discussion. The 34
rim sherds in this sample showed that three forms of lips were

PLATE 16. Connestee series ceramics from Garden Creek Mound No. 2 (Hw 2). a-e, Brushed; f-h, Cord Marked; i-l, Simple Stamped; m-o, Plain (and incised); p and q, Check Stamped.

present: rounded (53.0 percent), flat (41.1 percent), and chamfered (5.9 percent). More often than not, the lip was decorated. Decoration consisted of brushing (14.7 percent), notching (41.1 percent), or punctating (2.9 percent). The remaining 41.3 percent of the rims were plain. Lip thickness averaged 4.5 mm and had a range of 3 to 6 mm. Decorated lips were thicker than undecorated lips due to the compression produced on the lip by the decorative process. Rims were most often flaring (55.8 percent), but straight vertical rims were frequent (35.3 percent), whereas incurved rims (8.9 percent) were seldom encountered.

Walls of the vessels were generally thin, averaging 5.8 mm but with a range of 3 to 10 mm. The paste was compact and hard. No laminations or contortions were noted in the sample. Temper was composed of moderate amounts of sand which had a mean grain size of 0.5 mm. Colors ranged from dark gray to dark reddish brown. In exceptionally well oxidized sherds the color was light tan.

The brushed texture seems to have been produced by dragging a small bundle of sticks or the edge of a paddle across the damp surface of the vessel. One interesting feature of this type is that orientation of the lines of the brush marks was parallel to the vessel's mouth in 62.4 percent of specimens, but in the cord marked type this kind of orientation of lines occurred in only 2.6 percent of the observed cases.

Infrequently, a plain band ran from the lip of the vessel down the exterior to the shoulder. The shoulders of these vessels were rarely punctated with circular impressions or rectangular ticks (Plate 16b-e). Only a very few sherds (Plate 16n, o) of the entire sample of this series were incised. The incisions were uniformly fine and consisted of both rectilinear and curvilinear motifs. Incisions were restricted to the plain band described above. Only one of the incised sherds was sufficiently large to identify the surface finish as brushed.

Connestee Cord Marked (Plate 16f-b). Paste characteristics of Connestee Cord Marked were identical to Connestee Brushed. The cord that produced the impression was s-twisted, commonly was two-ply, and averaged about 2 mm in diameter. Flared rims were more frequently observed than in the Connestee Brushed type, but lips were thinner. This was due to the infrequent use of lip decoration on cord marked vessels in this series. As mentioned above, the axis of the cord impressions was quite different from the brushed impressions. The cord marks were placed perpendicular to the mouth of the vessel in 92.1 percent of the observations. Plain neck bands were comparable in frequency with those of the brushed type (about 10.5 percent). Shoulder punctations were present on less than 1 percent of the rim sherds. Bases indicated that tetrapods were less frequently on cord marked vessels than on brushed vessels, whereas conoidal bases had an opposite frequency. The sample of this type used for special study was made up of 182 body sherds, 56 basal sherds, and 47 rims sherds.

Connestee Simple Stamped (Plate 16i-l). Vessel forms and paste characteristics of Connestee Simple Stamped vessels are identical to other types in the series. Wall thickness was somewhat thinner on the average (about 5.4 mm), but this variation is probably not significant. Paddle marked lips were present on about 30 percent of the rims in the sample. Rims were usually flaring (58.9 percent). The plain band below the rim was present but, like shoulder punctations, was rare. Lands and grooves generally ran parallel to the vessel mouth (69 percent), but occasionally were placed diagonally to the mouth (23 percent) or perpendicular to the mouth (8 percent). Lands averaged 3.6 mm wide and grooves 2.6 mm wide. These dimensions were smaller than those found on comparable types in the Swannanoa and Pigeon series. Some of the sherds classified into this category could be classified as Turner Simple Stamped (Prufer and McKinzie 1965; Prufer 1968). Almost 300 sherds composed the sample from which the above notes were made. The relationship of Connestee ceramics and Prufer's (1968) Southeastern series of Hopewellian ceramics is discussed in a subsequent section of this monograph.

Connestee Check Stamped (Plate 16p and q). Connestee Check Stamped ceramics are identical to the other Connestee series types except for the surface finish. The checks tended to be much smaller on the average (5 × 4 mm) than those observed on Swannanoa Check Stamped (9 × 7 mm), but had the same mean size as Pigeon Check Stamped. In fact, without the distinctions in paste characteristics, or interior polish, it was difficult to separate Connestee and Pigeon Check Stamped body sherds.

Connestee Fabric Impressed. Less than 0.10 percent of the pottery studied matched the paste criteria established for the Connestee series and was fabric impressed. The fabric was a closely woven twined weave. Weft elements were generally two-ply cords between 1.5 and 2.0 mm in diameter. Warp elements were larger in diameter and spaced about 5 mm apart. The sample of five body sherds gave no evidence of vessel form or rim characteristics.

Connestee Plain (Plate 16m-o). The plain ware of the Connestee series was usually well smoothed, but could not be called polished or burnished. Vessel forms were identical to the brushed and cord marked types, but globular, necked jars seemed to occur more frequently. Operationally, it was impossible to distinguish between the rim sherds of this type and the plain banded rim sherds of the other types unless the sherd was quite large. For this reason, only eight rims were placed into this category with any degree of certainty. Although this size of a sample is inadequate to make generalizations, it did show that rims were straight or flaring, and lips were flat or rounded and were decorated with notches. Body walls were thinner on the average (5.3 mm) than other types of the series. The range, however, was identical. Incised sherds, some of which may belong to this type, are shown in Plate 16n and o.

Pigeon Series (Plate 17; see also Appendix)

Forty percent of the ceramics in the analyzed sample belonged to the Pigeon series, which was formally defined by Holden (1966: 64-67). The most frequent type observed was Pigeon Check Stamped, which composed 80.5 percent of the series. About 91 percent of the Pigeon pottery was recovered from the premound layer. Distributional data from the eight squares of this layer that were excavated in three arbitrary levels indicated that Pigeon ceramics were more common in the lower two-thirds of the midden than in the upper one-third. This distribution indicates that there is good reason to suggest temporal priority for the Pigeon series over the Connestee series.

Five hundred body sherds, 97 rim sherds, and 47 podal supports were selected as representing the range of variation in the series. This group of specimens is the basis for the following discussion of the types present at Hw 2. Profiles of rims, feet, and vessel reconstructions are shown in Plate 16n and o.

PLATE 17. Ceramics from Garden Creek Mound No. 2 (Hw 2). a-f, Pigeon
series: a and b, Check Stamped; c, Plain; d and e, Complicated Stamped
(Napier Stamped?); f, Simple Stamped podal support; g-m, Swannanoa series;
g and h, Cord Marked; i and j, Fabric Impressed; k, Plain; l and m, Simple
Stamped.

Pigeon Check Stamped (Plate 17a, b). The paste was compact, but not contorted or laminated. Temper consisted of crushed quartz. Examination with a 10X hand lens showed that the temper particles were quite angular with sharp edges and corners. The size range of the temper was from 1.5 to 3.5 mm with an average of about 3.0 mm. Occasionally large pieces of aplastic were observed, measuring over 6.0 mm in maximum dimension. Colors ranged from light brown to dark reddish brown. The lighter colors predominated, contrasting Pigeon series sherds with the darker-colored Connestee series. The checkered pattern was usually formed by rectangles which ranged in size from 9 × 7 to 2 × 4 mm with a mean size of 5 × 4 mm. Less frequently the checkered pattern was made of squares varying in size from 6 × 6 to 3 × 3 mm with a mean size of 4 × 4 mm. Wall thickness ranged from 4 to 8 mm and had a mean value of 5.3 mm. Lips were flat or rounded. Decoration of the rim at the lip was rare (19 percent) and consisted of paddle stamping along or on the edge of the lip. Notched lips were not present in the Garden Creek collection. In the cases observed, the incipient folded rim was the result of paddle marking the lip. This practice produced vertical compaction of the lip which gave the appearance of a small rim fold or everted lip. Bases were commonly flat and supported by tetrapods. However, simple open bowls had rounded bottoms and lacked podal supports. Tetrapods were large, ranging up to 45 mm long. The mean length of Pigeon pods (26.7 mm) was almost double the mean length (13.9 mm) of Connestee supports. More than 90 percent of the sherds studied have the characteristic sheen of this series.

Pigeon Simple Stamped (Plate 17f). Aside from the details of surface finish, other attributes of the type are identical to Pigeon Check Stamped. The surface finish was produced by carved paddles that had grooves 2 to 3 mm wide and lands 2 to 3.5 mm wide. In most cases the pattern created by the stamping was of lands and grooves oriented parallel to the mouth of the vessel.

Pigeon Plain (Plate 17c). This type was identical in ware characteristics and vessel form to the others described in this series except that the exterior surface was smoothed and showed the sheen so typically found on the interior surface of sherds of this series.

Pigeon Brushed. Only 1.7 percent of the Pigeon pottery in the sample had this type of surface finish. Brushing was generally fine, 0.5 to 1.5 mm in width, and vertical or diagonal to the orifice. No identifiable rim or basal sherds were present in the sample.

Pigeon Complicated Stamped (Plate 17d, e). Nine sherds of this category were found in the total ceramic collection. Six of these were decorated with rectilinear motifs similar to those occurring on Napier Stamped or Early Swift Creek as illustrated by Wauchope (1966:Figs. 12, 15). Two of the six sherds were rims, one of which had a plain band below the lip that was set off from the stamped body by an incised line. The remaining three sherds were stamped with curvilinear motifs, definitely of the Swift Creek style. It is possible that these sherds represent trade vessels, but their paste characteristics are remarkably similar to the Pigeon series and quite different from sherds of this type from north Georgia specimens on file at the Research Laboratories of Anthropology.

Swannanoa Series (Plate 17; see also Appendix)

This series accounted for less than 7 percent of the collection studied. The predominant type was Swannanoa Cord Marked, which made up 40 percent of the series. Other types were: Brushed (17.5 percent), Plain (16.5 percent), and Fabric Impressed (8.3 percent). The remainder was composed of simple stamped and check stamped types, which together totaled 5.2 percent, and eroded or otherwise unclassifiable sherds (12.5 percent).

This series most frequently occurred in the premound midden and in the fill of the secondary mound. The distribution of this series in the major stratigraphic units indicated that it preceded the period when Connestee ceramics were made, but no decision could be made concerning the temporal relationship between Swannanoa and Pigeon pottery from the evidence at Hw 2. The initial position of Swannanoa series in the Appalachian Summit Area Woodland sequence will be demonstrated in the next chapter.

One hundred seventy-eight Swannanoa sherds were measured and studied in detail. Beyond the distinctive surface finishes all types shared identical attributes. Temper was generally crushed quartz (60 percent) or coarse sand (40 percent). The prepared grit measured from 2.0 to 10 mm in maximum dimension and had a mean size of 4.5 mm. Occasionally, a piece of crushed quartz measured as much as 15 mm in one dimension. The coarse sand had a mean of 2.0 mm. Examination with a 10X hand lens showed the sand had rounded and abraded edges, but the crushed quartz had edges that were quite sharp.

One of the most easily recognized features of Swannanoa ceramics is its thickness. The range observed in the measured sample was 7 to 13 mm for wall or body sherds. Basal sherds often measured up to 22 mm thick. The mean body sherd thickness was 9.7 mm. For comparison, Pigeon series body sherds averaged 5.3 mm and the mean of Connestee body sherds was 5.6 mm.

No appendages were found on Swannanoa sherds. Bases were conoidal or flat, rims vertical or very slightly incurved or flaring, lips rounded or, more commonly, flattened. Colors were about the same as those found on Pigeon series sherds, i.e., red-browns, but the darker shades of red seemed to be most frequent.

Swannanoa Cord Marked (Plate 17g, h). This type has been described by Holden (1966:61-63) as "Early Cord Marked." Cord impressions were closely spaced and generally placed vertically to the mouth of the vessel. In a few cases, the cord was widely spaced. The cord was s-twisted. It ranged in diameter from 1.5 to 3.0 mm. A mean diameter of 2.5 mm made the cordage used by the Swannanoa potters a little larger on the average than that used by Pigeon or Connestee ceramicists. However, the ranges of cord diameters of all series overlapped; therefore, cord diameter is not a distinctive feature. Furthermore, the diameter of the cord is a function of the cord making process and probably has nothing to do with the size of cord impressions found on the various types of pottery.

Swannanoa Fabric Impressed (Plate 17i, j). The twined fabric used to produce this finish was, for the most part, heavier than the fabrics used in comparable types in the other series. This was probably a factor of the size of the cordage produced for other purposes and not an inherent part of the ceramic technological system. The warp elements measured approximately 5 to 12 mm in diameter with a mean of 8.9 mm. Not surprisingly, the weft elements had the same dimensions as the cords used to produce the cord marked type. A few sherds appeared to have been finished with untwisted fibers or perhaps sinew, since no clear cord twists could be seen. However, it is possible that the lack of visible cord twists was primarily due to the eroded condition of the sherds. Holden (1966: 63-64) has referred to this type as "Early Fabric Impressed."

Swannanoa Check Stamped. Only 31 sherds of this type were present in the sample used in the analysis. The checks were quite large, ranging in size from 6 X 8 to 7 X 10 mm (mean, 7 X 9 mm), which made them larger than those found on either Pigeon or Connestee Check Stamped types.

Swannanoa Simple Stamped (Plate 17l, m). This type made up 1.2 percent of the total collection studied. These sherds were thick, tempered with coarse sand or crushed quartz, and clearly stamped in a crisscrossed fashion. Phelps (1965) and Caldwell (1970) have pointed out similar early simple stamped types in northwestern Florida and on the Georgia coast.

Swannanoa Plain (Plate 17k). A sizable fraction (17.4 percent) of the Swannanoa series sherds had plain surfaces. Large open bowls and conoidal-based jars were represented by these sherds.

Trade Ceramics (Plate 18)

A small portion of the total ceramic collection was made of sherds derived from vessels imported from other areas of the eastern United States. All sherds derived from imported vessels were included in analysis. This produced some discrepancies in the percentage relationships between the local and imported types as given in Table 16 and Figure 19. The degree of distortion produced was not great since the total number of imported vessel fragments was not large when compared to the locally made ceramics. On the other hand, the imported vessel sherds show a much higher frequency than they warrant in the tables since all were included.

Three broad categories of trade vessel sherds were recognized. All of these belong to the Woodland period in their respective local sequences. Twelve sherds were from vessels most likely imported from vessels made in Tennessee, and 97 sherds from vessels possibly manufactured in Ohio.

Georgia Types (Plate 18). Five small eroded sherds which were tempered with fine sand and had complicated curvilinear stamped designs were recovered from the plowed soil (Plate 18a). These have been classified as Early Swift Creek Complicated Stamped following Wauchope's (1966:54-57) description of the type. Seven sherds tentatively identified as Napier Stamped (Wauchope 1966: 57-60) were present in the collection (Plate 18b).

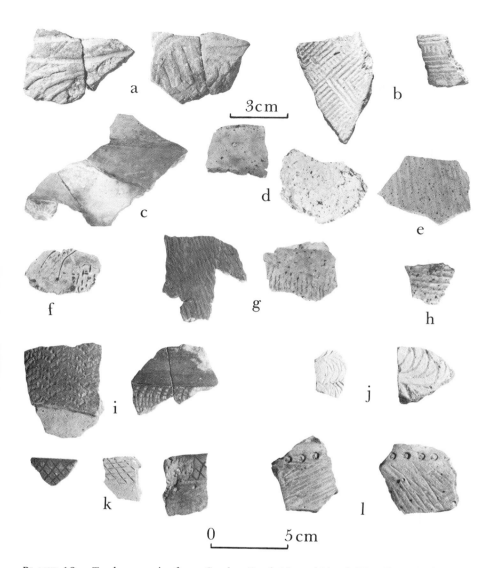

PLATE 18.   Trade ceramics from Garden Creek Mound No. 2 (Hw 2).   a, Early
Swift Creek Complicated Stamped; b, Napier Stamped; c, Crystal River Plain;
d, limestone tempered plain; e, limestone tempered simple stamped; f, limestone tempered zone punctated; g, limestone tempered cord marked; h, limestone tempered check stamped; i, Chillicothe Rocker Stamped, dentate rocked;
j, Chillicothe Rocker Stamped, plain rocked; k, Hopewell series cross-hatched
rims; l, Turner Simple Stamped—B.

The rarity of complicated stamped sherds in the Appalachian
Summit Area before the Pisgah period indicates that the influence
that produced the simple and check stamped ceramics of the
Swannanoa and Pigeon periods was not sustained after the introduction of complicated stamping in Georgia. The Appalachian
Summit Area participated in the ceramic interaction sphere of the
late Early Woodland period in the South, but this interaction virtually halted at the beginning of the Middle Woodland period.

Tennessee Types (Plate 18c-h). The 92 limestone tempered
sherds recovered from the excavations were considered to be the
remains of vessels imported from Tennessee, although other sources
were possible. All of the types present in the Hw 2 collection can
be found in the middle and upper reaches of the Tennessee River;
therefore, I have looked no farther afield for sources, except in one
instance. In this case, a highly burnished necked jar fragment
(Plate 18c) which was not typical of the eastern Tennessee area has
been tentatively assigned to the category "Crystal River Plain"
(Daniel T. Penton, personal communication). This is a type which
occurs on Swift Creek period sites in northern Florida.
    A variety of type names could have been used for the materials
in this class; however, in view of Faulkner's (1968a) comments concerning the confusion surrounding diagnostic attributes on Tennessee Woodland period ceramics, I have entered surface finishes
rather than type names in the tables. Table 16 shows that limestone-
tempered types were fairly evenly distributed in the premound midden. Over half (64 percent) of these sherds were found in the
premound layer. With the exception of the fabric impressed type,
all other limestone tempered types present at Hw 2 have been found
associated with a Connestee assemblage at the Icehouse Bottom
site, Tennessee (Chapman 1972; Table 2; and 1973). This site has
also produced Hopewellian prismatic blades and Hopewell series
ceramics.

Ohio Hopewell Types (Plate 18i-l). Almost 100 sherds belonged
to types which have been found in Hopewellian sites in Ohio. Olaf
H. Prufer (Prufer and McKinzie 1965; Prufer 1968) has intensively
studied the ceramics from Ohio Hopewell mounds and one village
site (McGraw). From these studies he has recognized three ceramic
series related to Ohio Hopewell. The Scioto series, primarily made
up of cord marked ceramics, was regarded as the utilitarian pottery,

but the Hopewell series and the Southeastern series were regarded as ceremonial wares. Both the Hopewell series and the Southeastern series were present at Hw 2. The presence of ceramics that had a Southeastern flavor in Ohio Hopewell contexts was reported as early as 1931 (Shetrone and Greenman 1931). Griffin (1945) pointed out Southeastern relationships in ceramics for the earlier Adena Culture in 1945.

In 1965 the only Hopewellian material known in the region was that found at Garden Creek Mound No. 2. However, since that time the author has recognized Hopewellian remains at three additional sites in North Carolina and two in eastern Tennessee. Undoubtedly, additional remains of the widespread Hopewellian trade network will be found in the area as investigators become aware of its presence in the area.

Chillicothe Rocker-stamped, dentate-rocked (Plate 18i). Sixty-six percent of the Hopewell series sherds were of this type. These sherds conformed to the published description (Prufer 1968:11-16) in all respects, and if a finer distinction is desired, they are Variety B. Sixty-eight percent of this type were recovered from the premound layer. Sherds were uniformly small, but six sherds showed that the dentate stamping was enclosed by incised lines. A minimum of four vessels was represented in the collection.

Chillicothe Rocker-stamped, plain-rocked (Plate 18j). Seven plain-rocked sherds, some of which had the rocker stamped area restricted by incised lines, were found. These specimens conformed to Prufer's (1965:29-30) description. These sherds were yellow-buff to orange-brown in color; they were tempered with sand and were sugary in appearance. Metric attributes of wall thickness fall within the defined range of 4 to 6 mm although the mean thickness of this small sample was a little greater than that given in the type description. No rim or basal sherds referable to this type were recovered. A minimum of two vessels is present.

Hopewell rims (Plate 18k). Three Hopewellian rims representing at least two vessels were present in the collection. Unfortunately all were quite small, and only two showed the lip, both of which were flat. All were crosshatched with fine incised lines, but only one specimen was large enough to display the characteristic row of punctates that separates the rim area from the vessel body. None of the rims could be matched with any of the other Hopewellian vessels represented by sherds in the collection.

Turner Simple-stamped (Plate 18l). Sherds so classified matched the published description (Prufer 1968:8-9). The temper was composed of fine sand or finely ground limestone. Paste texture was fine, colors were grays and blacks, lips were rounded or "knife-edged," and rims were flaring or incurved. Some of the sherds classified as Connestee Simple Stamped could have been relegated to this category, and it is possible that some sherds classified as Turner Simple-stamped should have been assigned to the Connestee group. One specimen was identical to the shoulder area attributes of a Turner Simple-stamped vessel recovered from Mound 13 at the Hopewell site (compare Plate 18l with Prufer 1968:Plate 11b). This sherd was classified as Connestee Simple Stamped. There is a close relationship between the Connestee series of the Appalachian Summit Area and certain Southeastern series types found in Ohio (Keel 1974).

Prufer (1968:9) suggested that Turner Simple-stamped types and Turner Check-stamped were related to the Mossy Oak and Deptford types of central Georgia. He, like other Midwestern specialists, has suggested a relationship that seems in error to this author. The view held here is that most, if not all, of the Ohio "Southeastern series" types are Middle Woodland types comparable to Connestee or Cartersville types, not Early Woodland Deptford and Mossy Oak types. The complicated stamped sherds that occur on Ohio Hopewell sites are most certainly Swift Creek Complicated Stamped. This relationship speaks for the contemporaneity of these ceramic series.

The Hopewell series ceramics from Hw 2 were examined in detail by a number of Hopewell specialists including Olaf Prufer, Raymond Baby, Douglas McKinzie, and James B. Griffin. All agreed that these ceramics were of the Middle Hopewell period, about A.D. 200 to 400.

FIGURINES (Plate 19a-c)

Eleven fragments of terra-cotta figurines were recovered. These fragments were divided into three categories.

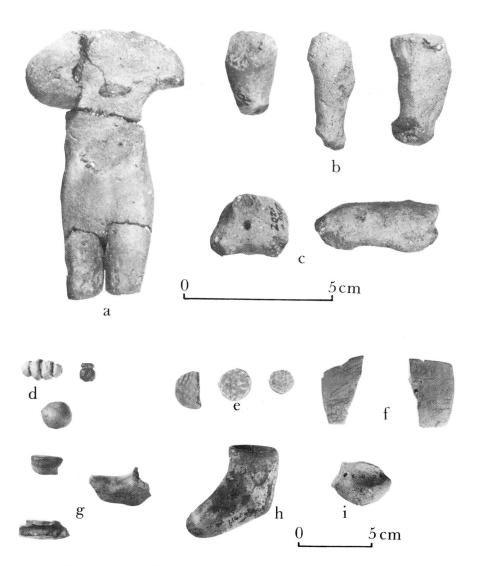

PLATE 19. Ceramic artifacts from Garden Creek Mound No. 2 (Hw 2).
a and b, anthropomorphic figurine fragments; c, zoomorphic figurine fragments; d, beads; e, discoidals; f, sherd gorget fragments; g, pipe fragments;
h, complete pipe; i, miniature pottery vessel.

Anthropomorphic Figurines (Plate 19a, b)

This class was composed of six fragments. Four fragments seemed to be portions of legs, one was an arm, and the other a torso with vestiges of legs, arms, and neck. The paste characteristics of these figurines were similar to the Connestee pottery, but the figurines themselves were made in the Hopewell style. Leg fragments, for example, showed the typical Hopewellian bent knee. The lower leg tapered gently from the knee to the foot, which was small and set at a right angle to the axis of the leg. The leg fragments measured from 29 to 40 mm long and 15 to 17 mm in diameter at the thickest point. All leg fragments were broken at the junction of the thigh and body. The arm fragment was 31 mm long and 13 mm in diameter.

The most complete fragment was a well-modeled torso recovered from Feature 30. The lower arms were missing, but scars on the body indicated that the right arm was folded across the chest and the left arm was folded across the abdomen. Scars on the abdomen showed that at least three of the fingers of the left hand were modeled. Two semicircular scars on the chest may have been caused by the removal of the breasts when the arms were broken off. If this was the case, the figurine would be a female representation. The legs were broken just below the flexed knees. There was no evidence of clothing on this specimen. The representation of garments is common on Hopewellian figurines, but not universal. The Turner site, Ohio, figurines (Willoughby 1922:71-74), the Knight site, Illinois (Griffin, Flanders, and Titterington 1970), and the Mandeville site, Georgia (Kellar, Kelly, and McMichael 1962), produced both "well-dressed" and unclothed figurines. The height of this fragment was 93 mm, but if complete, it would have measured between 140 and 150 mm. The width at the shoulders was 52 mm and at the hip 31 mm, and the maximum thickness was 20 mm.

Zoomorphic Figurines (Plate 19c)

Two specimens in this class represented the hind quarters of an animal. In both, the upraised tail and rear legs had been broken off, but the anus was realistically indicated by a conical punctation. The third fragment was a torso. It had small scars which indicated the position of the front and hind legs.

Amorphous Figurines

This class was made up of two nondescript pieces of baked clay that vaguely appeared to be parts of figurines. These fragments did not seem to be the tag ends of pottery coils.

Except for the anthropomorphic figurine torso which was found in Feature 30 and the zoomorphic figurine torso recovered from Feature 27, the figurines were retrieved from the premound midden.

OTHER CERAMIC ARTIFACTS

Twelve artifacts made of baked clay were recovered.

Two beads (Plate 19d) with paste characteristic of Pigeon ceramics were recovered from the premound midden. One was spherical and the other cylindrical with three encircling grooves. The former was 20 mm in diameter, and the latter was 30 mm long and 15 mm in diameter. A third specimen, found in the plowed soil, resembled Connestee ceramics in paste characteristics. It measures 13 mm long and 10.5 mm in diameter. At one end, a groove 2 mm deep and 3 mm wide was present around the circumference.

Three small ground-edged pottery discs (Plate 19e) were recovered from the plowed soil. All were made from Pisgah series sherds. Measurements on the two complete discs were 22 mm and 16 mm in diameter and 7 mm and 6 mm in thickness, respectively. The third disc had a maximum diameter of 27 mm and was 8 mm thick. Two fragments of what appeared to be a single sherd gorget (Plate 19f) were recovered from the premound level. These fragments were the end portions of a tabular object with expanding sides which have the general outline of Middle Woodland period expanded gorgets. The interior surfaces as well as the edges had been well ground. Faulkner and Graham (1966a:5-52; Plate 19g, h) have reported similar specimens in eastern Tennessee. The specimen was made from a limestone tempered sherd. Four small pipe fragments (Plate 19g) recovered from the plow zone were thin-walled and made of a very fine textured paste. One specimen was of sufficient size to suggest an obtuse-angled elbow form. The Valentine collection contained a complete pipe (Plate 19h) and one fragment. All pipe fragments and the complete specimen belong to the Pisgah phase. Approximately three-fourths of a shouldered miniature pot

(Plate 19i) which was decorated with a single row of circular punctates about 1 mm in diameter was found in the mound slump. This vessel, if complete, would have stood 30 mm tall. It was 37 mm in diameter at the shoulder. It was assigned to the Connestee phase on the basis of paste characteristics.

CHIPPED STONE ARTIFACTS

The collection of chipped stone artifacts recovered from the 1965-1966 excavations and the Valentine collection made in 1880 numbered 472 specimens. These have been classified into stylistic or morphological categories such as projectile points, knives, and prismatic blades and are described below.

Projectile Points

The collection of 472 chipped stone specimens contained 261 points or point fragments; of these 138 were classified into previously defined types or constituted the data for the new types defined below.

A wide variety of Archaic period projectile point types was recovered. These points were deposited on the site prior to the Woodland period, or brought to the site mixed with soil used to construct the mounds. Twelve projectile point types have been defined and assigned to the Woodland occupation of the site. The distribution of projectile points from the general excavations is given in Table 17.

Palmer Corner Notched (Plate 20a). Six specimens of this type (Coe 1964:64) were recovered. The estimated age of this form is 8000 to 9000 B.C. (Coe 1964:Fig. 116).

Kirk Types (Plate 20b, c). Four Kirk Stemmed, six Kirk Corner Notched, and one Kirk Serrated point were found. The Kirk complex is estimated to date from about 7000 to 5500 B.C. (Coe 1964: Fig. 116). These types were defined by Coe (1964:69-70) from stratified deposits in the Yadkin River Basin of Piedmont North Carolina.

Stanly Stemmed (Plate 20d). A single specimen of this type was found in the premound midden. Coe (1964:35) has used this type and its association with ground stone tools to designate the beginning of the Late Archaic period. Fowler has reported similar forms

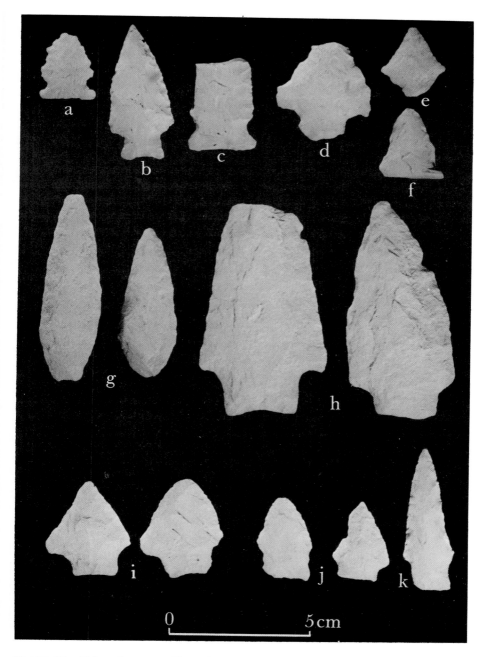

PLATE 20. Chipped stone artifacts from Garden Creek Mound No. 2 (Hw 2).
Projectile points: a, Palmer Corner Notched; b, Kirk Stemmed; c, Kirk
Notched; d, Stanly Stemmed; e, Morrow Mountain I; f, Morrow Mountain II;
g, Guilford Lanceolate; h. Savannah River Stemmed; i, Otarre Stemmed;
j, Plott Short Stemmed; k, Bradley Spike.

to be associated with ground stone tools in Illinois (Fowler 1957: Fig. 5n, o; 1959:Fig. 9c). The date of the Stanly complex has been given as about 5500 to 5000 B.C. (Coe 1964:Fig. 116).

Morrow Mountain Types. Five specimens classified as Morrow Mountain I (Coe 1964:37) were recovered (Plate 20e and f). Four specimens recovered from the premound midden were typed as Morrow Mountain II points (Plate 20f). All had "a long narrow blade with a long tapering stem" (Coe 1964:37). The Morrow Mountain complex has a suggested temporal span of 5000 to 4500 B.C. (Coe 1964:Fig. 116).

Guilford Lanceolate (Plate 20g). Three of the nine specimens of this type (Coe 1964:43) found were recovered from the premound layer. The other six specimens came from the mound fill or mound fill derived units. This substantiates the interpretation that the mound fill was derived from areas which had been occupied in earlier times.

Savannah River Stemmed (Plate 20h). A total of 30 specimens of this type (Coe 1964:44-45) was recovered. In the Savannah River Valley in the area around Augusta, Georgia, this type is associated with fiber tempered ceramics.

Otarre Stemmed (Plate 20i). Eighteen specimens of this type were recovered. This type was associated with the last preceramic level at the Warren Wilson site (Bn 29). The specimens recovered at Hw 2 exhibited the typical broad short blade and relatively large stem of the type which is described on pages 194-196.

Bradley Spike (Plate 20k). This type, defined by Kneberg (1956: 27) from the upper portion of the Tennessee Valley, has been regarded as an Early Woodland period form based on its reported association with the Upper Valley Side Notched point. Two specimens so classified average 55.5 mm long, 19 mm wide, and 11 mm thick.

Plott Short Stemmed (Plate 20j). The Plott Short Stemmed is herein defined. It is a small, short, square stemmed point with a broad triangular blade. Five specimens were recovered.

Form:
(1) Blade: Relatively broad and straight-edged. Width-to-length ratio, 1:1.5.
(2) Stem: Broad, parallel-sided or expanding.
(3) Shoulder: Generally slightly inclined to base of stem.
(4) Base: Straight or slightly incurvate.
(5) Tip: Usually quite sharp.

Size:
(1) Length: Range, 25-36 mm; mean, 30.5 mm.
(2) Stem length: Range, 3-8 mm; mean, 6.4 mm.
(3) Blade length: Range, 20-29 mm; mean, 25.5 mm.
(4) Stem width: Range, 10-20 mm; mean, 16.5 mm.
(5) Shoulder width: Range, 15-24 mm; mean, 19.3 mm.
(6) Thickness: Range, 6-9 mm; mean, 7.4 mm.

Material:
Generally made of quartzite, but occasionally this type was made of chert.

Technique of Manufacture:
Percussion-flaked with occasional pressure retouch along the blade and stem.

Comments:
This type was named for the Plott family who owned the site in the 1880s. Points from Hw 2, Bn 29, and Holden's Translyvania County survey were used in defining this type. Table 18 shows that all of the specimens recovered were found in the premound midden. At Bn 29, the Plott Short Stemmed type was associated with Swannanoa ceramics, and Holden found it on sites which yielded Swannanoa and Pigeon ceramics. It is similar to points described by Faulkner and Graham (1966a: 73) in eastern Tennessee that were associated with grit tempered, cord marked, and fabric impressed pottery.

Swannanoa Stemmed (Plate 21a). This type is a small thick triangular-bladed point with a relatively large stem. Fifty-three examples were recovered at Hw 2. At Bn 29 this type was associated with Swannanoa ceramics. The type is described on pages 196-198.

Pigeon Side Notched (Plate 21b). The Pigeon Side Notched is herein defined. It is a medium-sized triangular-bladed, shallow side notched point.

Form:
(1) Blade: Generally concave-sided, but occasionally straight-sided. Width-to-length ratio range from 1:1.7 to 1:2. The mean was 1:1.73.

PLATE 21.   Chipped stone artifacts from Garden Creek Mound No. 2 (Hw 2).
Projectile points: a, Swannanoa Stemmed; b, Pigeon Side Notched; c, Transylvania Triangular; d, Garden Creek Triangular; e, Copena Triangular;
f, Connestee Triangular; g, Haywood Triangular; h, South Appalachian
Pentagonal.

(2) Base: Usually incurvate or excurvate. About 10 percent of the specimens have straight bases. The base is always thinned by pressure flaking.

(3) Tip: The distal 6-8 mm of the blade is often rounded rather than pointed. One specimen exhibits crushing and wear at the tip and up both blade edges for a distance of 6 mm.

(4) Side notches: Very shallow, generally about 1 mm deep and 1 to 2.5 mm wide. The side notches are most frequently located about one-third of the way down the blade from the base.

Size:

(1) Length: Range, 28-39 mm; mean, 33.3 mm.

(2) Basal width: Range, 13-23 mm; mean, 18.8 mm.

(3) Internotch width: Range, 12-20.5 mm; mean, 15.8 mm.

(4) Thickness: Range, 6-8 mm; mean, 7.2 mm. The thickest part of the point is located at the approximate center of the blade.

Material:

Flint or chert. Only about 4 percent were made of quartzite. About one-third of the specimens show small patches of cortex.

Technique of Manufacture:

Direct percussion with pressure retouch along all margins. The side notches were produced by pressure flaking.

Comments:

The type was named after the Pigeon River in western North Carolina. Fifty-three specimens were recovered at Hw 2, and it is likely that a comparable number of broken specimens are represented in the unclassifiable category. The distribution of this type (Table 17) showed that 54.7 percent of these points were recovered from the premound layer. Points of this style were found in the Swannanoa midden at Bn 29 and Bn 9 and in the prehistoric layer at Jk 12. In northern Alabama this type occurs with grit tempered cord and fabric marked pottery (DeJarnette, Kurjack, and Keel 1973). Some specimens classified as Coosa Notched (Cambron and Hulse 1969:54) might fit the above description, but the Coosa Notched type shows a much more developed side notch.

Wauchope (1966:107-108) has included representatives of this type in his Medium Isosceles Triangular category and recognized they associate with Early Woodland ceramics. Gleeson (1970) reported this form in the Tellico Reservoir in eastern Tennessee under his provisional type P-11c. Here, too, they occur in Early Woodland contexts. Workers in the Tellico Reservoir have generally refrained from classifying examples of this style as Nolichucky points (Kneberg 1957:65; Lewis and Kneberg 1957:Fig. 14) except when well-executed specimens were found (Salo 1969).

Transylvania Triangular (Plate 21c). The Transylvania Triangular is herein defined. It is a large, thick, straight-bladed point with an incurvate or straight base.

Form:
    (1) Blade: Straight. Width-to-length ratio ranged from 1.2 to 1:2.6. The mean was 1:1.6.
    (2) Base: Straight or incurvate.
    (3) Tip: Quite pointed.

Size:
    (1) Length: 40-60 mm; mean, 55 mm.
    (2) Width: 24-35 mm; mean, 27 mm.
    (3) Thickness: Range, 10-18 mm; mean, 11.9 mm.

Material:
    Quartzite and felsite, with the former predominating.

Technique of Manufacture:
    Direct percussion.

Comments:
    This type was named for Transylvania County, North Carolina, where Holden (1966:54-56) included examples of it in her early triangular points. The above definition was based on specimens from Holden's survey and seven points recovered from Hw 2. All specimens recovered from Hw 2 were found in the basket-loaded fill of the last mound or in the overlying plowed soil. Such a position in the stratigraphy indicates that the type was an early style rather than a late one. This type compares reasonably well with Coe's (1964:45) Badin Crude Triangular. This was the earliest triangular point type found on the North Carolina Piedmont. Wauchope has included similar points in his Medium Triangular category and considered them to be Early Woodland points (Wauchope 1966:109-111). Similar points observed in the McClung Museum at the University of Tennessee were said to be related to Early Woodland assemblages of the Tennessee River Valley (Paul F. Gleeson and Charles H. Faulkner, personal communication).

Garden Creek Triangular (Plate 21d). The Garden Creek Triangular is herein defined. It is a long, narrow, concave-based isosceles triangle usually made of quartzite.

Form:
    (1) Blade: Straight. Only in 10 percent of the observations were one or both edges excurvate. Width-to-length ratio ranged from 1:2.8 to 1:3.4. The mean was 1:3.
    (2) Base: Concave.
    (3) Tip: Very sharply pointed.

Size:
  (1) Length: Range, 31-68 mm; mean, 48.1 mm.
  (2) Width: Range, 21-29 mm; mean, 24.3 mm.
  (3) Thickness: Range, 5-10 mm; mean, 8 mm.
  (4) Depth of basal concavity: Range, 3-5.5 mm; mean, 3.2 mm.

Material:
  Eighty percent of the specimens were made of quartzite, five percent of slate, and fifteen percent of chert.

Technique of Manufacture:
  Percussion-chipped preform was finished by pressure retouch along the edges and base.

Comment:
  On the whole, this group appears to be a larger-sized Connestee Triangular point. Individual points of this group might have been classified as Camp Creek or Greeneville points. The distribution of this type indicates that it was manufactured before the mounds were constructed. This type is considered to belong to the Late Pigeon and Early Connestee periods.

Copena Triangular (Plate 21e). Four examples were recovered. Three came from the premound humus layer and the fourth from the primary mound. These examples conform to the type description published by Cambron and Hulse (1969:26) except that they were somewhat smaller in size, barely within the defined metric ranges. The Hw 2 points ranged from 44 to 50 mm long with a mean length of 47 mm. They varied from 17 to 20 mm wide with a mean width of 18 mm. They had an average thickness of 7 mm. All were made of chert. This type was reported by Webb and DeJarnette (1942:176) as part of the Middle Woodland period Copena complex in northern Alabama. Charles H. Faulkner has reported Copena Triangular points in the Tims Ford Reservoir of southeastern Tennessee (Faulkner 1968b:177).

Connestee Triangular (Plate 21f). The Connestee Triangular is herein defined. It is a medium-sized isosceles triangle usually made of chert.

Form:
  (1) Blade: Usually straight, but 12 percent had incurvate blades and 18 percent had excurvate blades. Width-to-length ratio ranged from 1:1.3 to 1:2.7 with a mean of 1:1.8.
  (2) Base: 92 percent of the points had straight bases. Twelve percent of the points had cortex remaining on the base.

(3) Tip: Very sharp. About 20 percent had shattered tips.

Size:
- (1) Length: Range, 24-46.5 mm; mean, 32.5 mm.
- (2) Width: Range, 15-24 mm; mean, 17.6 mm.
- (3) Thickness: Range, 4.5-9 mm; mean, 6.9 mm. The thickest part of the point was near the base.

Material:
More than 90 percent of the specimens were made of chert. The remainder were made of local quartzites.

Technique of Manufacture:
Many of these points were made from decortication flakes. Percussion chipping was retouched by pressure flaking along the base and edges.

Comments:
Most of the points of this type were found in the premound midden. Their repeated association with Connestee ceramics makes it possible to assign this type to the Connestee phase. The Greeneville type of eastern Tennessee is a comparable type, but the range of variation within that type is much larger than permitted in the above definition. Both Salo (1969) and Gleeson (1970) have reported identical specimens from the Tellico Reservoir, and Faulkner and Graham (1966a:Plate 16) have illustrated comparable points found in the Nickajack Reservoir, Tennessee. Wauchope (1966:107-109) included examples of this form in his Medium Isosceles Triangular group. All evidence suggests that medium-sized isosceles triangular projectile points first appeared in the Middle Woodland period.

Haywood Triangular (Plate 21g). The Haywood Triangular is herein defined. It is a small, almost equilateral, triangular point with a straight or incurved base.

Form:
- (1) Blade: Straight or very slightly excurvate. Width-to-length ratio ranged from 1:1.1 to 1:1.4. The mean was 1:1.2.
- (2) Base: Straight or slightly incurved.
- (3) Tip: Well pointed and sharp.

Size:
- (1) Length: Range, 17.5-22 mm; mean, 20.4 mm.
- (2) Width: Range, 12-19 mm; mean, 15.7 mm.
- (3) Thickness: Range, 3-7 mm; mean, 4.8 mm. The thickest part was found to be about the center of the blade.

Material:
Chert.

Technique of Manufacture:
  Pressure flaking or decortication and subsequent flakes.

Comment:
  This type was named for Haywood County, North Carolina. At Hw 2 it
  was present in the premound layer and associated with Connestee ceramics. In general form and size, this type shows strong affinities to the Pisgah Triangular point (Dickens 1970:90). In Tennessee a number of type
  names have been applied to the triangular points of the Woodland and
  Mississippian periods. These names include Camp Creek, Hamilton, and
  Greeneville. Wauchope (1966:161-163) included all small triangular
  points found in northern Georgia in the category Small Triangular. Similar points found in southwestern Virginia are called Madison or Levanna
  Triangular (Holland 1970:Plate 17). Coe (1952, 1964) has reported
  points of comparable form in the Yadkin Basin. Haywood Triangular
  points probably belong to the latter part of the Connestee period.

South Appalachian Pentagonal (Plate 21b). South Appalachian
Pentagonal is herein defined. It is a small pentagonal point with a
straight base made of chert.

Form:
  (1) Blade: The blade is formed about two-fifths to one-half the way
      down the length from the base.
  (2) Sides: The sides of the point include about two-fifths to one-half
      of the total length and are parallel.
  (3) Base: Straight. The base is the widest part of this point. Width-to-
      length ratio averaged about 1:1.25.
  (4) Tip: Usually sharp, but may be rounded.

Size:
  (1) Total length: Range, 22-28 mm; mean, 25.6 mm.
  (2) Width: Range, 18-23 mm; mean, 20.2 mm.
  (3) Side length: Range, 9-15 mm; mean, 11.6 mm.
  (4) Blade length: Range, 14-21 mm; mean, 15.2 mm.
  (5) Thickness: Range, 5-6 mm; mean, 5.6 mm.

Material:
  Chert.

Technique of Manufacture:
  Direct percussion, but finished by pressure flaking.

Comments:
  Distributional data suggest a late premound appearance for this type. If
  such is the case, this type should be regarded as part of the Connestee
  assemblage.

Small Triangular Serrate. Two specimens, which averaged about 34 mm long, 9.5 mm wide at the base, and 4.5 mm thick, were recovered from the plowed soil. These specimens were made of black chert and were markedly serrated. One showed tip wear and polish.

OTHER MAJOR CHIPPED STONE ARTIFACTS

Small Oval Knives (Plate 22a).

Form:
  (1) Blade: Straight to slightly excurvate.
  (2) Base: Well rounded, may be slightly pointed.
  (3) Tip: Point angles averaged 60°

Size:
  (1) Length: Range, 32-42 mm; mean, 36.2 mm.
  (2) Width: Range, 15-24 mm; mean, 20.3 mm.
  (3) Thickness: Range, 8-13 mm; mean, 9.3 mm.

Material:
  Quartzite.

Technique of Manufacture:
  Direct percussion chipping.

Comments:
  Faulkner and Graham (1966b:53) have classified similar specimens as bifacial knives in the Nickajack Reservoir, Tennessee. Nine were recovered at Garden Creek Mound No. 2.

Triangular Knives (Plate 22f). Seven specimens of brownish gray flint were classified as triangular knives. The term *cache blade* is used in the Midwest for similar artifacts. These specimens were recovered from several proveniences. As a class, they were triangular in outline, characterized by rather large flat flake scars. Five of the specimens were fragmentary, but two were complete and will be described in some detail. The larger of these was 82 mm long, 35 mm wide, and 8 mm thick. It was made of brownish gray flint with light gray circular or oval inclusions. It had excurvate blades and a flat base. The corners were well defined and angular. The second complete knife was 56 mm long, 29 mm wide, and 5 mm thick. It was made of a gray flint with brownish mottled bands. The corners were round, and on one edge, near the tip, several flakes had been removed to form a deep notch. It had been used as a spoke shave, perhaps for shaping wooden shafts. These

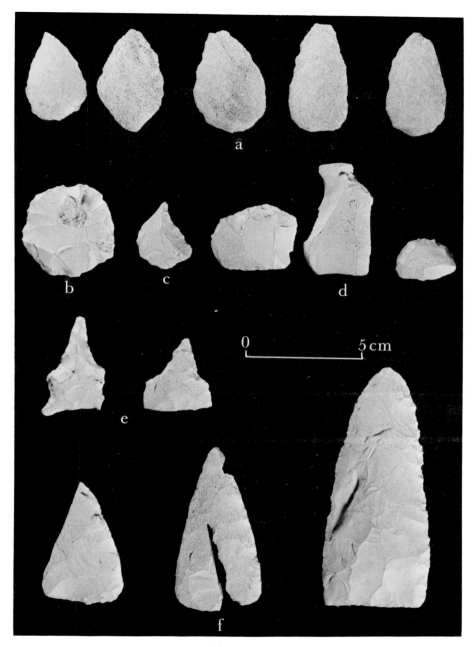

PLATE 22.   Chipped stone artifacts from Garden Creek Mound No. 2 (Hw 2).
a, small oval knives; b, disc; c, graver; d, scrapers; e, drills; f, triangular
knives.

specimens are comparable to bifaces recovered from the McGraw site, Ohio (Pi-Sunyer 1965:82), and to specimens recovered from the Turner site, Ohio (Willoughby 1922:Fig. 6). They are considered here as part of the Hopewell complex encountered at Hw 2.

Prismatic Blades (Plate 23). The 79 specimens recovered at Hw 2 make this one the largest collection yet reported in the Southeast. Thirty-three specimens were complete blades, and forty-six were proximal, dorsal, or middle sections. The metric attributes of the Hw 2 collection are compared with Ohio and Illinois blades as reported by Pi-Sunyer (1965) and White (1963; 1968) in Tables 19 and 20. These tables and Figures 17 and 18 suggest that the North Carolina blades are more similar to Ohio Hopewell blades than to Illinois Hopewell blades. The statistic "z" test indicated that there was no significant difference between the Hw 2 blades and Ohio blades, but that there was a significant difference between the North Carolina and the Illinois blades.

The prismatic blades were generally parallel-sided with one or more medial ridges on the dorsal surface. A positive bulb of percussion was present on the proximal end of all blades.

Form:
   Parallel-sided, slightly curved dorsally-ventrally in the distal portion of the blade.
   (1) Proximal section: The presence of a well-defined striking platform occurred on approximately one-half of the proximal sections. The angle between the striking platform and the blade was slightly less than 90°. Platform vestiges showed slight grinding in only a few cases. Thus, cores were not often ground before the blades were struck. Platforms measured from 0.5 to 4.0 mm ventrally-dorsally and from 2 to 4 mm wide. One complete and several proximal fragments indicated that natural planes were used occasionally for striking platforms. This observation was also made from cores recovered. The other half of the proximal sections showed well-marked positive bulbs of percussion although they lacked striking platforms.
   (2) Midsections: These showed typical ridged backs and parallel sides.
   (3) Distal sections: The distal ends of the blades showed slightly curved arcs and rounded tips. Thirty-three percent of the specimens had cortex present at the terminus of the blade.
   (4) Dorsal surface: The presence of a single ridge was noted on 18 percent of the specimens, while the remaining 82 percent had two or more medial ridges.

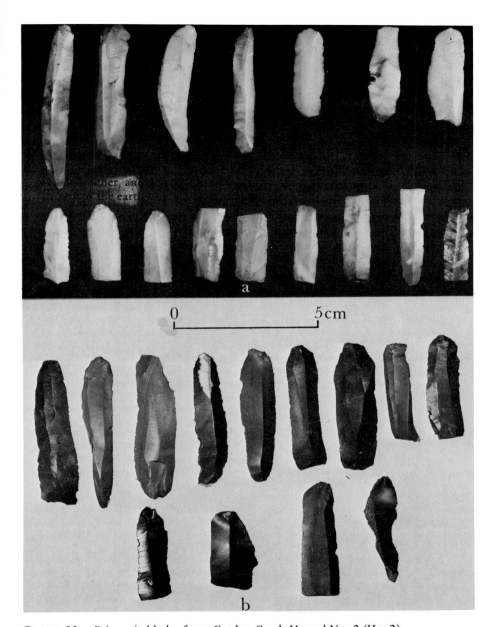

0   5cm

PLATE 23.   Prismatic blades from Garden Creek Mound No. 2 (Hw 2).
a, Flint Ridge, Ohio, chalcedony; b, gray and black chert.

TABLE 19. Distribution of prismatic-blade length classes from North Carolina, Ohio, and Illinois sites.

Class (mm)	Hw 2, N. C.	McGraw, Ohio	Turner No. 1, Ohio	Turner No. 4, Ohio	Snyders, Ill.
0- 5.0	25	2			
5.1-10.0	47	150	19	40	3
10.1-15.0	7	74	19	22	43
15.1-20.0		5	5	1	86
20.1-25.0		2		1	46
25.1-30.0					14
30.1-35.0					2
TOTALS	79	233	43	64	194
Mean	11.51	9.66	11.37	10.33	18.3
s	2.53	2.83	2.67	2.57	

TABLE 20. Distribution of prismatic blade width classes from North Carolina, Ohio, and Illinois sites.

Class (mm)	Hw 2, N. C.	McGraw, Ohio	Turner No. 1, Ohio	Turner No. 4, Ohio	Snyders, Ill.
20.1-25.0		1	1	1	
25.1-30.0	6	10	2	5	
30.1-35.0	5	11	4	10	14
35.1-40.0	7	12	8	18	20
40.1-45.0	4	10	11	21	43
45.1-50.0	6	8	8	5	41
50.1-55.0	4	3	3	4	27
55.1-60.0		4	1		27
60.1-65.0	1	1			8
65.1-70.0			1		6
70.1-75.0			2		4
75.1-80.0			2		4
TOTALS	33	60	43	64	194
Mean	40.15	39.65	45.58	39.73	48.7
s		9.63	12.04	6.67	
Width-to-length Ratio	1:3.49	1:3.70	1:40	1:3.85	

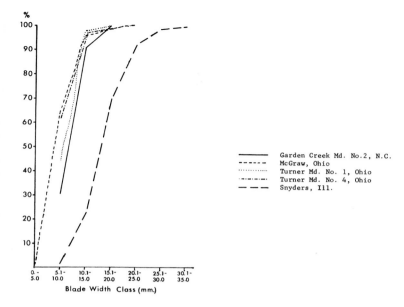

FIG. 17 (above). Comparison of width class distributions of blades from North Carolina, Ohio, and Illinois sites. FIG. 18 (below). Comparison of length class distributions of blades from North Carolina, Ohio, and Illinois sites.

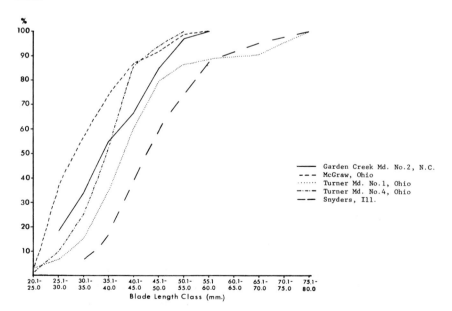

(5) Ventral surface: A positive bulb of percussion was present on all proximal sections. Crescentric ripples were present, but not well developed.

(6) Longitudinal axis: Complete blades were slightly curved toward the ventral surface. The curvature was most pronounced in the lower one-third of the length.

Technique of Manufacture:

In a few instances blades were flaked from flint pebbles which had natural striking platforms. This was observed on both blades and cores. In most cases, however, blades were struck from prepared cores. Cores recovered indicated that in some cases the platform was established by the removal of a number of flakes, and in one instance a core had been rejuvenated (E. H. Swanson, Jr., personal communication). The technique used to produce the blades must have been comparable to the Fulton technique. This term has been used by Anta M. White (1968:28) to describe the resulting blades, but she has not described the technique itself. The characteristics of the blades are similar to those produced by the soft hammer, direct-percussion technique (Crabtree 1968:457-458; White 1968:28-29; Swanson, personal communication). The striking platform was abraded in some cases; however, both blades and cores in the collection indicated that this was rare.

Material:

Black or gray chert (73 percent): This material may have been imported from Tennessee. Quartz crystal (2.3 percent) and chalcedony (24.6 percent): This was a variegated material which was identified as Flint Ridge, Ohio, chalcedony by Raymond Baby, Joffre Coe, James B. Griffin, Lee H. Hanson, and Olaf H. Prufer. A single blade in the Valentine collection was made of chalcedony.

Distribution:

Blades occurred in all stratigraphic units (Table 21). The premound midden contained the majority (62 percent) of the blades.

Comments:

Prismatic blades, although rare, do occur in the Woodland period of the southeast. In the study area, for example, they have been found at Kituhwa (Sw 2), Swain County (Museum of Anthropology Collection, University of Michigan), the Peachtree site (Ce 1), Cherokee County (Setzler and Jennings 1941:Plate 14, No. 6), and a site near Hendersonville, Transylvania County (Thomas Beutell, personal communication). Until 1970, the Mandeville site, Georgia (Kellar, Kelly, and McMichael 1962:336-355), Fu-14, near Atlanta (A. R. Kelly, personal communication), and 9 Dd 25, Tunachunnhee, Georgia (Jefferies 1974), were the nearest locations to the study area known to contain prismatic blades and other Hopewellian elements. However, on advice from the writer,

TABLE 21. Distribution of Hopewellian artifacts at Garden Creek Mound No. 2 (Hw 2).

Category	Plow Zone	2nd Mound	1st Mound	Premound	Features and Burials	TOTAL
Ceramics:						
Chillicothe Rocker Stamped, plain	1	4		2		7
Chillicothe Rocker Stamped, dentate rocked		1	6	15		22
Rims		2	1			3
Turner Simple Stamped		2	1	62		65
Figurine fragments				5	6	11
Prismatic blades	10	6	14	43	6	79
Cores				3		3
Triangular preforms (Cache blades)	3	1		3		7
TOTALS	14	16	22	133	12	197
Percent of total Hopewell per unit	7.10	8.12	11.16	67.51	6.09	99.98

Gleeson recommended that work at 40 Mr 23, Tennessee, be continued. Here, careful sifting and water screening of sediments have produced not only prismatic blades, but Hopewell series ceramics as well. These Midwestern elements are associated with a Connestee-Candy Creek component (Chapman 1973).

Backed Blades. A total of 28 specimens (35.4 percent) in the collection was classified as backed blades. This type of artifact was made by chipping one edge of the blade. Crabtree (1968:450, 453) and White (1968:93) have noted that edge wear is rarely found on prismatic blades. The dulling along one edge results from intentional chipping to convert a double-bladed knife into a more safely handled single-edged form. Backed blades are not common in Illinois Hopewell, but are found more frequently in Ohio Hopewell (James B. Griffin, personal communication).

Graver on Blade. Graver points were found on two specimens of prismatic blades. One had a graver point placed on one end. On the other specimen, the graver point was placed on the side of the blade by chipping away the surrounding area.

Polyhedral Cores (Plate 24a). Three polyhedral cores from which prismatic blades had been removed were recovered. Two of these were found in the premound midden and the other on the surface of the barrow area. The largest (Plate 24a, center) of the three was the best representative of the class. It was pyramidal in shape and measured 36 × 28 mm across the face of the platform. It was 25 mm high. The striking platform had been rejuvenated (E. H. Swanson, Jr., personal communication) by the removal of one large flake. This surface was further prepared by the removal of at least 17 medium-sized flat flakes. The striking platform, the point of impact for blade removal, showed no evidence of grinding along the edge for subsequent blade production. Cortex was present on the distal end of the core. Scars produced by the removal of blades indicated that step-and-hinge fractures were so common that the core was probably discarded as expended. The characteristics of the core correspond with those described by Crabtree (1968:457) for cores produced by direct percussion. One of the smallest cores (23 × 20 × 19.5 mm) did show edge grinding. On that specimen the striking platform was a natural flat surface. The other core measured 24 × 21.5 × 19.5 mm. All of the cores were made of

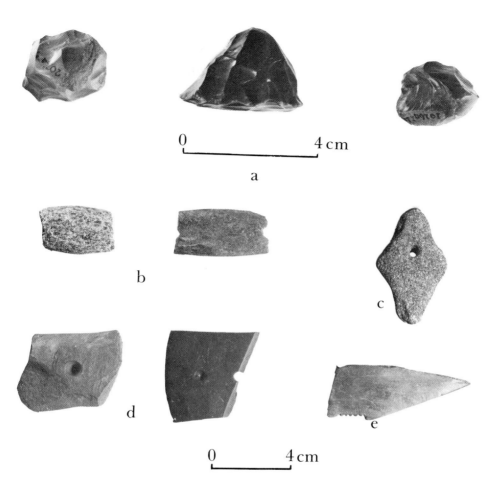

0   4 cm

a

b

c

d

e

0   4 cm

PLATE 24. Polyhedral cores and polished stone gorgets from Garden Creek Mound No. 2 (Hw 2). a, polyhedral cores; b, expanded-center gorgets; c, pendant gorget; d, tabular contracting-center gorgets; e, tabular pointed-end gorget.

gray-black flint. Comparable cores have been illustrated for Ohio Hopewell by Pi-Sunyer (1965:85) and Illinois Hopewell by White (1963:18-23, Fig. 34, Nos. 13 and 14; 1968:28-30, Fig. 8, No. 4).

MISCELLANEOUS CHIPPED STONE ARTIFACTS

A bifacially chipped stone disc (Plate 22b) was recovered from the surface of the primary mound. It measured 33 mm in diameter and had a thickness of 8 mm. The edge showed some evidence of pressure retouching and one area of slight polish. A graver (Plate 22c), made on a bifacially chipped blade fragment, was recovered from the premound midden. It measured 24 mm long, 16 mm wide, and 5 mm thick. The graver spur was 2.0 mm long and showed only slight polish from use. Five small flake scrapers made of black chert were recovered (Plate 22d). All were retouched at a steep angle along one edge, but none showed extensive use. Four were recovered from the premound midden and one from the secondary mound fill. The largest measured 31 mm long, 20 mm wide, and 4 mm thick, and the smallest measured 20 $\times$ 16 $\times$ 6 mm. Two drills (Plate 22e), one made from an early Archaic projectile point and the other from a triangular point, were recovered. Both specimens showed point wear and polish, and both were evenly patinated; thus, they do not appear to have been reworked and used as drills at a time much later than their original manufacture. Four large crude quartzite bifaces were recovered that may have been blanks for Savannah River Stemmed points. These bifaces, broken at midlength, averaged 69.5 mm wide and 29.7 mm thick. The three quartzite cores recovered were characterized by the removal of large, broad, flat flakes. They ranged in size up to 125 mm long and were probably related to the Savannah River complex; however, it is possible that the large flat flakes produced from these cores could have been used for the manufacture of the Woodland period triangular point types.

CUT, GROUND, AND POLISHED STONE ARTIFACTS

Cut Mica

The Valentine Museum collection contained several pieces of mica which had been cut. Neither the exact number of pieces nor their provenience could be ascertained. Feature 45 was a pit which had been lined with plates of mica, but none of the pieces was obviously worked.

Gorgets (Plate 24b-e)

One complete gorget and fourteen fragments of polished stone gorgets were recovered. These have been divided into four categories based on form. The plano-convex expanded-center form (Plate 24b) was represented by six specimens. This form is flat on one side and slightly to moderately convex on the other, the ends are pointed or rounded, and the center is expanded to a width greater than the ends. The complete gorget was recovered from Feature 7, and a similar fragment was also recovered from Feature 30, both Connestee phase hearths. The remainder was found in the premound midden. Two of the specimens were decorated with incised lines along the edges. Half of the gorgets of this class were drilled with biconical holes, and half were drilled with a single conical hole. The complete specimen (Plate 24c) measured 62.6 mm long, 36 mm wide, and 9 mm thick. Two tabular (Plate 24d) contracting-center gorgets were recovered from the premound midden. One, made of red banded slate, was similar to a specimen collected in Graham County, North Carolina, by the Valentine Museum. The other specimen, also made of slate, was unfinished in that the suspension holes were not completely drilled through. Two specimens of tabular expanded-center gorgets were recovered from the premound midden. This type differs from the plano-convex form only in being flat on both sides. Both were made of sandstone. A tabular pointed-end gorget (Plate 23e) was found in the area removed by the bulldozer. This specimen is similar to gorgets found in eastern Tennessee and assigned to the Middle Woodland period of that area (Smith and Hodges 1968:Plate XXXVII; Lewis and Kneberg 1957:Fig. 23a; Kneberg 1952:Fig. 103m). The gorget recovered at Hw 2 had polished grooves on one face. These grooves are similar to grooves found on gorgets and atlatl weights from eastern Tennessee. Faulkner and Graham have suggested that these grooves may have been formed by sharpening other tools (Faulkner and Graham 1966a:91-92). Four polished stone fragments were too small to be assigned to any of the above categories, but were probably fragments of gorgets.

Miscellaneous

The Valentine collection contained a finely polished white quartzite discoidal, or chunkey, stone which I consider to belong to the Pisgah phase. This specimen was 83 mm in diameter and 53 mm thick. The edge was beveled; one side was convex, and the other was flat. Three pipe stems and two pipe bowls made of steatite were recovered. One specimen (Plate 25a) of particular interest was a platform pipe comparable to those reported by Webb (1938:Plate 122b) and Caldwell (1952:Fig. 171b), attributed by them to the Middle Woodland period. Two of the stem fragments (Plate 25b) showed engraved lines and were probably similar in finished form to the complete pipe recovered at Tuckasegee (Jk 12) (see Plate 8a). A small fragment of red siltstone was classified as a semilunate atlatl weight. It was comparable to some Ohio and Kentucky specimens of the Late Archaic and Early Woodland periods. A broken pendant (Plate 25c) made of talc was recovered from the premound midden. This fragment was 29 mm long, 18 mm wide, and 9 mm thick. Faulkner and Graham (1966a:91-92) have reported a similar Middle Woodland specimen from the Westmoreland-Barber site, Tennessee. A single finely polished plummet (Plate 25d) made of chlorite schist was found in the fill of the secondary mound. This object measured 62 mm long and 36 mm thick, and had a diameter of 12 mm at the smaller end.

One complete celt and eighteen fragments were recovered (Plate 25c). Most came from the premound midden. The single complete celt was made from a water-rolled cobble. Only the bit had been altered by grinding and polishing. This celt was 79 mm long, 24 mm thick, and 50 mm wide at the bit. All of the fragments were well polished. Bits numbered 11, polls 2, and midsections 5 in the collection. The celts from Hw 2 showed the same general characteristics of Middle Woodland period forms as described by Robert Wauchope (1966:180-185) and discussed by James A. Ford (1969: 50-53). They were oval in cross section and had rounded blades and pointed polls. In some instances both front and back edges were ground flat.

Two stones were found that showed polished grooves or depressions on one face. One was made of Carolina slate and the other of quartzite. Both came from the northern part of the excavation where one occurred in the plowed soil and one in the secondary mound slump. Seven chlorite schist cobbles, packed in a tight cluster at the toe of the primary mound, implying a ceremonial cache,

a

b

c

d

e

e

f

g

h

0   5 cm

PLATE 25. Polished and pecked stone artifacts from Garden Creek Mound
No. 2 (Hw 2). a, platform pipe; b, pipe fragments; c, talc pendant; d, plummet; e, celt fragments; f, pitted hammerstones; g, pebble hammerstones;
h, cylindrical hammerstone.

composed Feature 35. Three of the stones had been cut and abraded. Several tabular stones showed abrasion and wear on the face or along the edges. These artifacts were probably used in the manufacture of ground stone objects; however, they might have also been used in the manufacture of blades, as suggested by Crabtree and Swanson (1968:50-58). The 15 hammerstones recovered were divided into three categories. Pitted hammerstones (Plate 25f) were represented by nine specimens. Five were pitted on both faces, while the remainder were pitted on one face. None had multiple pits. Three of the single-pitted specimens were similar to those described by Coe (1964:79) as Type III hammerstones. The other six specimens were fairly large, weighing up to 4 pounds. Their distribution was concentrated in the premound level.

Artifacts of this general type occur widely in space and time; however, they tend to cluster in the Archaic and Early Woodland periods. Faulkner and Graham (1966a:113-114 and Table 14) found similar specimens in both Early and Late Woodland period features at the Westmoreland-Barber site in southeastern Tennessee. There, one specimen was recovered from Feature 43 where it was associated with fabric impressed pottery. This feature was dated at 2290 ± 150 (340 B.C.). Two specimens also found at Westmoreland-Barber in Feature 50 were associated with plain, check stamped, simple stamped, and brushed pottery. Charcoal from this feature gave a date of 1325 ± 105 (A.D. 625). Quartzite pebble hammerstones (Plate 25g) were characterized by abraded or battered areas along one or more edges and occasionally on either or both faces. These hammerstones, as a class, were much smaller in size than the pitted type. The five specimens recovered weighed from 3½ to 10 ounces. One specimen of a cylindrical hammerstone (Plate 25h), weighing 7 ounces, was recovered from the slump of the secondary mound. It was made of a dark, fine-grained stone. Both ends had been altered by crushing and shattering.

Small crystals and lumps of graphite, of local origin most likely, were recovered in several excavation units.

The Valentine collection contained six lumps of hematite. One segment of a crinoid stem was found in the premound midden. This object may have been used as a bead. However, the characteristic wear around the perforation of beads that have been used for any period of time was absent.

COPPER ARTIFACTS

A number of copper artifacts were recovered from the site. By virtue of their position in the mound they cannot be considered as European in origin. A single bipointed specimen (Plate 26a), which was rectangular in cross section and measured 45 mm long, 4 mm wide, and 2 mm thick, was found in the premound layer. Artifacts of this type are known from Ohio Hopewell sites. A poorly preserved rolled-sheet bead was found in the fill of Burial 6. It was 4 mm long and 2 mm in diameter. Osborne collected two similar specimens in 1880. A small piece of sheet copper (Plate 26b), probably part of an ornament, was found in the mound slump. This fragment was 13 mm long, 12 mm wide, and less than 1 mm thick.

BONE ARTIFACTS

Bone preservation at Hw 2 could, at best, be considered as only fair. The illustrations of the burials (Plates 13, 14) indicate the general condition of the bone. Field observations indicated that deer was the predominant species encountered, but substantial amounts of bear, turtle, small mammal, and bird bones were also present.

One specimen of cut deer mandible (Plate 26c), found in the premound midden, was a left horizontal ramus. The ascending ramus had been cut away just behind the root of the M2 and the anterior portion of the horizontal ramus cut off 4 mm from the P2. The ventral surface was cut, or ground, away, exposing the root cavities. Overall, the specimen measured 69 mm long, 12 mm wide at the root of M3, 7 mm wide at the most anterior inferior point, and 16 mm high. Tooth surfaces showed no alteration.

Specimens of this type are rare, and only a few can be offered for comparison. Maxwell (1951:105 and Plate V) reported a very similar specimen from a Crab Orchard component at the Sugar Hill Camp site, Illinois. An almost identical specimen was recovered at the Camp Creek site, Tennessee (Lewis and Kneberg 1957:Fig. 10a). A deer mandible, which may represent an initial stage of manufacture of an artifact of this type, was reported by C. H. Faulkner and J. B. Graham (1965:33) from the Pittman-Alder site, Tennessee. Daniel T. Penton (personal communication) has recovered similar artifacts from Swift Creek components in northwest Florida. A

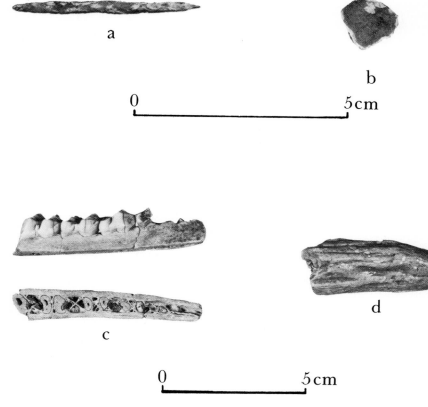

a

b

0   5cm

d

c

0   5cm

PLATE 26.   Copper, antler, and bone artifacts from Garden Creek Mound No. 2 (Hw 2). a, copper pin; b, piece of sheet copper; c, cut deer mandible; d, antler punch or drift.

total of five specimens of this type has been recovered at the Cane Creek site, North Carolina (Keel 1970). All of the above specimens are attributed to Woodland phases. The function of this artifact is unknown. A single antler drift or punch (Plate 26a) was contained in the Valentine Museum collection. This object was 51 mm long and 20 mm in diameter at the large end where it had been scored and snapped away from the rack. The distal end was battered.

SHELL ARTIFACTS

Shell, like bone, was not particularly well preserved at Hw 2. All specimens recovered in 1965-1966, except one columella bead, were found with burials. One decayed fragmentary gorget (Plate 27a, right), associated with Burial 2, was made from the wall of a whelk or conch shell. Osborne recovered two gorget fragments (Plate 27a, left and center) in his 1880 investigation. These gorgets were probably grave goods also. Gorgets of this type have been found with Pisgah phase burials on numerous occasions (Dickens 1970:118). Ten expanded-headed ear pins (Plate 27b) were present in the Valentine Museum collection. These ranged in size from 46 to 62 mm long and were from 12 to 19 mm in diameter at the head. This type of shell pin occurs frequently with Pisgah and Qualla phase burials throughout the study area. One small conch shell and fragments of eight others were recovered by Osborne in 1880. These objects were most likely grave goods. Such a provenience is strongly suggested because Dickens (1970:119) found similar small conch shells associated with a burial at the Warren Wilson site (Bn 29).

Three kinds of shell beads were found. The most common bead (Plate 27d) was made from *Marginella* sp. shells by grinding away the shell wall opposite the natural aperture to form a suspension hole. Six beads of this type were found with Burial 6, and approximately 500 were contained in the Valentine Museum collection. Disc beads (Plate 27c) were manufactured from the walls of mussels. Rectangular or square sections cut from the shell were ground into a circle and perforated in the center. Ten were associated with Burial 6, and ten were present in the Valentine collection. Columella beads (Plate 27e), made from the conch or whelk, were spherical or barrel-shaped. They measured from 13 to 26 mm in maximum dimension. The perforation was made by the junction of two conical holes bored from opposite ends of the bead. One was found in the bulldozed area in 1965, and Osborne recovered thirty-seven in

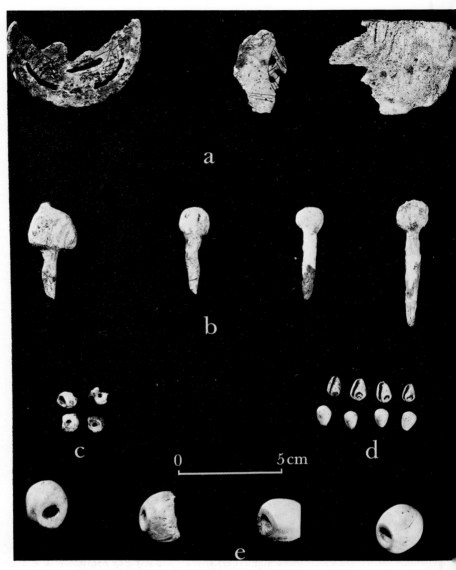

PLATE 27. Shell artifacts from Garden Creek Mound No. 2 (Hw 2). a, gorgets; b, ear pins; c, disc beads; d. *Marginella* sp. beads; e, columella beads.

1880. Beads of this form often accompany Pisgah and Qualla phase burials.

EURO-AMERICAN TRADE OBJECTS

A badly rusted clasp knife and four glass trade beads in the Valentine Museum collection were attributed to the Garden Creek Mound No. 2 (Hw 2). The presence of Qualla series ceramics in the plowed soil testifies to an occupation by the historic Cherokee. Furthermore, at Garden Creek Mound No. 1 (Hw 1) a fairly large collection of historic trade material was obtained associated with the Qualla component. The presence of these items does not alter the interpretation that Garden Creek Mound No. 2 was primarily prehistoric in time.

SUMMARY

The archaeological remains recovered at Garden Creek Mound No. 2 have been placed into several phases on the basis of their stratigraphic position (those belonging to the Historic, Mississippian, and Woodland periods) or on the basis of typological affinities (those belonging to the Archaic period). At this mound we recognized two stages of construction undertaken during the Middle Woodland period Connestee phase. The mound had been erected over an earlier village midden which contained Middle Woodland (Connestee phase), Early Woodland (Pigeon and Swannanoa phases), and some material that belonged to various Archaic phases. The most interesting and important discoveries found at this site were: (1) the mound, clearly a platform for the foundation of some type(s) of structure, was built during the Middle Woodland period, (2) the people who were responsible for its construction were in contact with Hopewellian peoples in Ohio, (3) the stratigraphic evidence allowed me to place the Connestee phase in its correct temporal position, and (4) the stratigraphic evidence brought about my first awareness that additional work regarding Middle Woodland cultures of the Middle South would prove worthwhile.

THE ARCHAIC PERIOD

The recovery of a variety of diagnostic Archaic tradition projectile point types from the premound midden and mound-fill units shows that the site was occupied intermittently over several thousands of years. The earliest tool type recovered was the Palmer Corner Notched projectile point, which Coe (1964:64) has suggested to appear on the Carolina Piedmont as early as 8000-9000 B.C. The latest Archaic tradition projectile point type recovered is the Otarre Stemmed type, which perhaps was in use as recently as 700 B.C. The time between the occurrence of the earliest and latest type is represented at Hw 2 by Kirk, Stanly, Morrow Mountain, Guilford Lanceolate, and Savannah River Stemmed points. Since none of the Archaic material occurred in a stratigraphic context commensurate with its known occurrence elsewhere, but rather mixed with later materials, no further comments seemed warranted.

THE WOODLAND PERIOD

A sequence from Swannanoa to Pigeon to Connestee phases is suggested by the distribution of ceramics associated with components of these cultural units. This distribution also indicates that the primary and secondary mounds were constructed by the Connestee folk sometime after they had occupied the site.

Before a summary of the Woodland components present at Hw 2 is offered, the distributional relationships between the ceramics assigned to these phases should be discussed. Figure 19a indicates the percentages of the various ceramic series as they occurred in the major stratigraphic units. This graph indicates a diminution in the amount of Pigeon series sherds through time, i.e., from the premound midden to the plowed soil. On the other hand, the amount of Connestee series ceramics increases. The Swannanoa series shows its highest proportion in the secondary mound unit, but it must be remembered that this unit was composed of soil dug from an old village area. Furthermore, four times as many Swannanoa sherds were in the premound midden as in the secondary mound fill. A second graph (Fig. 19b) even more clearly describes the relationship between the Connestee and Pigeon series in chronological terms. Although these percentage distributions do not as clearly as I wish illustrate the proposed relationship between that series and the Pigeon series, the earliest arbitrary levels contained the most

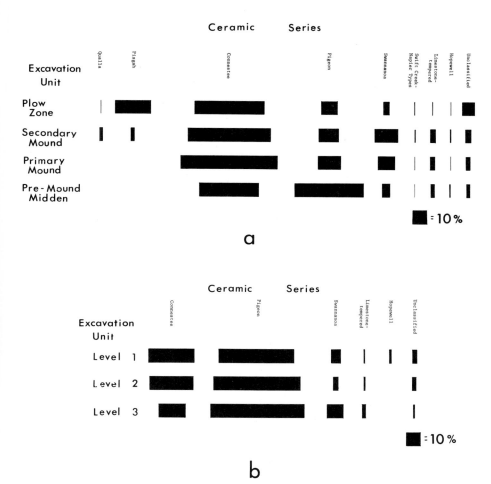

FIG. 19. Distribution of ceramic series at Garden Creek Mound No. 2 (Hw 2): a, general excavations; b, premound or Old Village midden units which were excavated in three arbitrary units.

Swannanoa sherds. A special point of interest is brought out in Figure 19b; Hopewellian ceramics except those associated with the mound were found only in the upper third of the premound midden.

Swannanoa Component

This component was represented by Swannanoa series pottery, Swannanoa Stemmed projectile points, expanded-center bar gorgets, elbow pipes made of steatite, pitted and pebble hammerstones, flake scrapers, and oval knives made of quartzite. Eighty percent of the Swannanoa ceramics were recovered from the premound midden and the secondary mound fill, which was derived from an early village area.

The presence of Transylvania Triangular points and the high representation of Swannanoa Check Stamped and Swannanoa Simple Stamped pottery types could be considered grounds for placing the Swannanoa component at Hw 2 near the end of the Swannanoa period.

Pigeon Component

This component was characterized by a typologically distinct group of ceramics, the Pigeon series. About 90 percent of this pottery was found in the premound layer. The fact that the Pigeon phase holds an intermediate position in the sequence from Swannanoa to Connestee periods will make it difficult to ascertain what other artifact types should be assigned to this culture until a relatively pure Pigeon occupation layer is excavated. It appears that Pigeon Side Notched, Transylvania Triangular, and Garden Creek projectile points are assignable to this manifestation. Expanded-center gorgets, celts, pebble and pitted hammerstones, and flake scrapers can be assigned to this phase with more certainty.

Connestee Component

The Connestee folk were responsible for the construction of the mounds at Hw 2. The earlier mound, a yellow clay platform measuring approximately 40 × 60 feet and 1.7 feet high, formed a platform for the construction of some type of building. Later, the primary mound was covered by a mantle of midden soil to form the secondary mound. Postholes found on the truncated surface of the secondary mound indicated that it also served as a structure platform. The construction of the mounds occurred prior to A.D. 805 ± 85 years.

The material culture of the Connestee component was primarily represented by the Connestee ceramic series. However, Connestee Triangular, Haywood Triangular, and possibly South Appalachian Pentagonal projectile points can be assigned to this assemblage. Other remains consisted of celts; polished-stone gorgets of several forms; pitted, pebble, and cylindrical hammerstones; elbow pipes, flake scrapers, and cut deer mandibles. Some of these types were also present in the earlier Woodland phases.

A Hopewellian-derived assemblage (Table 21) was associated with the Connestee occupation. Evidence for this association was found in the upper third of the premound layer, but more convincingly in the primary and secondary mounds. This assemblage consisted of prismatic blades, polyhedral cores, triangular knives (cache blades), sheet copper, copper beads, a bipointed copper pin, human and animal figurines, and certain pottery types. Only the figurines and, perhaps, some of the Turner Simple Stamped pottery could have been produced from local materials.

The association of this assemblage with the Connestee phase necessitates a reevaluation of Southeastern-Hopewell interaction (see Chapter 5 for further discussion). The thesis offered is that the apogee of this interaction occurred during the Middle and Late Hopewell-Connestee period, not in the preceding Early Hopewell-Mossy Oak-Deptford-Pigeon period.

THE MISSISSIPPIAN PERIOD

The Mississippian tradition is represented in the Southern Appalachians by the Pisgah phase (Dickens 1970; Ferguson 1971). During this period several burials were placed on the mound, and it is possible that the mound was enlarged. Cultural items representative of this phase recovered at Hw 2 include Pisgah series ceramics, ceramic pipes, cut mica (?), ground stone discoidal (chunkey stone), copper beads (?), shell gorgets, and beads.

THE HISTORIC PERIOD

The Qualla phase had scant representation at Hw 2—the historic Cherokee component was represented by only 22 sherds and a clasp knife and 4 glass beads present in the Valentine collection.

In regard to other sites at the Garden Creek locality the following comments are offered. Dickens (1970) and Ferguson (1971) have treated Garden Creek Mound No. 1 (Hw 1) in some detail in regard to their studies of the Pisgah phase and South Appalachian Mississippianism, respectively. My own examination of the specimens, publications, and unpublished photographs leads me to conclude that Garden Creek Mound No. 3 (Hw 3) was most likely a Pisgah phase mound, similar in some respects to Garden Creek Mound No. 1, and furthermore both had been erected on Connestee phase middens.

4. The Warren Wilson Site

INTRODUCTION

The Warren Wilson site (Bn 29) is situated on the northern floodplain of the Swannanoa River one mile west of Swannanoa, Buncombe County, North Carolina, on the campus of Warren Wilson
College (Plate 28; Fig. 20). The site was initially reported by
Harold T. Johnson as part of the statewide Works Progress Admin-
istration (WPA) sponsored archaeological survey directed by
Joffre L. Coe. This site is a stratified station. The lower levels
have yielded artifacts of two preceramic phases, and the upper
layers have produced remains of Woodland and Mississippian phases.
Roy S. Dickens (1970) conducted extensive excavations at the site
from 1966 through 1968 as part of a long-term project which will
continue for at least a decade. In his doctoral dissertation Dickens
thoroughly dealt with the Mississippian Pisgah component but
treated the earlier material only in a summary fashion (Dickens
1970). This early material, particularly that of the Early Woodland
period, is the primary subject matter of this chapter.

The stratigraphy of the site, which will be described in detail below, can be summarized in terms of the cultural components the
layers contained. Zone A contained the remains of the Pisgah component mixed with earlier remains. Zone B contained intrusive
Pisgah materials as well as earlier material, but primarily produced
specimens of the Swannanoa phase. Zones C and D produced *in
situ* artifacts of the Savannah River and Morrow Mountain phases,
respectively. Zone D has also produced a few nondiagnostic chips
of slate. Zones E, F, and G had produced no evidence of human
habitation as of 1970.

The definition of the Swannanoa phase is the chief objective of
this chapter. However, the stratigraphic relationships of this component and other components at the site are treated in some detail
since these relationships are critical to the cultural sequence developed in this study.

PLATE 28.   Aerial view of the Warren Wilson site (Bn 29).

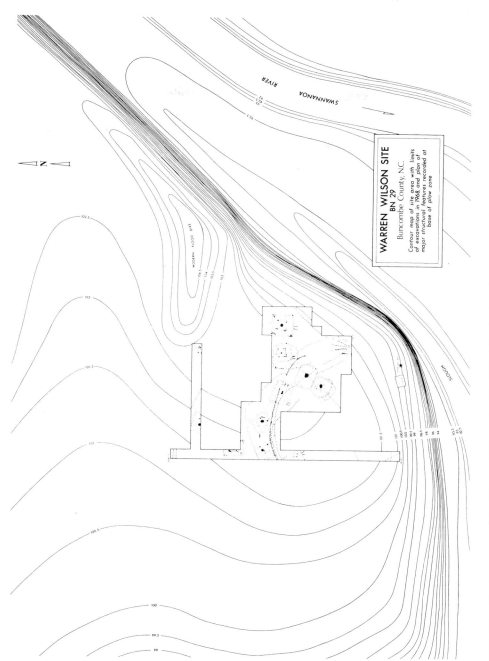

FIG. 20. Contour map of the Warren Wilson site (Bn 29). Pisgah phase houses and palisade lines indicated.

The cooperative research program between Warren Wilson College and the Research Laboratories of Anthropology at the University of North Carolina has served the purposes of both institutions remarkably well during the past nine years. The university has provided a supervisor to conduct the archaeology and teach a field methods course to students enrolled at the college. The college, in turn, has provided the bulk of the labor as well as quarters and subsistence for university personnel. The excavations conducted in 1966, 1967, and 1968 were supervised by Dickens; in 1969 by James J. Reid; in 1970, 1971, and 1972 by Thomas Loftfield; and by Traywick Ward in 1973 and 1974.

GEOLOGY

Bn 29 is situated on the floodplain of the Swannanoa River. The site is bordered by the river on the south and east and by Bartlett Mountain on the north. Village debris extends westward along the river for some 200 yards. The upper 4 feet of the deposit which composes the site was formed by overbank flooding during the last 7,000 years.

In 1968 the author collected two soil monoliths from one deep test pit (Square 120R330). One of these was prepared and stabilized by Dr. Frank C. Leonhardy and is now in the stratigraphic collection of the Laboratory of Anthropology, Washington State University. The other monolith was submitted to Dr. Stanley W. Boul, Soils Department, North Carolina State University, Raleigh, for study. Dr. Boul classified this soil as Tusquitee series, a loam which occurs in northern Georgia, the Carolinas, eastern Tennessee, and Virginia (Table 22). The soil profile is illustrated in Figure 21b.

Dickens described the stratigraphic units (Fig. 21; Plate 29) along the 130 line as follows:

> There is a plow zone [Zone A] 0.8 to 1.2 feet deep which contained mixed remains of the Pisgah, Connestee and Pigeon Cultures. . . . on reaching the bottom of the Plow Zone, an undisturbed tan-colored sand [Zone B] is encountered. Within this zone, which is 0.5-0.8 foot thick, are found *in situ* remains of Swannanoa Culture. Below the Swannanoa zone are two successively older preceramic zones [Zones C and D], and below these there is sterile river sand [Zone E], and finally gravel [Zone F] [Dickens 1970:8].

The archaeological zones described correspond so closely to the soil horizons described by Boul that apparently the archaeological

TABLE 22. Description of the soil profile at the Warren Wilson site (Bn 29).

Soil Horizon	Depth below Surface	Description
AP	0.0-0.65 ft (0-20 cm)	Very dark grayish brown (10YR 3/2) moist to grayish brown (10YR 5/2) dry; sandy loam; moderate fine to medium granular structure; about 5 percent mica flakes; abrupt smooth boundary
A3	0.65-1.9 ft (20-58 cm)	Dark brown (10YR 3/3) moist to brown (10YR 5/3) dry; sandy loam; massive; about 7 percent mica flakes; gradual wavy boundary
B one	1.9-3.15 ft (58-95 cm)	Dark yellowish brown (10YR 3/4) moist to yellowish brown (10YR 5/4) dry; sandy loam; weak medium subangular block structure; about 5 percent mica; gradual wavy boundary
B2t	3.15-4.2 ft (95-128 cm)	Yellowish brown (10YR 5/4) moist to light yellowish brown (10YR 6/4) dry; clay loam; moderate medium to coarse subangular blocky structure; gradual wavy boundary
B31t	4.2-4.7 ft (128-146 cm)	Brown to dark brown (7.5YR 4/4) moist to brown (7.5YR 5/4) dry; with common medium reddish brown (5YR 4/4) moist clay films; light clay loam; moderate to medium coarse subangular block structure; 5 percent mica; gradual wavy boundary
B32t	4.7-5.4 ft (146-165 cm)	Brown to dark brown (7.5YR 4/4) moist to brown (7.5YR 5/4) moist; with common medium reddish brown (5YR 4/4) moist clay films; weak coarse subangular block structure; 5 percent mica; gradual wavy boundary
C one	5.4-6.1 ft (165-185 cm)	Brown to dark brown (7.5YR 5/4) moist to brown (7.5YR 4/4) moist; few, medium reddish brown (5YR 4/4) moist clay films; loamy sand; weak coarse subangular block structure; 10 percent weathered granite increasing with depth

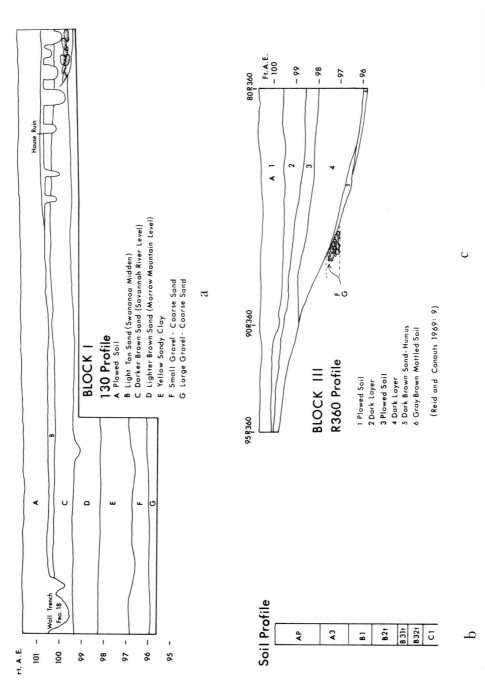

rt. A.E.

101 —
100 —
99 —
98 —
97 —
96 —
95 —

A

House Ruin

B

Wall Trench
Fea. 18

C

D

E

F

G

BLOCK I

130 Profile

A Plowed Soil
B Light Tan Sand (Swannanoa Midden)
C Darker Brown Sand (Savannah River Level)
D Lighter Brown Sand (Morrow Mountain Level)
E Yellow Sandy Clay
F Small Gravel - Coarse Sand
G Large Gravel - Coarse Sand

a

95R360   90R360   80R360

Ft. A.E.
— 100
— 99
— 98
— 97
— 96

A 1
2
3
4
F
G
5

BLOCK III

R360 Profile

1 Plowed Soil
2 Dark Layer
3 Plowed Soil
4 Dark Layer
5 Dark Brown Sand - Humus
6 Gray Brown Mottled Soil

(Reid and Canouts 1969: 9)

c

Soil Profile

AP
A3
B1
B2t
B31t
B32t
C1

b

FIG. 21. Stratification and soil profiles of the Warren Wilson site (Bn 29): a, 130 profile view is to the north; b, the soil pro-

A
B
C
D
E
F
G

PLATE 29 (above). Stratification of the Warren Wilson site (Bn 29) as shown in the R130 cut. PLATE 30 (below). Feature 12, a Swannanoa phase hearth, Warren Wilson site (Bn 29).

zones defined by Dickens were soil horizons rather than cultural middens. The stratigraphy of the main part of the site as illustrated by the 130 profile is contrasted with the cut and fill situation (Feature 141) along the R360 profile at the southern margin of the site (see Fig. 21a, c). J. J. Reid and Valetta Canouts identified six distant stratigraphic units in Feature 141. These units have been denoted by arabic numerals in Figure 21c to avoid confusion with the previously described stratigraphic units. They described the stratigraphy in the following manner:

1. Plow soil
2. Top dark layer or Midden I
3. Layer similar to plow soil
4. Bottom dark layer or Midden II
5. Dark brown
6. Gray brown mottled

These layers were given the following interpretation:

1. This is the present plowed soil
2. This is a disturbed midden layer deposited through plowing and erosion.
3. Old plow soil
4. This is the bottom midden, thought to be undisturbed and dating from Pigeon/Connestee times. The depth of this layer is less the result of refuse accumulation and more the deposition of flood sand
5. Original river bank humus
6. Mushy gunk usually associated with the mud and trash of river banks [Reid and Canouts 1969:9].

Feature 141 (Block III) undoubtedly represents a cut and fill process which occurred sometime after the Pisgah occupation because Pisgah ceramics were found in Zone 5 (Table 25). The ceramic analysis of Zone 4 (Table 25) clearly indicates that this zone was not a Pigeon-Connestee midden as suggested by Reid and Canouts, because this zone contains over 50 percent Pisgah series ceramics. A layer of gravel and coarse sand observed in the walls of the Feature 141 excavation is equated with Zones F and G elsewhere on the site.

EXCAVATIONS

The site was divided into 10 X 10 feet squares by grid lines running east to west and north to south. The plowed soil was excavated by shovel in two levels of equal thickness. This soil, as were all sediments, was sifted through ½-inch-mesh screen. The plow scars were removed from the top of Zone B. The surface of Zone B was troweled to reveal pits, postholes, and burials. Postholes, except in squares which were excavated deeper, were not cleaned out. Large pits, such as burials, hearths, tree stumps, and refuse pits, were always excavated. All soil removed from these was sifted through window screen or subjected to flotation recovery. Zones B, C, D, and E were subdivided into 0.2-foot-thick levels, except the bottom level of each zone was adjusted in thickness to avoid crossing stratigraphic boundaries (Dickens 1970:8-14).

The plowed soil (Zone A) contained the bulk of the Pisgah phase material found. Additionally, specimens belonging to earlier periods were recovered in the plowed soil. These specimens had been brought to this zone by both aboriginal digging and recent cultivation. The data recovered from Zone A and from the intrusive features in Zone B were used by Dickens (1970) in his study of the Pisgah Culture. Neither in his analysis covering materials excavated during the 1966, 1967, and 1968 seasons nor in my analysis of materials excavated in 1969 and 1970 did we find any material of aboriginal manufacture postdating the Pisgah occupation. The treatment of the Pisgah phase in this study is restricted to the remains of this culture contained in the areas used for analysis. A summary of the character of this Mississippian phase is presented in Chapter 5.

Zone B contained extensive remains of the Swannanoa phase. In some areas of the site this zone could almost be characterized as a "pure settlement" of the Swannanoa phase. Only a small amount of Pisgah phase material in this layer was found in what must be considered unrecognized intrusions. Likewise, very few Pigeon or Connestee remains were encountered. In Zone B 5,500 square feet had been excavated as of 1970; of this, 1,800 square feet was analyzed.

Zones C and D have been less extensively exposed. A total surface area of 4,700 square feet of Zone C was excavated, but only 2,200 square feet of Zone D had been dug by 1970.

EXCAVATION UNITS USED IN ANALYSIS

By the end of the 1970 season the equivalent of more than one full year had been spent at the site by a crew which averaged eight workmen. Approximately 21,300 square feet of surface area was explored during this period. As an indication of the abundance of material accruing from these excavations, the following quantities of specimens had been processed by the end of 1969: 5,997 artifacts; 366,684 potsherds (roughly 1.6 tons by weight); 12,497 animal bones; 490 ethnobotanical samples; 17,300 miscellaneous items.

The site was divided into block units for analysis (Fig. 22) because, first, the interest of this particular study in establishing a cultural sequence for the Appalachian Summit Area dictated that only those areas which had been excavated at least through Zone B should be included since only such units could be used for sequence ordering. This criterion substantially reduced the area to select units for analysis in terms of the total area excavated. Second, a very practical consideration in selecting units for analysis was the availability of specimens which had been washed and cataloged and could therefore be studied at the time. This consideration restricted the analysis to the Feature 141 materials from the 1969 excavations. The units used in this study were excavated prior to 1970. They covered a total surface area of 7,500 square feet and reached depths from about 1 foot to over 6 feet.

The 200 Trench, 10 feet wide and 120 feet long, was excavated through Zone C. One square, 200R300, was excavated through Zone D. The total ceramic collection and all artifacts were studied from this 1,200-square-foot area (Tables 23 and 24). Block I was a rectangular area with an L-shaped extension to the east and south, covering 3,100 square feet. Nine hundred square feet of this area had been excavated through Zone C. All ceramics and artifacts from Zones B and C were classified in addition to the ceramics from Zone A (Tables 23 and 24). Block II was composed of 22 squares (2,200 square feet) located in the southern portion of the 1968 excavations. In this section all ceramics and artifacts from both Zones A and B were analyzed (Tables 23, 24). Block III was made up of the area covering Feature 141 (see page 166). All of the remains below the plowed soil were analyzed and are presented in Tables 25 and 26.

In addition to the general excavation units described above, 22 features which had associated cultural materials were selected for inclusion in the analysis (Table 27). Twenty features were rock-filled pit hearths, one was a cache of twenty-five Otarre Stemmed points, and the other was a ceremonial cache. Nine of the features were found in Zone C; the remainder was found in Zone B. The

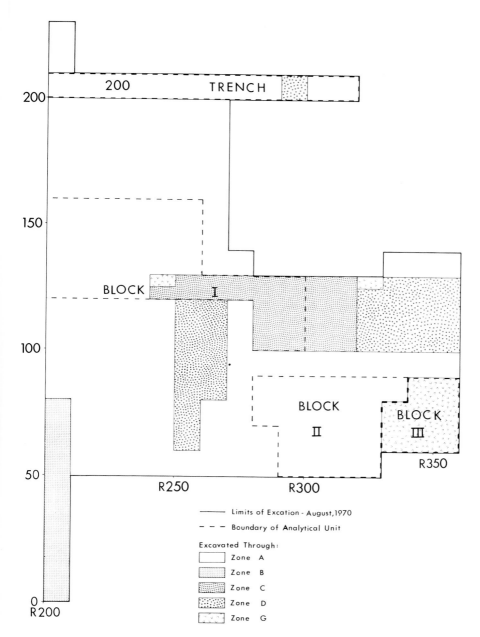

FIG. 22. Plan of units used in analysis, Warren Wilson site (Bn 29). Scale:
1 inch = 40 feet.

TABLE 23. Distribution of pottery types, Warren Wilson site (Bn 29).

ANALYTICAL UNITS

Column key — Tr = 200 Trench; I = Block I; II = Block II. Each unit has No. and % columns; values are No. / %.

Type	Tr Zone A No.	%	Tr Zone B No.	%	Tr Zone C No.	%	I Zone A No.	%	I Zone B No.	%	I Zone C No.	%	II Zone A No.	%	II Zone B No.	%	TOTAL No.	%
Pisgah Series																		
Rectilinear Complicated Stamped	2466	47.59	104	7.44			5368	40.15	98	4.13			3787	48.56	219	15.10	12042	37.84
Curvilinear Complicated Stamped	43	.83	2	.14			118	.88	1	.04			55	.71	1	.07	220	.69
Check Stamped	218	4.21	11	.79			644	4.82	30	1.26			295	3.78	8	.55	1206	3.79
Cob Marked							2	.01									2	.01
Cord Marked	2	.04											2	.03			4	.02
Reed or Quill Impressed	2	.04					4	.03									6	.02
Plain	1912	36.90	97	6.94			4933	36.90	148	6.23			2901	37.20	217	14.97	10208	32.08
unclassified	34	.66	4	.29			77	.58	8	.34			85	1.09	1	.07	209	.66
Total Pisgah Series	4677	90.27	218	15.60			11146	83.37	285	12.00			7125	91.37	446	30.76	23897	75.09
Connestee Series																		
Cord Marked	3	.06					3	.02	16	.67			2	.03			21	.06
Brushed							10	.07	15	.63			1	.01			26	.08
Simple Stamped			4	.29			5	.04	21	.88							30	.09
Check Stamped																	3	.01
Plain	14	.27					51	.37	12	.51			15	.19	3	.21	95	.30
unclassified							1	.01	1	.04							2	.01
Total Connestee Series	17	.33	4	.29			70	.51	65	2.73			18	.23	3	.21	177	.54
Pigeon Series																		
Check Stamped	69	1.33	19	1.36			420	3.15	80	3.38	6	3.77	9	.12	3	.21	606	1.91
Simple Stamped	24	.46	5	.36			162	1.21	18	.76	1	.62	8	.10			218	.69
Complicated Stamped	1	.02	1	.07			4	.03	1	.04			4	.05			11	.03
Plain	27	.52	11	.79			147	1.10	49	2.06	6	3.77	6	.07	4	.27	250	.79
unclassified	4	.07	2	.14			38	.28	7	.30			2	.03			53	.17
Total Pigeon Series	125	2.40	38	2.72			771	5.77	155	6.54	13	8.16	29	.37	7	.48	1138	3.59
Swannanoa Series																		
Cord Marked	145	2.80	612	43.81	20	21.50	334	2.49	860	36.23	39	24.53	402	5.15	535	36.90	2947	9.26
Fabric Impressed	12	.23	14	1.00			26	.19	42	1.77	1	.62	12	.15			107	.33
Check Stamped	2	.04	17	1.22	2	2.15	21	.16	14	.59	7	4.40	1	.01			64	.20
Simple Stamped	13	.25	19	1.36	2	2.15	76	.57	157	6.61	9	5.66	10	.13	12	.83	298	.94
Plain	6	.12	248	17.75			41	.31	173	7.29	14	8.81	24	.31	64	4.41	570	1.79
unclassified	56	1.08					236	1.77	307	12.93	1	.62	102	1.31	258	17.79	960	3.02
Total Swannanoa Series	234	4.52	910	65.14	24	25.80	734	5.49	1553	65.42	71	44.64	551	7.06	869	59.93	4946	15.53
Miscellaneous Types																		
Catawba Plain	9	.17					23	.17					1	.01			33	.11
Dan River Net-Impressed	1	.02					1	.01	2	.08			1	.01			5	.02
Pee Dee Complicated Stamped	2	.04	1	.07			4	.03					2	.03			9	.02
Pee Dee Fabric	1	.02					6	.05					1	.01			8	.02
Etowah Stamped	1	.02					1	.01									2	
Woodstock Stamped	4	.07	1	.07			7	.05	2	.08			1	.01			15	.04
Total Miscellaneous Types	18	.34	2	.14			42	.32	4	.17			6	.06			72	.21
Steatite Vessel Fragments	25	.48	133	9.52	69	74.20	130	.98	181	7.62	69	43.40	56	.72	94	6.48	757	2.38
Unclassified	86	1.66	92	6.58			476	3.56	131	5.51	6	3.77	14	.18	31	2.14	836	2.62
TOTAL	5182	100.00	1397	99.99	93	100.00	13369	100.00	2374	99.98	159	99.97	7799	99.99	1450	100.00	31823	99.96

TABLE 24. Distribution of artifact types, Warren Wilson site (Bn 29).

Category	Zone A	Zone B			Zone C			Zone D	TOTALS
	L-162	L-3	L-4	L-5	L-6	L-7	L-8	L-9	
Projectile Points									
Lecroy Bifurcated Stem	1								1
Morrow Mountain I Stemmed	1	1	1			2	2	2	10
Guilford Lanceolate	1	3	1	1	1				5
Savannah River Stemmed	1	2	2	2	1				8
Otarre Stemmed	2	7	9	7	11	1			36
Swannanoa Stemmed		60	24	2					88
Plott Short Stemmed		6							6
Pigeon Side Notched	2								2
Haywood Triangular	1								1
Garden Creek Triangular	1	4							5
Pisgah Triangular	5	2							7
Unclassified	3	34	13	4	2	2		1	59
Polished Stone									
Celt	1								1
Grooved axe		4						1	7
Gorget		4			2				4
Discoidal	5	2	1	1					9
Beads, steatite			1						2
Vessel plugs				2	1				2
Miscellaneous Stone									
Crude biface		1		1					3
Flake Scrapers	2	17	1	1		1			21
Pebble hammerstone		11		2	2	1			15
Pitted hammerstone	2	2	1		3				8
Metate		2		1	1				4
Pestle		1		1					2
Polishing stone	1	2	1	4		1			6
Graphite		1							2
Limonite		1							1
Ceramic Artifacts									
Bead	1								1
Discoidal	6	2							8
Pipe, Pisgah	4	2							6
Pipe, Swannanoa		4							4
Bone Artifacts									
Shark tooth pendant	1								1
Cut turtle shell				1					1
TOTALS	41	174	55	29	24	7	2	4	336

TABLE 25. Distribution of pottery types, Warren Wilson site (Bn 29).

Type	Stratigraphic Units								TOTALS	
	Zone 2		Zone 3		Zone 4		Zone 5			
	N	%	N	%	N	%	N	%	N	%
Pisgah Series										
Rectilinear Complicated Stamped	1686	65.30	528	70.40	533	51.75	1	2.63	2748	62.45
Curvilinear Complicated Stamped	27	1.04	9	1.20	4	.39			40	.91
Check Stamped	67	2.60	24	3.20	36	3.50			127	2.87
Woven Reed/Quill	2	.08							2	.04
Cord Marked			1	.13	2	.19			3	.07
Plain	151	5.85	49	6.53	17	1.65			217	4.93
Unclassified	16	.62	2	.27	8	.78			26	.59
TOTAL	1949	75.48	613	81.73	600	58.26	1	2.63	3163	71.86
Connestee Series										
Cord Marked	17	.66	2	.27	22	2.14	1	2.63	42	.95
Fabric Impressed					2	.19			2	.04
Brushed	12	.46			6	.58	5	13.14	23	.52
Check Stamped	22	.85			15	1.46	2	5.27	39	.89
Simple Stamped	5	.19			6	.58			11	.25
Plain	21	.82	7	.93	13	1.26			43	.98
TOTAL	77	2.98	9	1.20	64	6.21	10	26.31	160	3.63
Pigeon Series										
Check Stamped	3	.12	8	1.07	22	2.14	10	26.31	43	.98
Complicated Stamped (Barred-Diamond)	2	.08			11	1.07			13	.30
Complicated Stamped (Line Block)	3	.12			2	.19			5	.11
Complicated Stamped (?)					10	.97			10	.23
Plain	69	2.66	15	2.00	158	15.34			242	5.50
TOTAL	77	2.98	23	3.07	203	19.71	10	26.31	313	7.12
Swannanoa Series										
Cord Marked	16	.61	5	.67	35	3.40	11	28.94	67	1.52
Fabric Impressed	2	.08	1	.13	1	.09			4	.09
Check Stamped	10	.39	3	.40	6	.58			19	.43
Simple Stamped	5	.19	1	.13	4	.39			10	.23
Plain	31	1.20	23	3.07	13	1.26	1	2.63	68	1.55
Unclassified	12	.46	3	.40	13	1.26	2	5.27	30	.68
TOTAL	76	2.93	36	4.80	72	6.98	14	36.84	198	4.50
Miscellaneous Types										
Catawba Plain	1	.04	2	.27					2	.04
Catawba Complicated Stamped	1	.04							1	.02
Dan River Net-Impressed					3	.29			4	.09
PeeDee Complicated Stamped					3	.29			4	.09
PeeDee Fabric-Impressed	7	.27			1	.09			8	.18
Etowah Stamped										
Woodstock Stamped	3	.12			3	.29			8	.18
TOTAL	12	.46	2	.27	10	.96			27	.60
Unclassified	388	15.03	64	8.53	79	7.67	2	5.27	533	12.11
Steatite Vessel Fragments	3	.12			2	.19	1	2.63	6	.14
TOTAL	2582	99.98	750	100.00	1030	99.98	38	99.99	4400	99.96

TABLE 26. Distribution of artifact types recovered from Block III at the Warren Wilson site (Bn 29).

Category	Zone				TOTALS
	1	2	3	4	
Projectile points					
Pisgah Triangular	1	1	1		3
Garden Creek Triangular	2	1			3
Haywood Triangular		1			1
Swannanoa Stemmed			2		2
Savannah River Stemmed			2		2
Lecroy		1			1
Unclassified	2	3	2		7
Polished stone					
Celt	1				1
Discoidal	5	8	2		15
Miscellaneous stone					
Flake scraper	2	3	3	1	9
Pebble hammer	1	1			2
Pitted hammer	1	1			2
Polishing stone	1				1
Pottery					
Animal effigy				1	1
Ladle	1				1
Pisgah pipe	8	4	1		13
Discoidal	6	4			10
TOTALS	31	28	13	2	74

TABLE 27. Feature data, Warren Wilson site (Bn 29).

Feature Number	Category	Location of Center	Dimensions (ft.)	Shape	Stratigraphic Unit	Cultural Phase
12	Rock-filled pit hearth	129R309	2.2x1.9x.25	Circular	Zone B	Swannanoa
13	Rock-filled pit hearth	127R300	2.7x2.5x.15	Circular	Zone B	Swannanoa
15	Projectile Point Cache	122.5R295.8	0.7x0.6x.10	Circular	Zone C	Savannah River
23	Rock-filled pit hearth	124.75R267.5	3.5x3.0x.25	Circular	Zone C	Savannah River
30	Rock-filled pit hearth	128.5R282.5	2.9x1.9x.30	Oval	Zone C	Savannah River
31	Rock-filled pit hearth	122.8R288.35 121.75R293.5	1.5x1.4x.40	Circular	Zone C	Savannah River
34	Rock-filled pit hearth	125.5R306.5	2.1x2.1x.20	Circular	Zone C	Savannah River
35	Rock-filled pit hearth	127.5R305.5	2.5x1.3x.20	Oval	Zone C	Savannah River
36	Rock-filled pit hearth	115.5R307.7	2.3x2.1x.25	Circular	Zone B	Swannanoa
39	Rock-filled pit hearth	112.15R303.85	2.9x2.8x.10	Circular	Zone B	Swannanoa
50	Rock-filled pit hearth	107.5R301	4.0x2.5x.40	Oval	Zone B	Swannanoa
69	Rock-filled pit hearth	114.25R288.5	3.0x2.2x.40	Oval	Zonc C	Savannah River
89	Rock-filled pit hearth	64.0R260	1.8x1.4x.30	Circular	Zone B	Swannanoa
100	Rock-filled pit hearth	130R325.25	2.0x1.3x.90	Oval	Zone C	Savannah River
126	Rock-filled pit hearth	97.75R318	3.8x3.5	Circular	Zone B	Swannanoa
129	Rock-filled pit hearth	106R326	5.7x3.7x1.10	Oval	Zone B	Swannanoa
130	Rock-filled pit hearth	106.5R321	3.4x2.7x1.00	Oval	Zone B	Swannanoa
133	Rock-filled pit hearth	201.2R294.6	3.1x2.6x.30	Oval	Zone C	Savannah River
142	Rock-filled pit hearth	82.0R256.3	3.9x2.5x.80	Oval	Zone B	Swannanoa
160	Rock-filled pit hearth	91.75R262.5	2.6x2.5x.80	Circular	Zone C	Savannah River
162	Rock-filled pit hearth	113R265.5	3.0x2.6x.40	Oval	Zone B	Swannanoa
164	Cache	75.5R203.7	0.7x0.3x.10	Oval	Zone B	Swannanoa

Zone C features belonged to an Appalachian subphase of the Savannah River phase. Features found in Zone B were assigned to the Swannanoa phase. All associated artifacts are tabulated in Table 28, and the associated ceramics are tabulated in Table 29.

The distinction between the Late Archaic period hearths and those assigned to the Swannanoa period was made on the basis of stratigraphy and, in some instances, on the basis of associated cultural remains. Ceramics of the Swannanoa series occurred only in Zone B features, whereas steatite vessel fragments occurred in both Zone B and Zone C features. Both groups of hearths were the rock-filled pits. Features 12 and 160 are illustrated (Plates 30, 31) to show the general appearance of this hearth type. As a class the hearths ranged in size from 5.7 × 3.7 × 1.1 feet to 1.5 × 1.4 × 0.4 feet. The mean size was about 3.0 × 2.3 × 0.4 feet, which also closely approximated the median of 3.0 × 2.2 × 0.4 feet. The rocks used to fill the pits were local river cobbles of schists and quartzite. Many were fire-cracked and heat-spalled. The sparse amount of bone recovered from these features was either calcined or very poorly preserved. Charcoal was abundant in some hearths but virtually absent in others.

Feature 15 (Plate 32) was a cache of 25 Otarre Stemmed points found in Zone C. This cache was located near a number of rock-filled pit hearths and could have been associated with one of them. The field notes indicated that Feature 164 (Plate 33) was found in the lower part of Zone B. It was described as an ellipsoidal stain of burned clay and pebbles containing a gorget and cord marked sherds lying on top of a deposit of yellow and red ochres.

Features 31 and 34 were dated by radiocarbon determination. Feature 31, a circular, rock-filled hearth measuring 1.5 × 1.4 × 0.4 feet, was one of the few features from Zone C that contained both sufficient carbon for dating purposes and associated diagnostic stone tools—in this case a Savannah River Stemmed projectile point. The age of the carbon from this feature was determined to be 4865 ± 280 years, or 2915 ± 280 B.C. (GX2274). Although Feature 34 contained no diagnostic chipped stone implements, it did contain two hammerstones, a pestle, and sufficient carbon for Carbon 14 analysis. Since the feature was contained in Zone C, we felt that it would give an age for that zone and consequently the Savannah River component which was found there. The age determined for Feature 32 was 3515 ± 140 years, or 1565 ± 140 years B.C.

TABLE 28. Distribution of artifact types, Warren Wilson site (Bn 29).

Category		13	15	22	23	30	31	34	35	36	39	50	100	129	130	133	142	160	164	TOTALS
													Feature Number							
Projectile Points																				
	Swannanoa Stemmed	1									1						1			3
	Otarre Stemmed		25										4	1						30
	Savannah River Stemmed						1							2						3
	Lecroy									1										1
	Unclassified																	1		2
Polished Stone																				
	Grooved Axe													1						1
	Gorget																		1	1
Miscellaneous Stone																				
	Pigment																		2	2
	Pitted Hammer			1	1			1			2	2								7
	Pebble Hammer				3			1				2		4						10
	Pestle					1														1
	Metate	1												1	1	1				5
	Flake Scraper								1											1
	Crude Biface										1									1
Pottery																				
	Swannanoa Pipe										1									1

TABLE 29. Distribution of pottery types recovered from some features at the Warren Wilson site (Bn 29).

Type	Feature Number												Total
	12	13	36	69	89	126	129	130	142	160	162	164	
Pisgah series													
Rectilinear Complicated Stamped	2												2
Swannanoa series													
Cord Marked	36	15	9	10	67	50	63	5	10		2	5	272
Fabric Impressed		2											2
Check Stamped					1								1
Simple Stamped		2	2	7		7	4						22
Plain	2	14		4		38	87	3		2	2		152
Unclassified		4				15			5	2	1	3	30
Steatite vessel fragments	1	1		1	2				1				6
TOTAL	41	38	11	22	70	110	154	8	16	4	5	8	487

PLATE 31 (above).   Feature 160, a Savannah River phase hearth, Warren Wilson site (Bn 29).   PLATE 32 (below).   Feature 15, a cache of 25 Otarre Stemmed points found in Zone C, Warren Wilson site (Bn 29).

PLATE 33. Feature 164, a "ceremonial cache," consisting of an unfinished gorget, burned clay, pebbles, Swannanoa series sherds, and yellow and red ochre, found in Zone B, Warren Wilson site (Bn 29).

These dates from features in Zone C may bracket the Savannah River occupation at Warren Wilson. Although the 2915 ± 280 B.C. date from Feature 31 seems early to me for this phase, it falls within one standard deviation of the 2750 ± 150 B.C. (M-1279) date for the phase at Stallings Island, Georgia. Furthermore the Warren Wilson date is in agreement with the Savannah River date of 1780 ± 150 B.C. (M-1278) at Stallings Island (Bullen and Greene 1970:11-12).

To be sure, many additional dates for the Savannah River phase in the Southern Appalachians are needed before we can fully understand its chronological duration.

ARTIFACTS

The total specimen collection from the site amounted to more than 402,968 items when the cataloging of the 1969 season's work was completed. Over 90 percent of this collection was potsherds. In the present analysis only about 10 percent of this collection was potsherds. In the present analysis only about 10 percent of the total collection has been utilized. The reasons for restricting the size of the sample and the nature of the units from which the sample was taken were discussed earlier. The excavation units chosen for study produced about 37,200 cultural items including more than 36,700 vessel fragments. The analysis of these specimens and their distribution indicates that the distribution of artifact types correlates well with the stratigraphic units previously described.

CERAMICS

A small fraction of the total sherds could be classified as fragments of trade vessels. The pottery types representing imported vessels are shown in Tables 23 and 25. With the possible exception of the Catawba Complicated Stamped, Catawba Plain, and Dan River Net Impressed types, the other trade wares were related to the Pisgah occupation of Bn 29. The Catawba and Dan River series are found on the Carolina Piedmont in association with Euro-American trade goods. Their earliest appearance, however, may predate contact with the whites. On the other hand, the repeated association of Pisgah ceramics with Pee Dee series ceramics at Bn 29 and at Hw 1, as well as the presence of Pisgah-like ceramics at the

Pee Dee type site (Reid 1967:Plate VIII), suggests the contemporaneity of these series. The Etowah and Woodstock Stamped types recovered at the site indicate contact with the south during the early part of the Pisgah phase. The relations shared by the Pisgah culture with other cultures have been adequately discussed by Dickens (1970:58-78).

Catawba Series

A total of 35 Catawba sherds were present in the sample studied. All had the characteristic crushed steatite temper. Thirty-four of the sherds were polished Plain ware. There was one complicated stamped sherd of the "sloppy" variety which constitutes the bulk of the Catawba Complicated Stamped type (Keeler 1971).

Dan River Net Impressed

J. L. Coe and Ernest Lewis (1952) reported Dan River Net Impressed as the principal type in the ceramic assemblage of the Saura (Cheraw) tribe of the upper Carolina Piedmont. The surface finish of this grit tempered ware usually shows not only the mesh of the knotted net, but frequently impressions of the knots as well. The earliest appearance of this type is probably in the 16th century A.D., thus making it contemporary with the latest Pisgah ceramics. Only nine sherds referable to this type were recovered. Six of them were found in the plowed soil.

Pee Dee Series

Twenty-nine Pee Dee series sherds were recovered. J. J. Reid (1967) described the series from specimens excavated from Town Creek Indian Mound (Mg 2), Montgomery County, North Carolina. The compact, granular, "sugary" appearing paste, the fabric impressions, and the stamped motifs of the Warren Wilson specimens are quite similar in detail to those from the type site. In addition, specialized attributes typical of the Pee Dee ceramics such as punctates near the rim and appliqued rosettes surrounded by punctates were present on the Bn 29 specimens (*vide* Dickens 1970:Plate 23).

Etowah Stamped

The Etowah Stamped type is represented by two sherds, both with the "nested diamond" motif (Wauchope 1966:64).

Woodstock Stamped

Twenty-three sherds referable to the Woodstock Stamped type were recovered. All but one were found in the plowed soil. The single exception was found in Zone B in the 200 Trench. The Woodstock period is considered to predate the Etowah period in Georgia. A radiocarbon date of AD 928 ± 40 was associated with Woodstock ceramics at 9-Mu-103 (Hally 1970).

Pisgah Series (Plate 34)

The Pisgah series, divided into seven types, constituted 75 percent of the pottery studied from Zone A in the 200 Trench and Blocks I and II and 71.86 percent of that found in Block III (Tables 23 and 25). Only two sherds of this series occurred in the features analyzed. Pisgah series ceramics occurred in Zone B in percentages as high as 30.76 (Block II), but these sherds are considered intrusive. The high frequency of the series in all zones in Block III (Feature 141) indicates that the stratigraphic situation there was not comparable to the rest of the site.

Roy S. Dickens (1970:27-88 and 273-274) has described the series in great detail, and his summary of the series' characteristics has been quoted herein (page 47). In his study of type frequencies within the series, he analyzed six house units, fifty 10 × 10 feet squares of plowed soil, and all burials and features excavated through 1968. The frequencies of types showed no significant differences from one unit to the next. Such a distribution suggests that Pisgah occupation at Bn 29 was relatively brief, or that surface finish does not reflect temporal distinctions, at least during the Pisgah occupation of the site. The present analysis in no way alters this conclusion. Of the 36,710 sherds included in this analysis, 27,062 (73.7 percent) are referable to the Pisgah series.

Connestee Series (Plate 35a-c)

At the Warren Wilson site, Connestee series sherds constituted only 0.54 percent of the pottery analyzed from areas outside of Block III, where it had a frequency of 3.63 percent. The types belonging to this series present at Bn 29 were the same as those described in Chapter 3. Connestee Plain was the most common type (41.5 percent), followed by Connestee Simple Stamped (20.5 percent), Connestee Cord Marked (18.7 percent) and Connestee Brushed (14.5 percent). Connestee Check Stamped,

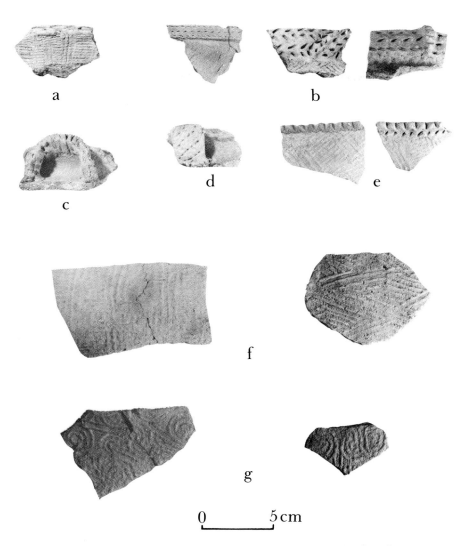

a

b

c

d

e

f

g

0   5 cm

PLATE 34.   Ceramics from the Warren Wilson site (Bn 29). Pisgah series:
a, thickened rim; b, collared rims; c, appliqued arch; d, loop handle;
e, straight rims; f, Rectilinear Stamped; g, Curvilinear Stamped.

0   10 cm

PLATE 35. Ceramics from the Warren Wilson site (Bn 29). a-c, Connestee series: a, Simple Stamped; b, Check Stamped; c, Plain; d and e, Pigeon series: d, Check Stamped; e, Plain; f-i, Swannanoa series: f, Cord Marked; g, Fabric Impressed; h, Plain; i, Simple Stamped.

Connestee Fabric Impressed, and unclassifiable sherds made up the remaining 4.8 percent of the Connestee series sample.

Pigeon Series (Plate 35d, e)

The Pigeon series was the third most numerous ware in the study collection. The ubiquitous Pigeon Check Stamped type made up 44.8 percent of the series sample. The remainder was composed of Pigeon Simple Stamped (15 percent), Pigeon Plain (33.9 percent), Pigeon Complicated Stamped (2.7 percent), and unclassified sherds (3.6 percent). Like the Connestee ceramics, Pigeon series sherds found at Bn 29 were identical to their counterparts elsewhere in the Southern mountains.

Pigeon Complicated Stamped was similar to the complicated stamped sherds of this series found at Hw 2. However, no good Swift Creek-like motifs were present at Bn 29. Instead, the designs were made up of triangles bound by grids, converging ladder-like motifs surrounded by parallel lines, or variations on these themes.

Swannanoa Series (Plate 35f-i)

The Swannanoa series, earliest of the Woodland phases, was characterized by heavy, thick, grit or sand tempered pottery. The ceramic series that represents this phase was named for the Swannanoa River, which flows by the Warren Wilson site. The types composing this series are described in the Appendix.

My observation (based on the Hw 2 sample of Swannanoa pottery) that the series was composed of very thick walled vessels was supported by the measurements made on 195 body sherds from Warren Wilson. Wall thickness in this sample ranged from 6 to 12 mm with a mean thickness of 8.1 mm. Temper was composed of crushed quartz grit (56 percent of the sample) and coarse sand (44 percent of the sample). Many sherds seemed to have been tempered with a mixture of both kinds of aplastic. However, in such instances these sherds were classified as grit tempered since the large pieces of quartz were more apparent. The size of the crushed quartz ranged from 3 to 19 mm. One particularly large piece of crushed quartz, measuring 17 X 12 X 7 mm, was noted in one sherd. The mean size of the sand temper was 2.1 mm. This tempering material has a size range of 1.5 to 3.0 mm. Colors were red, reddish brown, and light brown.

Vessel forms were restricted to hemispherical bowls and conoidal jars with vertical or slightly incurved rims. No elaboration in rim treatment was present. Although a few lips were notched, or had cord impressions on them, most were rounded or flattened. Decoration was almost nonexistent; less than ten sherds in the sample of more than 5,000 were incised. The incising was poorly executed. The lines were either narrow or wide, but always shallow. Usually they extended only a short distance down the rim. In one instance, a series of incised X's formed a band around the rim of a vessel.

Swannanoa Cord Marked (Plate 35f). The cord used to finish the surface of this type was usually thick, ranging from 1 to 3.5 mm in diameter with a mean of 2.1 mm, although some was a very fine two-ply cord less than 1 mm in diameter. The cord was generally applied at a right angle to the mouth of the vessel. Occasionally it was placed diagonally. This type made up approximately 58 percent of the series.

Swannanoa Fabric Impressed (Plate 35g). About 2 percent of the Swannanoa pottery was fabric impressed. Dickens (1970:16) stated that the fabric marked type was second only to the cord marked variety in frequency. However, analysis of the selected sample did not indicate this to be the case. Possibly the difference between Dickens' observations and the present analysis was due to the nature of the samples studied. Most of the former was from the plowed soil, while the latter sample included a great amount of material from Zone B. The distribution of types found associated with features (Table 23) suggests that fabric impressed sherds were rare in this context also.

Swannanoa Plain (Plate 35h). Sherds of a red-brown to tan-colored, smooth-surfaced, conoidal-based jar or hemispherical bowl made up about 10 percent of the Swannanoa sherds. Swannanoa Plain was second only to Swannanoa Cord Marked in frequency.

Swannanoa Simple Stamped (Plate 35i). A simple stamped type of Swannanoa pottery was present. The land was occasionally as wide as 7 mm, but generally averaged 2 to 3 mm wide. Groove width was of a size similar to the land width. Grooves were always deep, as much as 2.5 mm, but averaged 1.5 mm. The application of the carved paddle was haphazard. Many sherds appeared to have been purposely cross-stamped.

Steatite Vessels

A large number (763) of fragments of carved steatite vessels and one complete bowl were recovered. The majority of the fragments was recovered from Zone B (48 percent). Zone A produced the second largest number (32 percent). The remainder (20 percent) was from Zone C. The high frequency of steatite vessel fragments was the result of sample size rather than a measure of true frequency. If the number of stone vessel fragments from each zone is divided by the number of square feet excavated of that zone, then a frequency of vessel fragments per square foot results. Such a manipulation produced the following frequencies: Zone A, 0.02; Zone B, 0.05; Zone C, 1.3. These frequencies are probably more accurate than the percentage of the total count. There is little doubt that the majority of the steatite vessels was made by the Savannah River folk, but the manufacture of this type of container probably continued for some time after the introduction of ceramic technology.

The stone vessels at Bn 29 ranged in capacity from about 2 to 3 gallons down to 2 quarts. Walls were quite thick, 10 to 25 mm, and bottoms were even thicker, ranging from 18 to 40 mm. Rims were vertical and lips predominantly rounded, although some were flat. Appendages consisted of lip flanges or knobby lugs located below the rim. Decoration was rare, occurring only as incised lines forming V's across the lip.

A single complete vessel (Plate 36) was recovered from Zone C. It was a small pot with a rounded bottom and not well finished, for the exterior and interior still retain the cut marks of the initial shaping. This vessel was 111 mm in height and had a maximum diameter of 144 mm and a minimum diameter of 118 mm. Wall thickness varied considerably (12 to 22 mm) from place to place on the vessel. The rounded base was 36 mm thick.

OTHER CERAMIC ARTIFACTS

A single clay bead was found in the plowed soil of Square 60R340. This specimen was disc-shaped, 15 mm in diameter, and 9 mm thick. The hole, 1.5 mm in diameter, was made prior to firing. This specimen belonged to that class of artifacts described by Dickens (1970:107) as Pisgah clay beads.

The torso of a zoomorphic figurine was recovered from Block III (Square 70R350, Zone E). This fragment was similar to the clay

3 cm

PLATE 36. Complete steatite vessel from the Warren Wilson site (Bn 29), Zone C.

deer effigies described by Dickens (1970:106-107) for the Pisgah
Culture. This specimen was 35 mm long and 13 mm in diameter.
The hind legs seem to be virtually complete. They were quite short
and knobby, measuring only 5 mm long. A very short tail, 1 mm
long, was raised at an angle of 45° from the axis of the body. It did
not resemble the animal figurines recovered at Hw 2. A fragment of
what appeared to be a ladle with two separate bowls was recovered
from Zone B in Block III. The paste and general surface finish suggested Pisgah ceramics. A total of 18 clay discoidals, all made from
sherds, was in the sample analyzed. The sizes of these discoidals
were quite variable, ranging in diameter from 50 mm to as small as
10 mm. The mean diameter was 27.5 mm and the mode about
30 mm. Thickness, which was a function of the wall dimension of
the vessel, ranged from 4 to 9 mm. Dickens (1970:106) has discussed these objects and suggested that they were used as gaming or
counting pieces. It should be pointed out that ceramic discs have
not been found in contexts earlier than the Pisgah period in the
study area.

Of the 28 pottery pipes in the sample, 24 were Pisgah phase pipes
(Plate 37a-c); the others were Swannanoa pipes (Plate 37d, e), two
of which were reasonably complete specimens. The characteristics
of Pisgah pipes have been summarized as follows:

> These are small elbow-shaped pipes on which the stems are usually slightly
> shorter than the bowls. The bowls flare at the top and may be decorated
> with ridges, incised lines or nodes. Some pipes have highly burnished sur-
> faces while others are only lightly smoothed. Tempering particles are of
> smaller size and are less abundant in the clay used to make pipes than in
> the clay used for pots [Dickens 1970:106].

The Swannanoa pipes are entirely different forms. First, they are
thick-walled. Second, the surface was not burnished nor are knobs
or other embellishments present. Finally, and more distinctly, they
are tubular rather than elbow-shaped. The two virtually complete
pipes were quite similar in form and length. The larger of these was
80 mm long and had a maximum diameter of 40.5 mm about mid-
way down the tube. It was well smoothed, but not nearly as well
as the Pisgah type. The smaller pipe was 75 mm long. The widest
point (28 mm) was at the bowl orifice. The surface seems to have
been marked with evenly spaced cord impressions. Other Swannanoa pipes were represented by thick bowl fragments.

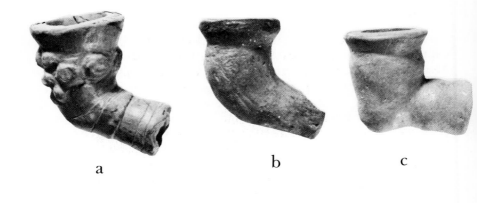

a   b   c

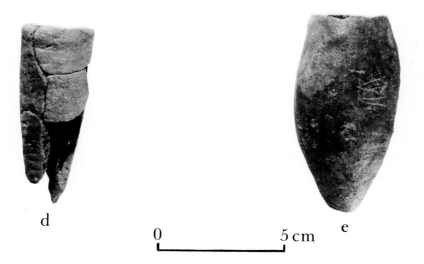

d

0   5 cm

e

PLATE 37.   Ceramic pipes from the Warren Wilson site (Bn 29). a, b, and c,
Pisgah phase elbow pipes; d and e, Swannanoa phase tubular pipes.

All of the Swannanoa pipes were found in Zone B. The Pisgah pipes were restricted to Zone A on the main part of the site and were found in the plowed deposits of Block III.

CHIPPED STONE ARTIFACTS

Stone artifacts produced by percussion or pressure flaking were common at Bn 29. In the sample analyzed such objects were placed in a small number of major categories: projectile points, crude bifaces, and flake scrapers. The distribution of projectile point types (Table 24) followed a much neater pattern in terms of the stratigraphic sequence than expected, especially in view of the great amount of aboriginal digging and other disturbances that originated in what is now plowed soil and in Zone B.

Projectile Points

Types such as Pisgah Triangular, Haywood Triangular, Garden Creek Triangular, and Pigeon Side Notched were found in Zone A or in the upper 0.2 foot of Zone B; Plott Short Stemmed and Swannanoa Stemmed were virtually restricted to Zone B; but the Savannah River Stemmed type had a much broader distribution, occurring in Zones A, B, and C. The Otarre Stemmed point was repeatedly associated with rock-filled pit hearths in Zone C. A small number of earlier point types were recovered. These included Lecroy Bifurcated Stem, Morrow Mountain I Stemmed, and Guilford Lanceolate types.

Lecroy Bifurcated Stem (Plate 38a). The Lecroy Bifurcated Stem type, as described by Kneberg (1956:27-28) from eastern Tennessee material, was suggested to have a temporal range from ca. 1500 B.C. to A.D. 500. However, more controlled work in other areas now indicates a much earlier date for the type. Cambron and Hulse (1969:72) have suggested a date prior to 5000 B.C. for this form in northern Alabama. Broyles (1968:11) recovered the type at the St. Albans site, West Virginia, in Zones 6 and 8. Zone 6 was dated to 6300 ± 100 B.C. Jefferson Chapman's 1974 excavations at Rose Island, Tennessee (40Mr44), have produced dates of 6850 ± 270 years B.C., 6750 ± 360 years B.C., and 6110 ± 350 years B.C. for early bifurcated base points (personal communication).

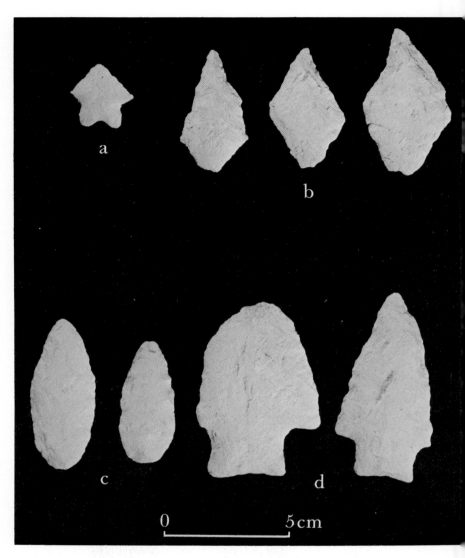

PLATE 38.   Chipped stone projectile points from the Warren Wilson site
(Bn 29). a, Lecroy Bifurcated Stem; b, Morrow Mountain I Stemmed;
c, Guilford Lanceolate; d, Savannah River Stemmed.

The Lecroy points recovered at Bn 29 were found in Zone B. The two complete specimens measured 22 mm and 32 mm long and 20 mm and 22 mm wide at the shoulders, and had stem widths of 15 mm and 16 mm, respectively. Both were made of black flint. The sides of the stems and the basal concavities were well ground.

The presence of these types in the relatively recent Zone B calls for explanation. The specimen that occurred in Block III can be considered redeposited. However, on the terrace, several hypotheses can be offered: redeposition by the river from a site further upstream, aboriginal digging into a yet unidentified early deposit, or perhaps the activity of some prehistoric collector (see Weigland 1970:365-367).

Morrow Mountain I Stemmed (Plate 38b). Ten relatively small triangular-bladed points with short pointed or rounded stems referable to the Morrow Mountain I Stemmed type were recovered from the units selected for analysis. One was found in the plow zone, two in Zone B, five in Zone C, and two in Zone D. The position of the majority of these points below the Savannah River Stemmed type replicates the stratigraphic occurrence of the type on the North Carolina Piedmont (Coe 1964:55 and Fig. 117).

All of the specimens were made of quartzite. They ranged in length from 40 to 57 mm, and the mean was 48.6 mm; width ranged from 19 to 36 mm with a mean of 26.4 mm; thickness ranged from 6.5 to 15 mm with a mean of 10 mm. Basal grinding was present on two specimens.

Guilford Lanceolate (Plate 38c). The smaller variety of the Guilford Lanceolate type was represented by five specimens in the units studied. Their occurrence at Bn 29 was not in their known stratigraphic position, i.e., between Morrow Mountain and Savannah River materials, but in Pisgah or Swannanoa contexts (Zones A and B), suggesting the redeposition of them in later times. Coe (1964: 43-44) described the type from stratified deposits on the Yadkin River in central North Carolina. Based on carbon 14 dates from the Gaston site, Coe (1964:118) estimated a date for the Guilford complex of about 4000 B.C.

The four complete specimens in the collection measured from 40 to 55 mm long, 19 to 22 mm wide, and 9 to 10 mm thick. Three were made of quartzite and the other of slate. Two of the points were slightly ground along the basal edge, and one was well ground on the base.

Savannah River Stemmed (Plate 38d). Few points of the Savannah River Stemmed type were present in the units studied. They are large, wide forms identical to the published description (Coe 1964:45). The most complete specimen of this type measured 88 mm long, 44 mm wide, and 15 mm thick. One edge of the blade was worn, suggesting that it was utilized as a knife.

Otarre Stemmed (Plate 39). The Otarre Stemmed type is herein defined. It is a medium-sized triangular-bladed stemmed point with the following characteristics.

Form:
    (1) Blade: Variable, straight, convex, or concave edges. The average width-to-length ratio was 1:1.6.
    (2) Stem: Generally parallel, but some are rounded or contracting. Edges were often ground.
    (3) Base: Straight, rounded, or concave. Usually thinned, but 8 of the 25 points of this type from Feature 15 were thick, still retaining the striking platform.
    (4) Shoulder: Generally inclined from the widest part of the point to the base of the stem, but occasionally straight (15 percent). Shoulders were frequently asymmetrical.
    (5) Tip: Well pointed or rounded. Resharpening of the tip area produced a pentagonal blade outline in 16 percent of the points studied.

Size:
    (1) Length: Range, 37-70 mm; mean, 51.4 mm.
    (2) Stem length: Range, 9.5-20 mm; mean, 15.7 mm.
    (3) Blade length: Range, 27-58 mm; mean, 35.2 mm.
    (4) Stem width: Range, 9-20 mm; mean 14.9 mm.
    (5) Shoulder width: Range, 22-44 mm; mean, 30.5 mm.
    (6) Thickness: Range, 7-10 mm; mean, 9.9 mm.

Material:
Slate, 64 percent; chert, 18 percent; quartzite, 18 percent.

Technique of Manufacture:
Percussion chipping of a large flake. Edges of the stem were often ground smooth. Flake scars were generally flat and broad. The stem was usually thinned, but in about 30 percent of the sample the remains of a striking platform was present on the stem. Most of the points of this type had rather narrow short stems. Attempts to thin the bases of these points often resulted in breakage at the stem. A large number of blade fragments

0   5 cm

PLATE 39.   Chipped stone projectile points from the Warren Wilson site (Bn 29).   Otarre Stemmed.

in the unclassified projectile point category may have been produced by attempted thinning of stems of this type.

Comments:
This type is considered to be the latest point type produced in the Southern Appalachians prior to the introduction of ceramics. It is the lineal descendant of the Savannah River Stemmed point. Smaller points of the Savannah River Stemmed type have been noted in numerous collections, e.g., the Doerschuck and Gaston sites, North Carolina (Coe 1964), and Stallings Island (Claflin 1931), but the larger forms were much more common, as evidenced by the mean of both length and width (100 mm and 50 mm, respectively). The Otarre Stemmed point represents a continuation of the Archaic tradition of stemmed projectile points, a tradition which was important even after the introduction of ceramics. The type name is from the Cherokee word for "mountainous" as given by James Adair (1940).

Swannanoa Stemmed (Plate 40a). The Swannanoa Stemmed type is herein defined. It is a small, thick, triangular-bladed point with a relatively long stem.

Form:
(1) Blade: Triangular, edges straight or convex. Width-to-length ratio averaged 1:1.6.
(2) Stem: Contracting, may lack good definition and appear as a contracting base rather than as a proper stem.
(3) Base: Flat, rounded, or concave bases occurred in about the same frequencies.
(4) Shoulder: Generally symmetrical; usually inclined to the base of the stem, but on rare occasions flat.
(5) Tip: Most commonly quite sharp, but occasionally rounded.

Size:
(1) Length: Range, 21-43 mm; mean, 32.6 mm.
(2) Blade length: Range, 11-36 mm; mean, 21.8 mm.
(3) Stem length: Range, 9-14 mm; mean, 11.3 mm.
(4) Stem width: Range, 9-18 mm; mean, 12.6 mm.
(5) Shoulder width: Range 9.5-24 mm; mean, 19 mm.

Material:
Chert, 73 percent; quartzite, 14.5 percent; slate, 12.5 percent.

Technique of Manufacture:
Direct percussion accompanied infrequently by pressure retouch along the stem and blade. The striking platform was present on the stem of 23 percent of the specimens. Approximately 15 percent of the specimens were made on old flakes, as evidenced by differential weathering.

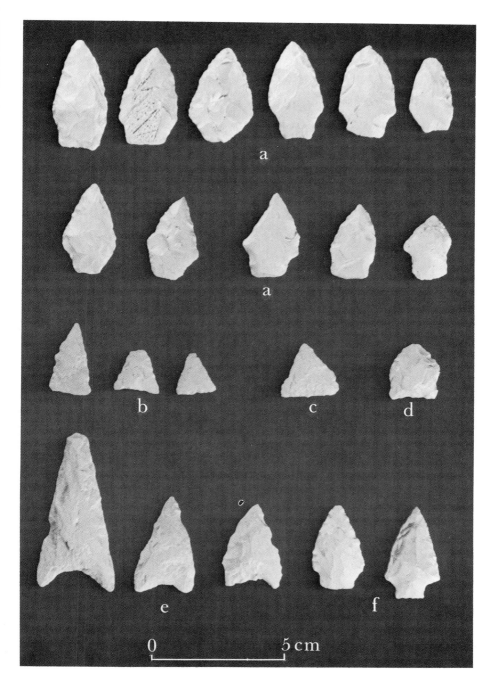

PLATE 40. Chipped stone projectile points from the Warren Wilson site (Bn 29). a, Swannanoa Stemmed; b, Pisgah Triangular; c, Haywood Triangular; d, Pigeon Side Notched; e, Garden Creek Triangular; f, Plott Short Stemmed.

About one-fourth of the specimens had thick bases, and like the Otarre
Stemmed points, failure to reduce the thickness of the stems was probably due to the frequency of breakage when thinning by percussion was
attempted.

Comments:

The presence of 84 (95 percent) of the 88 points of this type in Zone B
of the 200 Trench, Blocks I and II, and their association with Swannanoa
ceramics in Features 13 and 142 make this point type assignable to the
Swannanoa phase. Points of this type occurred at Hw 2 in the premound
midden. Similar points have been recovered from the Rankin site, Tennessee (Smith and Hodges 1968:Plate VIII), from the Nickajack Reservoir
(Faulkner and Graham 1966a:Plate 19), and from the Tellico Reservoir
(Salo 1969:Plate 28f). In all cases, the investigators assigned them to a
Woodland occupation characterized by the Tennessee equivalents of
Swannanoa pottery. Wauchope (1966:123-140) included points of this
type in his Stemmed and Shield-shaped category. Holden (1966:56-57)
described similar points in surface collections from Transylvania County,
North Carolina, as Stemmed Points, Variety X.

Plott Short Stemmed (Plate 40f). The Plott Short Stemmed type,
described in Chapter 3 (see page 126), was represented by six specimens, all from Zone B. This type was a minor form in the Swannanoa phase.

Pigeon Side Notched (Plate 40d). Two Pigeon Side Notched
points were present in the collection. Both occurred in Zone A.
While the evidence is inconclusive, this type likely belongs to the
Pigeon phase. The type has been described on page 127.

Haywood Triangular (Plate 40c). This small triangular arrowpoint referable to the Haywood Triangular type was associated
with the Connestee phase at Hw 2. At Bn 29 one point of this type
was recovered from Zone A in Block II and another in Zone C of
Block III. The type description, based on specimens recovered at
Hw 2, can be consulted on page 132.

Garden Creek Triangular (Plate 40e). Eight specimens referable
to the Garden Creek Triangular type from Zones A and B were
present in the sample studied. This type is said to be associated
with Early Woodland ceramics in eastern Tennessee, where it is included in the range of the Greeneville type (Kneberg 1957:64-65).
It may have appeared during the Swannanoa period, but it seems

to have been more popular in later times and continued in use throughout the Pigeon period. The type is described on page 130.

Pisgah Triangular (Plate 40b). Ten Pisgah Triangular points were present in the sample studied. Dickens (1970:90) described the type as "a small isosceles or equilateral triangle, . . . bases were flat or concave." He gave the length range as falling between 16 and 30 mm with a mean of 24.5 mm and the width range from 11 to 21 mm with a mean value of 15 mm. On the average the type is somewhat longer and narrower than the Madison point which was associated with Qualla ceramics at Jk 12.

OTHER CHIPPED STONE ARTIFACTS

Four heavy crude bifaces were present in the sample. Two were from the Zone C general excavation; one from Zone C, Feature 55; and one from Zone B, Block II. These bifaces are typical of specimens found at Savannah River phase sites. One broken specimen of slate was comparable to Coe's (1964:50-51) unspecialized quarry blade Type II. The three complete specimens were made of quartzite. All were fairly large; the smallest measured 63 × 53 × 30 mm, and the largest measured 120 × 65 × 33 mm.

Thirty-one scrapers, most found in Zone B, were in the collection analyzed. They were generally made by chipping the edge or edges of small flakes of chert, although some made from slate and quartzite were found. Typically, the edge of a primary flake was altered by the removal of small flakes to form an edge. Edge angles were not measured for all of the specimens, but the majority had angles ranging from 45° to 75°. As a class, flake scrapers were small, averaging about 35 mm in maximum dimension, but some specimens were 50 mm long. The specimens illustrated in Plate 41 were typical of this class of artifacts.

GROUND AND POLISHED STONE

Gorgets in the collection were of two forms: the expanded-center bar type (Plate 42a) and the boat-shaped type. Only one specimen of each type was complete. The complete expanded-center bar gorget made of slate found in Feature 164 (Zone B) was 203 mm long, 100 mm wide, and 20 mm thick (Plate 33). The boat-shaped gorget recovered from Zone B was made of a

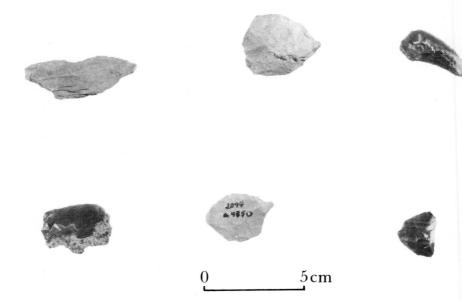

0 _____ 5 cm

PLATE 41 (above).   Flake scrapers from the Warren Wilson site (Bn 29).
PLATE 42 (below).   Polished-stone gorgets from the Warren Wilson site
(Bn 29). a, expanded-center bar gorget; b, boat-shaped gorget.

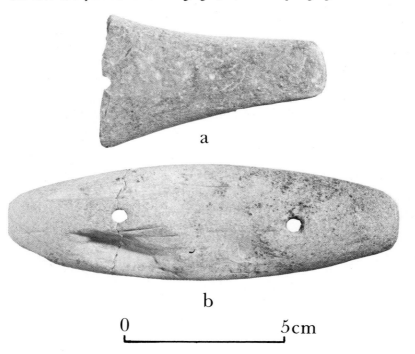

a

b

0 _____ 5 cm

fine-grained metamorphic stone and was 121 mm long, 37 mm wide, and 9 mm thick (Plate 42b). It was concave-convex in cross section, was well polished, and was decorated with a series of short engraved lines on the concave side along each edge near the ends. The three additional gorget fragments were also found in Zone B. All are attributable to the Swannanoa phase. Two fragments of polished stone celts, assigned to the Pisgah phase, were present in the sample utilized in this study. Dickens described a much larger sample of Pisgah celts:

> The form is basically rectangular with the bit-end some what larger than the butt-end. In cross-section they are flat to bi-convex. Some specimens are roughly pecked, with only the bit-ends being polished. Others are ground all over and a few rather well polished [Dickens 1970:95-96].

Fragments very similar to these were recovered from pre-Pisgah context at Hw 2. This was not surprising, since James A. Ford (1969: 49-53) pointed out that celts of this type had a long time span of use, approximately from as early as 300 B.C. to as late as A.D. 1700.

Seven specimens of fully grooved axes were recovered (Plate 43c). Four of these came from Zone B, two from Zone C, and one from Zone D. They exhibited surfaces ranging from roughly pecked to well polished. The larger of two nearly complete examples measured 136 × 118 × 31 mm. The smaller was 110 mm long, 95 mm wide, and 23 mm thick. The pecked grooves ranged from a faint indication to well-defined grooves up to 22 mm wide and 7 mm deep. The occurrence of a grooved axe in Zone D, although rewarding, was not a surprise since, like celts, these existed over a long span of time. J. L. Coe (1964:122) has suggested that they appear on the Carolina Piedmont sometime prior to 4000 B.C. Grooved axes were part of assemblages from east Tennessee, dating as late as the beginning of the Christian era (Rowe 1952). Paul F. Gleeson (1971) has reported that an axe of this type was found during the 1970 excavation in a historic period Cherokee feature at the Chota site, Tennessee.

Twenty-four small ground stone discoidals were present in the collections (Plate 44a). The majority of these were made from schist, but others were made of quartzite, gabro, and serpentine. Twenty were found in definite Pisgah contexts. Although three were recovered in Zone B, the Swannanoa midden, they, like the one found in Zone C, are considered to be intrusive. This class of

PLATE 43. Pecked stone artifacts from the Warren Wilson site (Bn 29).
a, pitted hammerstones; b, pebble hammerstones; c and d, grooved axes;
e, abrading stone; f, pestle.

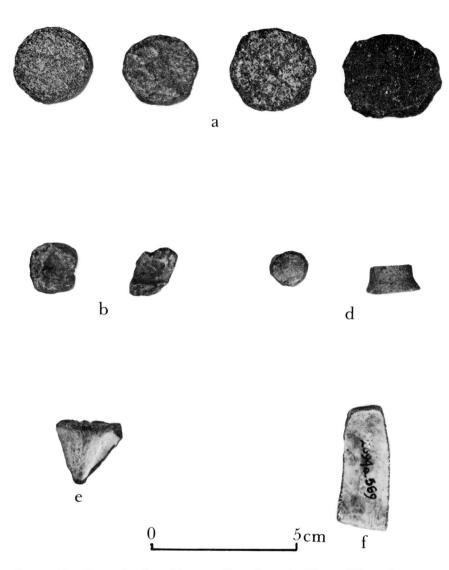

PLATE 44. Stone, fossil, and bone artifacts from the Warren Wilson site (Bn 29). a, stone discoidals; b, unfinished steatite beads; c, steatite vessel plugs; d, perforated fossil shark's tooth; e, cut turtle shell.

artifact was identical to the ceramic discoidals described earlier, insofar as the limits of the raw materials would allow. The principal difference in the two classes is in thickness. The ceramic discoidals were limited by the original thickness of the vessel wall, but the stone discoidals were limited by natural agencies and the reluctance of man to grind down hard stone. The stone discoidals ranged in diameter from 12 to 57 mm with a mean of 31.5 mm and in thickness from 7 to 25 mm with a mean of 13.5 mm. Their use as gaming or counting devices has been suggested.

Two small steatite beads, both about 20 mm in diameter, were recovered from Zone C (Plate 44b). One was broken in half, and the other was not completely perforated. Beads of this general form occur sporadically in Late Archaic period contexts (Ford 1969:57-61; Lewis and Kneberg 1946:117; Webb 1938:30). Two small steatite plugs were recovered from Zone C (Plate 44c). The larger specimen measured 19 × 14 mm at one end and 15 × 12 mm at the other and was 11 mm thick. The smaller specimen measured 13 × 14 mm on one end and was 11 mm in diameter at the other. It was 7 mm thick. Objects such as these have been referred to as laberettes or nose plugs. However, at the Coker Ford site, Cherokee County, Alabama, DeJarnette (DeJarnette, Kurjack, and Keel 1974) recovered two steatite vessels which had been plugged with identical objects. In both cases the plugs were placed in holes in the bottoms of the vessels with the larger end to the interior.

Three pestles were found in Block I—two in Zone C and one in Zone B. The Zone B specimen was cylindrical, was made of a dark mafic stone, and measured 121 mm long and 51 mm in diameter at the working end, which showed crushing and abrasive wear. It weighed 15.5 ounces. The complete specimen from Zone C was 83 mm long and had a pentagonal working face that measured 90 × 86 mm in maximum dimensions; it was made of granite and weighed 41 ounces (Plate 43e). The edge of the specimen at the base was flared around the circumference, giving it the "bell" shape that frequently occurs on Early Woodland and Late Archaic pestles. The other specimen, a fragment, was a large spall from the side of another bell-shaped pestle.

OTHER STONE ARTIFACTS

Two types of hammerstones occurred in the collection: pitted hammers (Plate 43a) and pebble hammers (Plate 43b). These types have been described on page 148. Three of the twenty pitted hammers had multiple pits on one face; one had three pits, and two were double-pitted. The remainder of the pitted stones corresponded to Coe's (1964:79) Type III hammerstone.

The other hammers were small cobbles or large pebbles which correspond in all details to Coe's (1964:79) Type II hammerstones. Like those he described, some also were used as manos.

The pebble hammers found in Zone B ranged in weight from 5 to 10.5 ounces and had a modal distribution which peaked at the lower end of the weight range. On the other hand, pebble hammers from Zone C were much heavier, ranging in weight from 14.5 to 42 ounces, with the typical specimen weighing about 24 ounces. The differences between the weights of the two groups of hammerstones may reflect technological aspects of chipped stone manufacture.

Nine fragments of what appeared to have been shallow mortars or metates were recovered. These were generally made of quartzite. None was large enough to estimate complete size. The ground depressions were quite shallow, being only about 7 to 10 mm deep. Six were found in Zone B and three in Zone C. Six examples of elongated tabular stones showing polish and abrasion were recovered. These objects seem to have been used in the manufacture of other ground stone tools such as celts, axes, and gorgets. Five of the specimens were found in Zone C, and one was recovered from Zone A (Plate 43d).

Five examples of pigment or pigment-producing minerals were noted. Deposits of red and yellow ochre were found in Feature 164 in Zone B. Two polished and abraded graphite pebbles and a small piece of limonite also occurred in Zone B. Sources for these "paint" stones can be found in the adjacent counties, if, indeed, they are not locally available. Graphite occurs in McDowell and Yancy counties, and limonite is found in Madison County (Stuckey 1965: 391 and 311).

BONE AND FOSSIL ARTIFACTS

A fossil shark tooth (Plate 44d) perforated at the root was found in the plowed soil. A likely source for this specimen is the extensive Cenozoic deposits of the Carolina Coastal Plain (Stuckey 1965:193). Sharks' teeth were recovered by Heye (1919) at Hw 3.

A single cut and polished fragment of turtle shell (Plate 44e) was found in Square 120R250 in Zone C. This specimen was intrusive into this level.

ETHNOBOTANICAL STUDIES

Two studies have been made on plant remains from Bn 29. Dr. Richard A. Yarnell (1970) analyzed a sample of material from Pisgah features, and Patricia Sanford (1970) studied samples from two features, one of which (Feature 141) contained a large quantity of pre-Pisgah ceramics. Unfortunately, the deposit dated no older than the Pisgah period. These studies, although they were made on materials much later than those with which the present study is concerned, are of interest since the species present at the time of the Pisgah occupation were also presumably available to earlier inhabitants of the site.

Food plants identified by Yarnell included hickory, walnut, butternut, acorn, *Iva* (sumpweed or marsh elder), persimmon, maypop, grape, black cherry, and chestnut. Pine, oak, locust or honey locust, poplar, and possibly birch were identified from wood charcoal.

The size of the *Iva* seeds suggests that this plant was cultivated. If this interpretation is correct, this makes the cultivation of sumpweed at Bn 29 the most recent and most eastward occurrence yet found. The presence of maize, squash, and beans in the Pisgah period remains was not surprising. However, no indication of these cultigens has been observed in the Connestee or earlier phases.

Sanford's study of the material from Feature 141 indicates the remains of a number of edible plants in the redeposited sediments along the riverbank. These included *Chenopodium*; *Solarum carolinse*; a clover, *Polygonum* sp.; and unidentified nut fragments. All these remains except the nut fragments were possibly recent condiments (Sanford 1970:39-41). All of the plants mentioned were probably used by the Woodland peoples, and, in fact, it would not be surprising if others are found when botanical analysis is undertaken.

ETHNOZOOLOGICAL STUDY

As part of his work on the Pisgah Culture, Roy S. Dickens submitted a sample of bones from Bn 29 to Dr. E. S. Wing (1970) for study. In this sample Dr. Wing reported that a minimum of 208 individuals representing more than 30 species were present. All the species identified would have been available to earlier people. Only two of the species, the bobcat and mountain lion, are locally extinct at the present time. The following fauna identified at Bn 29 have been modified from Wing (1970:297) to illustrate the variety of faunal remains.

Mammals:
  White-tailed deer
  Black bear
  Gray fox
  Bobcat
  Mountain lion
  Beaver
  Woodchuck
  Raccoon
  Rabbit
  Gray squirrel
  Fox squirrel
  Opossum
  Least weasel
  Deer mouse
  Unidentified rodent

Turtles:
  Box turtle
  Snapping turtle
  Terrapin

Snakes:
  Brown water snake
  Mud snake
  Whip snake
  King snake
  Hognosed snake
  Crotalidae (?)
  Unidentified *Colubridae* spp.

Amphibians:
  Auran
    Frog (*Rana* sp.)
    Toad
    Hellbender

Birds:
  Turkey

SUMMARY

Extensive excavations at the Warren Wilson site (Bn 29) have demonstrated that four stratigraphically separable culture units were present. The most recent of these was termed the Pisgah Culture by Roy S. Dickens (1970). This phase was represented by remains found in the plowed soil (Zone A) and by intrusives in Zones B and C. Zone B, a brown sandy loam, contained the material culture of the Early Woodland Swannanoa phase, but earlier materials had been introduced into this layer by several agencies. The most important cause of mixing was the enormous amount of digging by the Pisgah phase inhabitants of the site. These people dug numerous pits, postholes, and burials into earlier deposits. Zone C, another layer of sandy loam, contained the remains of a Middle Archaic period complex in the lower part. This complex, the Morrow Mountain phase, was also represented by a few projectile points found in the upper part of Zone D.

Along the old riverbank, the remains of cultural units intermediate in time between the Swannanoa period and the Pisgah period were encountered. These deposits resulted from aborigines throwing debris over the side of the bank and, subsequently, from plowing and erosion.

The frequencies of the ceramic series found in the 200 Trench and Blocks I and II (Fig. 23) indicate the dichotomous distribution of the Swannanoa and Pisgah ceramic complexes. Figure 24 illustrates that even during the initial deposition of the riverbank deposits, a sizable number of Pisgah ceramics were being discarded along the bank of the river in the area of Block III.

THE ARCHAIC PERIOD

Several projectile points—Lecroy Bifurcated Stem and Guilford Lanceolate types—indicated that the site had been occupied during the Archaic period. However, only two components of this period were isolated stratigraphically.

The Morrow Mountain Component

The Middle Archaic Morrow Mountain phase was recognized by the presence of Morrow Mountain I Stemmed projectile points found in the bottom of Zone C and the top of Zone D. Points of this type occurred in other layers at the site, but only in the base of Zone C and the top of Zone D were they found to the exclusion of other types. Their position at Bn 29 in these zones is comparable to their positions at other sites, i.e., below Savannah River points.

Morrow Mountain points were first identified in their correct stratigraphic position by Coe at the Doerschuk site (Coe 1964:54). Before this stratigraphic information was available, he had suggested that points of this type formed part of the Badin focus (Coe 1952: Fig. 163, L). His candid assessment of his interpretations prior to the excavation of stratified sites along the Yadkin River should be studied by all archaeologists in order to avoid some "logical" deductions (Coe 1964:6-8).

Unfortunately, little is known in detail about the Morrow Mountain phase. Coe (1964:54) has indicated that aside from the distinct point style, the Morrow Mountain complex artifact inventory was essentially the same as the Stanly complex. This would include, then, a variety of scrapers, hammerstones, and mortars, but he

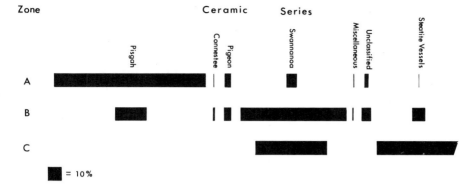

FIG. 23 (above).   Distribution of ceramic series, 200 Trench, Block II, and Block III by stratigraphic zones; Warren Wilson site (Bn 29). FIG. 24 (below). Distribution of ceramic series Block III by stratigraphic zones; Warren Wilson site (Bn 29).

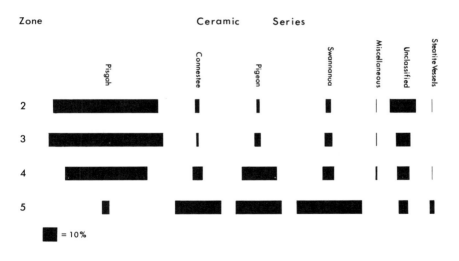

indicates that no atlatl weights occurred in Morrow Mountain contexts. The presence of spear thrower weights, however, is highly probable.

There are no radiocarbon dates for the Morrow Mountain phase in North Carolina. Coe (1964:Fig. 116) has suggested a date of between 4000 and 5000 B.C. Griffin has reported two dates from charcoal associated with Morrow Mountain points at Russell Cave, Alabama, as 3970 ± 200 B.C. (I-823) and 4290 ± 190 B.C. (I-702). The details of the Morrow Mountain occupation at Russell Cave have not yet been published.

The Savannah River Component

The Savannah River phase was represented by stemmed projectile points (Savannah River Stemmed and Otarre Stemmed), ground stone axes, large bifaces, steatite bowls, and hearths. The bulk of the material assigned to this manifestation was recovered from Zone C. The Savannah River Stemmed point was originally described by Claflin (1931:33-39) from the Stallings Island site, Columbia County, Georgia. A number of workers (Coe 1952:305-306; Fairbanks 1942; Miller 1949) have considered the Savannah River phase to be the latest Archaic complex in the Southeast.

Typical Savannah River Stemmed points were present at Bn 29, but the most common Late Archaic type was a much smaller stemmed point named the Otarre Stemmed point. As a group these points averaged about half the size of the Savannah River points. Radiocarbon dates for the Savannah River occupation were 2914 ± 280 B.C. and 1565 ± 140 B.C.

The only evidence of habitation areas of this period recognized at Bn 29 was the numerous rock-filled pit hearths and some rectilinear patterns of stones discovered in 1969 (Reid and Canouts 1969). These stone patterns measured 9 × 5 feet, 10 × 6 feet, and 8 × 4 feet in size.

WOODLAND PERIOD

The Swannanoa Component

The Swannanoa phase was represented by an assemblage of artifacts which was isolated below the Pisgah, Connestee, and Pigeon phase materials and above the Savannah River midden (Zone C). The ceramics inclusive in Zone B and associated with the rock-filled pit hearths originating in this zone belonged to the Swannanoa series. Some Pisgah materials were recovered from Zone B, but these were intrusive. The distribution of Swannanoa series ceramics in Zone B is evidence to support the hypothesis that this ceramic assemblage is the earliest in the Appalachian Summit Area. The presence of numerous stone vessel fragments in Zone B cannot be totally attributed to the earlier Archaic occupation of the site. Some must have been manufactured during the Swannanoa phase. In addition to the thick-walled grit or sand tempered, predominantly cord marked pottery and stone bowls, other items such as small stemmed points (Swannanoa Stemmed), large triangular points (Transylvania Triangular), expanded-center bar gorgets, boat-shaped gorgets, grooved axes, celts, metates, manos, bell-shaped pestles, tubular smoking pipes, and flake scrapers belong to the Swannanoa component.

The Pigeon Component

Evidence of the Pigeon phase was rarely encountered at Bn 29. This evidence, such as it was, consisted almost exclusively of ceramics. Pottery of the Pigeon series made up only 3.6 percent of the ceramics analyzed. The numerical majority of this series was found in the main part of the site, but the highest relative frequency occurred in Zone 5 of Block III. The types present at Bn 29 were identical to those described from Hw 2. Check stamping was the most common surface finish at both sites. Other elements of the Pigeon assemblage were difficult to identify. The inclusion of projectile points such as the Pigeon Side Notched, Garden Creek Triangular, and possibly the Haywood Triangular seems reasonable. Such items as expanded-center bar gorgets, celts, grooved axes, flake scrapers, smoking pipes, mortars, manos, several kinds of hammerstones, and polishing or abrading stones also might be associated since all these items were present in the earlier Swannanoa phase and many were still fashionable in the subsequent Connestee phase.

The Connestee Component

The Connestee phase was represented by about 1 percent of the pottery analyzed and two Haywood Triangular projectile points. Little else can be said about this manifestation from evidence collected at Bn 29.

MISSISSIPPIAN PERIOD

The Pisgah Phase

Remains of the Pisgah phase from Bn 29 have already received monographic consideration (Dickens 1970); they are summarized briefly in the subsequent chapter. The Pisgah occupation, which was limited to what is now the plow zone and to intrusive features in Zones B and C, formed the capstone of the cultural sequence at Bn 29.

5. Appalachian Summit Archaeology: *A Summary*

Archaeologists begin their summaries either by starting with the earliest remains and proceeding to the latest or by using the direct historical approach (Steward 1942) which proceeds backward in time by presenting information related to the historic period and then the less well known earlier periods. I have chosen the latter approach.

There is no doubt that the Qualla phase represents the material culture and abstracted associated behaviors of the Cherokees in the Appalachian Summit Area from the 16th century until it was replaced through the process of acculturation to a basic Euro-American material and economic culture in the 19th century. The ethnic or tribal affiliation of the prehistoric peoples of the area will, in the final analysis, never be ascertained. Fortunately, during the last quarter century tribal, or even linguistic, identification of prehistoric peoples has ceased to be a major goal of archaeological research in the eastern United States. This is due to the realization that, except in very special cases, such identities are not to be found on potsherds, arrowheads, or other material remains.

The mechanics of culture change as recognized in the archaeological record have also received innumerable treatments. In fact, every archaeologist who deals with more than a single component deals with variability in one aspect or another. Insofar as the archaeological record goes, this is a form of culture change—regardless of the level of abstraction. Such variability in the archaeological record may be interpreted in two frames of temporal reference. If viewed synchronically, these changes may be the results of diffusion, independent invention, or even migration. However, if viewed diachronically, such changes may be due to evolutionary modifications in traditional forms. Dealing with the mechanics of cultural change as seen in the archaeological record is a difficult task. Attempting to isolate causal factors of such change is even more difficult. Consequently, those prehistorians who favor *in situ* theories of development for a historically documented culture seem to me to stand on firmer ground than those who prefer migration theories when it is impossible to divide the prehistoric remains of an area into totally different cultural units. If a unit is documented as completely different from a preceding unit, then migration is a reasonable hypothesis. Of course, each case for *in situ* development or migration must be considered individually. I favor an *in situ* development hypothesis for Cherokee Culture because the phases I have defined in this study have great numbers of elements in common, although many of them may have appeared first elsewhere. The persistence of culture traits almost obscures distinctive elements to the point where phase separations sometimes seem to be arbitrary. The continuity of traits through time and the similarity between one unit and another reinforce the interpretation of an evolutionary continuum in the area.

The substantive sections of this monograph (Chapters 2-4) have described extensive investigations conducted at three archaeological sites in the Appalachian Summit Area. These chapters also presented analyses of the data recovered from these sites. In this chapter this information will be used to describe the prehistory of the area as it is presently understood by the author. This account will summarize the available evidence for their relative as well as absolute ages. I will discuss some of the problems of producing a chronology for the area.

This study has also dealt with the broader relationships between phases in the Appalachian Summit Area and other manifestations and events in the Southeast and the Midwest. Further, the relationships each of the phases had with its mountain environment will be discussed in this section.

QUALLA PHASE

The Qualla phase is the archaeological manifestation of the protohistoric and historic period Cherokee. The Research Laboratories of Anthropology have been investigating this archaeological entity over the last nine years. Considerable data have been collected and are presently under study. Other than to point out several obvious and general characteristics would be premature since a detailed presentation of these data will be made at a future time.

Qualla phase remains formed the bulk of the collection at Tuckasegee (Jk 12). Here they were found stratigraphically above the remains of the Pisgah, Connestee, Pigeon, and Swannanoa cultures. At Garden Creek Mound 2 (Hw 2), Qualla ceramic types were found mixed in the plowed soil with Pisgah ceramics. These were superpositioned above Connestee and earlier remains. At Garden Creek Mound No. 1 (Hw 1), Qualla ceramics, Madison points, and trade goods were found in post-Pisgah contexts. No Qualla remains were found at Warren Wilson (Bn 29). This evidence clearly indicates that the Qualla phase is the latest unit in the area and that it was preceded by the Pisgah phase. The ceramics of the Qualla phase can be considered an Appalachian Summit Area manifestation of the Lamar style horizon. Ceramics made during this period (ca. 1500-1908) by the Cherokee were characterized by complicated stamping and bold incising. Egloff (1967) has given the particulars of these ceramics, which have been described in Chapter 2 also.

Projectile points were small, thin, well-made triangular forms used as arrow tips. Other lithic items included flake scrapers, side scrapers, and small chipped stone drills. Occasionally, gunflints of native manufacture were found.

Celts were the most common ground stone objects made during this period, but stone pipes did occur. The only other items of ground stone found with any frequency were discoidals, both large chunkey stones and small counters. The smaller discoidals had ceramic counterparts, generally made from sherds. A few expanded-headed pins (hair or ear pins) of stone have been recorded. These also had both ceramic and shell counterparts.

The shell industry of the Qualla phase was restricted to ornamental forms: beads, gorgets, hair or ear pins, masks, and ceremonial dippers. Both native and imported shells were used. One utilitarian item of shell was the pottery scraper.

Architecture was complex and can only be treated in the briefest manner at this time. Circular and rectangular structures were used as religiopolitical buildings as well as habitations. Civic buildings were usually placed on mounds which were purposely constructed as foundations for them. By the end of the 18th century the log cabin made of horizontal logs, heavily chinked with clay, had been introduced to the Cherokees along the English frontier.

Burial practices were not complex. Grave goods occur, but only rarely. During the early historic period (ca. 1725) they were restricted to aboriginal items. Burials were flexed. The shaft-and-chamber type of grave was used, but the more frequent form was a simple pit (Coe 1969).

Trade relationships with Europeans were well established by the beginning of the 18th century. In return for furs and hides, English and French traders exchanged guns, blankets, knives, axes, hoes, tomahawks, beads, paint, a variety of hardware, and, of course, liquid spirits.

The development of this level of Cherokee Culture was based on an efficient cultural adaptation to the local environment. The occurrence of sites situated in all of the microenvironments present in the area indicates that these people made the most of the natural resources available. Hunting and gathering stations or camps were recorded during our surveys in the mountain gaps and along stream heads. Scattered farmsteads were found in the intermountain zones, and villages were established in association with town house mounds. The lack of extensive expanses of floodplains in the mountains seems to argue against the large concentrations of population that were common in other areas of the eastern United States. What apparently developed was a pattern of dispersed farmsteads or hamlets linked to small ceremonial centers. Such a pattern of settlement and resource utilization made it possible for the Cherokee population to expand to the sizable numbers reported by English traders. At the same time such a dispersion of the population may account for the lack of development of a centralized political organization. The development of such a political organization did not come about until dealing with European powers became a necessity. The evolution of Cherokee political development from a primary priest state to a political state has been treated by Fred Gearing (1962) and is highly recommended for study.

During the period of time when the Qualla phase was developing out of the earlier Pisgah phase in the Appalachian Summit Area, comparable developments were taking place in other parts of the South Appalachian Province. In the Ridge and Valley area of eastern Tennessee the Dallas Culture was developing into the Overhill Cherokee complex, and Lamar was taking its final form by replacing the Wilbanks-Savannah phase in Piedmont Georgia. Similarly, Lamar ceramic elements would also begin to appear in the Piedmont cultures of the Carolinas.

PISGAH PHASE

The culture unit preceding the development of the Qualla phase has been termed the Pisgah Culture (Dickens 1970). The transition from Pisgah style ceramics to Qualla series pottery is at present not clearly understood. Nonetheless, a gradual evolution from the earlier to the later forms can be seen from material collected at the Coweeta Creek site (Ma 34), Garden Creek Mound No. 1 (Hw 1), and the Warren Wilson site (Bn 29). The characteristic Pisgah vessel was stamped with a rectilinear complicated stamp, the rim was collared, and the vessel was shouldered. The rim received a special treatment of linear rather than circular punctates; loop handles, lugs, and castellations were frequently present, and bases were slightly pointed or rounded. Other artifacts made of clay were pipes, discoidals, animal head effigies, beads, and miniature or toy vessels.

Arrowpoints were triangular and were generally longer than the later Qualla forms. A variety of microtools, gravers, perforators, and drills were made of chipped stone. Flake scrapers were common.

The ground stone industry contained celts, pipes, and discoidals. By virtue of their polish, some pebbles were used to burnish pottery. The inventory of the shell industry is identical to that of the Qualla phase and includes gorgets, ear pins, beads, and dippers. Gorgets in the Lick Creek style and Citico style were present as well as the elongated "mask" type. The Lick Creek style seems to be earliest and the mask type latest. Furthermore the mask style is the most common type found during the Qualla period.

Wooden or vegetal implements are rarely recovered in the humid Southern Appalachians; however, cane matting has been found as well as impressions of matting on benches, in graves, and on pottery. Evidence of the textile industry rests solely on cord impressions found on pottery. Wooden digging-stick impressions were often revealed by careful cleaning of grave walls. Bone tools include ulna awls, splinter awls, pins, and needles. Necklaces made of rabbit pelves and scapulae occurred, and in one instance, six panther (*Felis concolor*) phalanges were included as *beigraben*. Turtle shell rattles also were used as grave gods.

Mica, in cutout forms, has been recovered from Pisgah contexts. Numerous examples of pigment such as red ochre, yellow ochre, and graphite have also been found.

The Pisgah folk constructed earth lodges and substructure mounds topped with rectangular civic buildings. Dwellings were rectangular with wall trench entrances and raised clay fire basins. Villages were enclosed by log palisades. The settlement pattern was similar to that of the Qualla phase—ceremonial centers complete with platform mounds and sometimes semisubterranean earth lodges—but the majority of the population was most likely dispersed into farmsteads and farming hamlets. Wild foods secured from small upland hunting and gathering camps supplemented the agricultural produce of the floodplain.

Usually a burial was flexed and the individual placed in a simple pit. Less frequently interments were made in shaft-and-chamber graves. Both types of grave were usually dug into the floor of a dwelling. Grave goods were rare and usually consisted of items of personal adornment. Dickens (1970:266) has pointed out that mortuary practices of the Pisgah folk were similar to those used during the Qualla phase in North Carolina, the Wilbanks period interments of north Georgia, and the Siouan burials of the Carolina Piedmont. Additionally, he has pointed out the striking overall similarities between the Pisgah Culture and the Dallas focus of eastern Tennessee (Dickens 1970:281).

Presently the Pisgah phase is thought to date from A.D. 1000 to A.D. 1550 (Dickens 1970:21). Stratigraphic evidence at Hw 2 and Bn 29 clearly demonstrates that the Pisgah phase was preceded by the Connestee phase.

The origin of the Pisgah phase is a vexing problem. As I have pointed out earlier, Dickens (1970) and Ferguson (1971) have noted the basic similarity between the Pisgah phase and the Dallas phase of eastern Tennessee, but neither has been able to unequivocally account for the origin of the ceramic complex. Dickens (1974) has suggested that this unique ceramic industry was the result of the *blending* of collared- and thickened-rim forms having loop handles and/or castellations which were moving along an expanding Mississippian frontier *with* rectilinear complicated stamping modes of surface finish diffusing northward from the Georgia Piedmont. He considers these and other Mississippian traits to have been accepted and elaborated on by peoples having a basic Woodland culture base. In my opinion, the archaeological complex in the area which immediately precedes Pisgah is empirically unknown (see discussion below).

CONNESTEE PHASE

The Connestee phase is the latest of the Woodland tradition segments presently defined in the Southern Highland region of North Carolina. Dates for the temporal span can only be estimated. As will be more fully discussed below, I consider a likely duration of approximately 400 to 500 years between A.D. 100 or A.D. 200 and A.D. 600 for this manifestation.

The ceramics of the Connestee phase differ in detail from the ceramics of both the subsequent Pisgah and preceding Pigeon phases. The ceramics of the Connestee phase are relatively thin in comparison with both earlier and later pottery. Surface finish was variable, but brushed, simple stamped, or plain surfaced conoidal or hemispherical vessels with constricted necks and flaring rims were most common. Small, flat-based conoidal jars were frequent. Some had flat bases and were supported by four small pods. The lips of Connestee vessels were punctated, notched, and incised.

A number of attributes indicate the continuation of ceramic ideas from the preceding Pigeon phase or the even earlier Swannanoa phase. All surface finishes used during the Connestee phase were present earlier, although the frequency relationships changed. The footed vessel form inherited from the Pigeon phase was made during the early part of the Connestee phase, but it seems to have been displaced in favor of the small, globular, necked jar.

The chipped stone assemblage consisted of at least three, and perhaps four, types of triangular arrowpoints: Haywood Triangular, Connestee Triangular, and Pigeon Side Notched. I offer the opinion that the sequence of projectile-point development within the Connestee phase was from Pigeon Side Notched to Haywood Triangular with Garden Creek Triangular and Connestee Triangular as intermediate forms. Flake scrapers, gravers, and chipped stone discs were also part of this assemblage.

These local artifact forms pose quite a contrast to imported items such as prismatic blades, polyhedral cores, triangular knives or cache blades, Copena Triangular points, and copper ornaments and pins. Some of these items indicate influence, probably in the form of trade, from Hopewellian centers to the north.

Ground and polished stone tools and ornaments such as pentaloid celts, tabular gorgets, and pipes are viewed as continued developments of earlier forms. A number of other items such as plummets, pendants, and grooved stones might be the remains of Connestee culture. Little difference between the various phases of the Woodland tradition can be seen in the rough-stone-tool category. Pebble and pitted hammerstones occurred in all phases. The only noticeable difference was the reduction in size of pebble hammers from the lowest to the higher zones at Bn 29. Well-made cylindrical hammerstones seem to have been a product of Connestee folk.

Bone was poorly preserved, and little can be said about this industry. Splinter awls, antler drifts, and cut deer jaws were all that were found. Cut animal jaws, primarily those of carnivores, are generally restricted to Middle Woodland contexts, but are known to occur in Mississippian cultures (Fairbanks 1956:31).

The data throw no direct light on the shell or wood industry of the phase. For the latter there is indirect evidence of cordage, woven fabric, and carved wooden paddles from the ceramic industry. The presence of the bow and arrow is indicated by the small triangular projectile points. We can probably expect shell beads of several varieties, gorgets, spoons, dippers, and pins to turn up in the excavation of other Connestee phase sites.

Nothing is known of the burial practices of the Connestee folk. No interments referable to this phase have been found.

Excavations at Hw 2 produced some architectural information concerning structures of the phase. First, in the old village, a rectangular posthole pattern measuring 20 × 21 feet showed that houses were constructed by setting posts in individual holes instead of trenches. Wall and roof coverings seemed to have been composed of perishable materials since there was no evidence of wattle and daub construction. If clay plaster had been used, some of this debris surely would have been present. No interior fireplace or hearth was present; thus if this was a domestic structure, cooking must have occurred outside the house. I have suggested that the structure was removed in order to build the first mound at Garden Creek.

This early mound consisted of at least two constructions. The earlier was a yellow clay platform measuring 1.7 feet high which had estimated horizontal dimensions of 40 × 60 feet. On top of this a building, or buildings, probably similar to the premound structure was constructed. At some later time a second mound was built directly on top of the first platform. This mound also served as the foundation for several buildings, one of which was circular.

The height of this mound in 1965 was just over 3 feet. It was estimated to have covered an area 60 × 80 feet at the base.

At the present time, I view the Connestee phase as a development from earlier local manifestations. The strong Southern influence apparent in the preceding Pigeon phase diminished, and interaction seems to have been directed to the West and Northwest.

If this hypothesized change of involvement is apparent in any aspect of Connestee culture, it is the ceramics. The basic forms and surface finishes had already been used in earlier ceramics of the area, and it is the continued use of these forms—particularly the surface finishes—that distinguishes Connestee ceramics from contemporary ceramics in middle Georgia, the Carolina Piedmont, and, to a degree, Virginia. In Georgia, at least in the central, coastal, and southern parts, complicated stamped pottery was making its appearance and spreading. However, in the Southern Appalachians proper, including northern Georgia, complicated stamped pottery did not become important until about A.D. 1000, Wauchope (1966:59-60) notwithstanding.

Ferguson (1971:58-86) has recently reviewed the archaeological knowledge of north Georgia. He points out that Wauchope's (1948) proposed sequence was unduly influenced by A. R. Kelly's previous work on the Macon Plateau. Unfortunately, many of Wauchope's suggestions relating to the ceramic sequence of north Georgia became accepted as fact. For example, Wauchope considered Napier ceramics to be the transitional link between Woodland and Mississippian manifestations; yet only 902 sherds of this type were found among the 105,812 sherds collected by the north Georgia survey (Ferguson 1971:67). Approximately half (497) of these sherds were recovered from the Towaliga site, which ought to be considered as being in central Georgia. Even more surprising, sites north of a line drawn from east to west through Atlanta produced only 81 Napier sherds out of a total of 89,880 sherds. In spite of this scanty representation in north Gerogia, a considerable discussion of the role of Napier pottery in ceramic development of the region has occurred (Wauchope 1948; Sears 1952). The role of Napier ceramics in north Georgia prehistory is still debatable. However, its position in time in central Georgia is clearly late Middle Woodland or Early Mississippian.

Joseph Caldwell (1958:Figs. 7-8 and pp. 9-70) most clearly presents another picture of Southern Appalachian pottery in northern

Georgia between 200 B.C. and A.D. 700—his charts are blank! This of course does not imply that this area was uninhabited, but that the data have been misunderstood. Following the same manner of cross dating used by Wauchope, and assuming ceramic progression, Caldwell neatly sidestepped the problem of north Georgia. He tells us little about what succeeds the Cartersville focus in that area, although he states that the Hamilton focus of eastern Tennessee occurred later in time than Cartersville (Caldwell 1958:46). In other areas about A.D. 500 (his date) "Hamilton, Decatur, Wilmington, McKelvey, and Miller II cultures were flourishing" (Caldwell 1958: 46). In northeast Georgia the earliest prehistoric occupation of the Lower Cherokee town of Tugalo contains pottery with both Napier (rectilinear) and Middle to Late Swift Creek Stamped (curvilinear) designs. Furthermore, a similar combination is characteristic of the Woodstock focus in north central Georgia (Caldwell 1958:47). While these combinations precede the historic period in north central and northeastern Georgia, they are not necessarily temporal equivalents of Middle Woodland foci. In fact, a recent carbon 14 date (Hally 1970) of A.D. 928 ± 40 years for a Woodstock component indicates that they are much too late.

Caldwell failed to spell out in 1958 what was obvious to him from his work in the Allatoona Reservoir (Caldwell 1950:17), for he indicated that there *was* a considerable time span represented by such ceramics as the Cartersville and Kellog series. It is at this juncture Caldwell committed the same error that Wauchope had made earlier. He failed to realize that in north Georgia the culture complex identified as the Cartersville focus continued to exist with only a few modifications, in ceramics at least, until about A.D. 700.

The sand tempered ceramics from the Tunacunnhee site (9Dd25) which were associated with Hopewellian materials and carbon 14 dated at A.D. 150 ± 95 and A.D. 280 ± 125 are virtually identical to Connestee pottery of the Appalachian Summit Area. This association argues for a date for the beginning of Connestee of at least A.D. 200.

In the western foothills of the Appalachians in the Tennessee Valley region, the Candy Creek focus (Kneberg 1961) was synchronous with the Connestee phase. As I have pointed out, Connestee phase ceramics were largely brushed, simple stamped, and cord marked. Cord marking predominates the Candy Creek series vessel finishes, but simple stamped and brushed surfaces are present. Vessel forms were also identical. Recent work by Paul Gleeson (1970 and personal communication) and Jefferson Chapman (1973) on the lower reaches of the Little Tennessee River indicates that such ceramic types as Connestee Simple Stamped and Connestee Brushed are present there and, except for temper, are identical to types found in the main valley. At least at Icehouse Bottom they are associated with Hopewellian materials.

My task is not to reinterpret the various eastern Tennessee units, but to point out the more obvious relationships between them and the North Carolina materials. In addition to the ceramics, projectile point forms are identical. In fact, the majority of the North Carolina specimens seem to be made of types of chert which occur in Tennessee. Gorgets, celts, scrapers, hammerstones, awls, and other items are also identical. Settlement patterns seem to have been similar since the larger sites are located along the major streams or on the larger tributaries; smaller sites were located on lesser water courses. Many other aspects of these cultures probably would be comparable if data from the mountains were as complete as that from the Tennessee Valley. Unfortunately we know nothing of burial practices and the shell industry and much too little about the bone industry of the Connestee phase. Until such information is collected, no more than speculation can be offered.

Looking to the north, in southwestern Virginia, Holland (1970) has not isolated any cultural unit containing ceramics dating earlier than about A.D. 1000. This date is applicable to the Lee series, which is identical to the Pisgah ceramics of the Appalachian Summit Area. Until earlier material is reported, no further consideration of southwestern Virginia is possible. It can be interjected that, with the exception of the Lee-Pisgah relationship, no connection is apparent between southwestern Virginia and the study area after the end of the Archaic period.

Although a great deal is known about the prehistory of the eastern edge of the Carolina Piedmont, where Joffre L. Coe has carried out extensive research over the last three decades, virtually no details are known about the western edge of the Piedmont. Several investigations made on the northwestern Piedmont (Thomas 1887: 61-76; Keel 1963; Polhemus n.d.) indicate that the upper Yadkin Basin, like southwestern Virginia, neither was overly influenced by events taking place in the southern Blue Ridge, nor was an influence upon Blue Ridge cultures. The picture is somewhat different farther to the southeast along the escarpment. Brief surveys conducted by the writer in this area indicate an extension of mountain culture area materials. Robert Keeler conducted a survey of the upper Catawba River in the summer of 1970 and found that Pisgah, Connestee, and Swannanoa ceramics diminished in quantity as distance to the escarpment was increased.

Proceeding further eastward to the lower Yadkin Basin, Coe's (1952, 1964) Yadkin and Badin complexes are of some interest. These complexes have been estimated to occupy the time span from a few centuries B.C. up to about the 16th century A.D. (Coe 1964: Fig. 116). The earlier of these, the Badin complex, seems to have evolved into the Yadkin complex at about the time the Connestee phase became a recognizable entity. The Yadkin complex follows the same direct tradition, slowly changing into the Uwharrie complex. The ceramics of these phases show no direct influence from the western part of North Carolina. The similarities between the two areas in ceramics were the result of the common Woodland tradition which they shared. The Badin and Yadkin ceramics retain the style of the northern Woodland tradition throughout their existence. Even though check stamping made up about 4 percent of the total analyzed sample of the Yadkin series at the Doerschuk site, Coe suggested that this was a unique occurrence.

Yadkin projectile points compare well with types such as Garden Creek Triangular and Connestee Triangular found in the mountains (compare Fig. 21d with Coe 1964:Fig. 42b, and Fig. 21f with Coe 1964:Fig. 42a). These similarities are viewed as part of the general Southeastern post-Archaic projectile point development rather than as indicators of historical connections between the two areas.

One other trait of the Connestee phase deserves added attention. I have assigned the Garden Creek Mound No. 2 to this phase for the reasons given in Chapter 3. The recognition of this platform mound as an element of Connestee culture is another addition to the slowly accumulating corpus of similar structures of early date. To make an involved case for the inclusion of this platform substructure mound into a Middle Woodland time slot is unnecessary. Mounds of this form have been known, though not fully appreciated, from Kelly's (1938) work on the Macon Plateau. Ferguson (1971:159-165) has discussed this problem in relation to his concept of South Appalachian Mississippianism. He noted that the Garden Creek Mound No. 2, the Swift Creek Mound, and probably Stubbs Mound were substructure mounds. The flat-topped mounds at Mandeville and the large mound at Kolomoki are of similar form, but their use as substructure mounds is uncertain. Since Ferguson's discussion,

R. S. Dickens (personal communication) has examined the Annee-wakee Creek Mound and reported a 7th-century date for its construction. Prufer (1964:50, 80-81) has pointed out that platform mounds are associated with the Hopewell complex at several sites (Marietta, Newark, Ginther, and Cedar Banks, Ohio) which he considered to be late Hopewell on other grounds. Whether or not these mounds served as bases for structures was not discussed. However, Reed (1969:37-39) has indicated that some Hopewell platforms had structures built upon them. Although the function of the structures built on Garden Creek Mound No. 2 will never be known, the evidence for structures is unequivocal.

I have indicated in Chapter 3 that the Hopewell complex specimens recovered from Garden Creek Mound No. 2 were associated with the Connestee phase and have pointed out the relationship of some of the Connestee ceramics to types recovered in Ohio which are considered to be of Southeastern origin. The occurrence of these materials together at sites in Ohio and North Carolina is proof of contact. The approximate date of this contact is estimated to fall between A.D. 200 and A.D. 400.

Since 1972 my understanding of the absolute dates of the Connestee phase has undergone considerable revision. At that time I conceived Connestee to have developed during late Hopewell times ca. A.D. 300-A.D. 400 according to the midwestern chronology and lasted until ca. 1000 A.D. At that time it seemed to be the only way to reconcile the dates from Garden Creek Mound No. 2 (Hw 2) of A.D. 805 ± 85 years and Icehouse Bottom (40Mr23) of A.D. 585 ± 90 years and A.D. 605 ± 90 years. However, this alignment no longer seems tenable in view of more recent excavations by others. The development of the Connestee phase must be pushed back at least to the 2nd century of our era to account for the relationships present in the ceramic assemblages at Mandeville (9Fu14), Georgia; Tunacunnhee, Georgia; Garden Creek Mound, North Carolina; and Icehouse Bottom, Tennessee; as well as the Hopewellian trade pieces found at these sites. The terminus of Connestee ought to fall about A.D. 600-A.D. 650. The three or three-and-a-half centuries between these dates and A.D. 1000 when Pisgah phase is considered to be established is a period of time where data are lacking. Hypothetically, during this 300 to 350 years Connestee society was being transformed into a sedentary agricultural life-style. Southern complicated stamped surface finishes were being applied to vessels which had rim forms originating in the Oliver phase of Indiana.

Most likely these archaeologically perceivable attributes arrived late during this period. And until their presence was felt, the rate of archaeologically observable change was slow.

The details of the Connestee settlement pattern are yet to be fully described. The survey data indicate that, like the other phases we have discussed, the Connestee folk were not particularly specialized in their use of the environment. Sites representing this phase are found in all of the microenvironments within the mountains. Connestee phase sites seem to be more numerous in the uplands than Pisgah and Qualla phase stations. On floodplain topography they are much smaller in size. As I noted in Chapter 3, no evidence of agriculture has been observed for the Connestee phase. Even if present, agriculture was not as important to the economy as it would become after the appearance of the Pisgah phase. Sites such as Gashes Creek (Bn 9) and Garden Creek Mound No. 2 (particularly the upper portion of the premound village midden) indicate that these people were certainly semisedentary. Such a settlement stability should not be unexpected when we recall that the mountains and their valleys are a rich naturally diverse environment where several microenvironments can be exploited by moving only a short distance vertically, i.e., up or down the mountainside.

PIGEON PHASE

Unfortunately, little beyond the ceramics of the Pigeon phase is known with any certainty. In several places in this study I have described the pottery in detail. It contrasts well with the more recent Connestee series and is distinctive from the earlier Swannanoa series. Little, if any, confusion between the three is likely.

Pigeon Check Stamped was the predominant type in the series. Only at the Tuckasegee site (Jk 12) was it surpassed in frequency by another type in the series. There Pigeon Plain made up 33.8 percent of the series, while Pigeon Check Stamped had a frequency of 32.6 percent. At the Warren Wilson site (Bn 29) Pigeon Check Stamped made up 44.7 percent of the series, and at Garden Creek (Hw 2) it amounted to 80.5 percent of the series.

Pigeon ceramics were characterized by crushed quartz temper. The paste was compact, but neither contorted nor laminated. Colors were typically light brown to reddish brown. Vessel forms were conical jars, open hemispherical bowls, and shouldered jars with slightly flaring rims, flat-based with four conical or wedged-shaped feet. Little elaboration was present in the form of decoration, although a few lips were notched or paddle marked.

As I have remarked earlier, Pigeon ceramics were the earliest major Appalachian Summit Area manifestation of the pan-Southeastern carved paddle horizon style. This technique of finishing the surface of vessels was so unique that it led W. H. Holmes (1903:131) to establish the South Appalachian Ceramic Province. At the time that Holmes was writing, no appreciable time depth was accorded to any remains found in the area. Consequently, he made no distinction between early and late carved paddle stamped ceramics. It was not until A. R. Kelly's (1938) work at Ocmulgee National Monument that any time depth, albeit much less than is known today, was given to South Appalachian pottery.

The ceramics of the Pigeon phase can be equated with a number of other ceramic complexes in the immediate area. The ancestral type for all carved paddle stamped types may be what Caldwell (1970) has recently called Deptford Cross Stamped, which is found on the Georgia coast. Another possible ancestor may be the type defined by Phelps (1965) as Norwood Simple Stamped, which occurs on the northwest coast of Florida. The temporal priority of one of these types over the other has yet to be demonstrated. Nonetheless, one of them is probably the earliest carved paddle stamped pottery in North America.

There has been a tendency for students of prehistoric Georgia to equate automatically the earliest check and simple stamped pottery found in any area of that state with a Deptford time level (cf. Fairbanks 1962:9-17, and Wauchope 1966:Table 12, for two examples). Betty Anderson Smith (1972) in attempting to clarify the Deptford tradition has observed that in northern Georgia considerable confusion exists concerning check stamped pottery. Based on her study of the literature, unpublished manuscripts, and collections at the University of Georgia, she points out that there is a shift in pottery type frequencies through time. The Kellog focus ceramic assemblage is composed almost exclusively of the Dunlap Fabric Marked type. The Post-Kellog focus (Forsyth period) ceramic assemblage is composed of both Dunlap Fabric Marked and Cartersville Check Stamped types. The Cartersville focus subsequent to the Forsyth period is recognized, ceramically at least, by the disappearance of the Dunlap Fabric Marked type, the appearance of the Cartersville Simple Stamped type, and the continuation of the Cartersville

Check Stamped type. There is a basic inconsistency between Caldwell's (n.d.) work in the Allatoona and Buford reservoirs if the Post-Kellog and Forsyth periods are considered to be contemporary. In the Allatoona Reservoir Caldwell (n.d. 290) indicates that during the Post-Kellog period the major type was Dunlap Fabric Marked, but in the Buford Reservoir during the Forsyth period the predominate pottery was check stamped—fabric marked pottery was rare or absent. Confusion in Georgia ceramic typology continues to cause problems when Smith indicates that a major Cartersville site, 9Fu14, is recognized on the basis of simple stamped pottery, "Deptford and Mossy Oak," and "minor amounts of Cartersville Check Stamped, fabric marked, and Swift Creek ceramics" (Smith 1972: 31).

Thirty years ago such a practice may have been logical in view of Kelly's pioneering work at Ocmulgee National Monument. But the continued use of check and simple stamping *per se* to indicate contemporaneity with Deptford has led to a great deal of confusion. In most archaeology in Georgia since 1938, the line of thought seems to have been: the earliest check or simple stamped pottery must *a priori* equate with the Deptford series, and since, as everyone knows, Deptford is replaced by complicated stamping in central Georgia, then check and simple stamping is replaced by complicated stamping elsewhere in the state. Check stamping and simple stamping do reoccur, but only in the latest cultures.

The case being made here should now be obvious. Check stamping and simple stamping do not serve *a priori* as temporal determinants. Other attributes such as vessel form, rim treatment, lip form, the presence of appendages, and the kind of appendages are just as important.

It appears to me that the Pigeon phase ought to be considered as a slightly later manifestation of the classic Deptford style. However, the Cartersville focus should be only partially so considered. As I have shown, the Connestee phase occurs later in time than the Pigeon phase in North Carolina. Furthermore, the Connestee phase ceramics compare rather well with some of the ceramics of the Cartersville focus, but not with those of the Deptford complex. The data presented in this study make it logical to assume that when most of Georgia was adopting the fashion of complicated stamped pottery, which succeeded the spread of simple and check stamped ceramics, northern Georgia, southwestern North Carolina, and eastern Tennessee formed their own interaction sphere. Here the earlier forms of pottery were continued. If such an interpretation is valid, then a number of conflicting situations are brought into accord. Such an arrangement would make the Post-Kellog complex, part of the Forsyth complex, the early Cartersville focus, Deptford, and the Pigeon phase synchronic manifestations. The later part of the Cartersville focus, the Early Swift Creek focus, the Connestee phase, and Prufer's Middle and Late Hopewell in Ohio would be roughly contemporaneous. The oversimplified chronological placements based on simple and check stamping as determinant attributes would be laid aside and the carbon 14 determinations brought into closer accord.

Other traits of the Pigeon phase have been hard to identify since no pure Pigeon component has been isolated to date. Because a number of traits were shared by both the Swannanoa and Connestee phases, it seems reasonable to assume they were present in the intervening Pigeon period. These would include flake scrapers, awls of bone as well as antler drifts, hammerstones of several varieties, stone and ceramic pipes, and celts. I have suggested that Pigeon Side Notched and Garden Creek Triangular points may belong primarily to this phase.

Sites producing typical Pigeon series ceramics occur less frequently than those of the later periods, but are found on all topographic forms. This distribution indicates that a broad range of exploitative activities was necessary to provide subsistence for the people of this culture.

That the Southern Appalachian region came under the influence of Piedmont Georgia during the time of the Pigeon phase cannot be denied. Cultures at the same latitude to the east and west continued their orientation to the earlier Northern tradition, while phases in eastern Tennessee seemed to have been even more influenced from the South than were those of Piedmont North Carolina. As I have pointed out earlier in discussing the development of Connestee ceramics, it is apparent that neither north Georgia nor southwestern North Carolina continued to follow the developments taking place in middle Georgia after the initial spread of carved paddle stamping of pottery. But with eastern Tennessee, northern Georgia and southwestern North Carolina formed an interaction sphere which was maintained until it was replaced by the advent of South Appalachian Mississippianism.

SWANNANOA PHASE

Components of the Swannanoa phase were recognized at all of the sites discussed in this study. At the Tuckasegee site (Jk 12) Swannanoa material, principally ceramics, was mixed with the remains of the later phases in the old midden zone; at Garden Creek (Hw 2) it occurred principally at the base of the premound midden; and at the Warren Wilson (Bn 29) it was stratigraphically isolated from the remains of the later phases and from earlier Archaic phases.

The ceramics of this phase reflect most strongly Northern relationships in ceramic manufacture. Cord marked or fabric impressed conoidal jars and simple bowls were the common forms of vessels. Other surface treatments occurred: simple stamping, check stamping, and smoothed plain, but not too frequently and evidently toward the end of the phase. The rare decorated sherd was always sloppily incised with vertical or oblique lines originating near the lip and continuing down the side for only a short distance.

Swannanoa ceramics are comparable in form and style to the pottery of the Kellog focus of northern Georgia (Caldwell n.d.), the Greenville complex of Tennessee (Larson 1959), and the Watts Bar focus and at least part of the Candy Creek complex of southeastern Tennessee. Comparisons which could be made to phases further removed geographically would show not only similar Northern tradition elements in ceramics but the similar occurrence of other traits which have been assigned to the Swannanoa phase. Among these would be small stemmed points, bar gorgets, continued but less frequent use of soapstone vessels, bone awls, pitted and pebble hammerstones, ochres, and net weights.

Permanent structures are presently unknown. However, postholes present at the Warren Wilson (Bn 29) indicate that some type of fairly permanent housing was present.

Contacts with the Adena Culture of the Ohio Valley seem to be lacking during the Swannanoa period or the later Pigeon phase. To be sure, the tubular pipes recovered at Warren Wilson and some gorget forms found at a number of sites may resemble artifacts found at Adena sites, but I believe these represent generalized Early Woodland concepts rather than unique Adena ideas. The vexing problem of Adena was treated in a special symposium in 1970 (Swartz 1971). The problem of Adena has yet to be resolved to my satisfaction.

Settlements during the Swannanoa period are present in all micro-environments, indicating a broad adaptation to local resources.

In western North Carolina the Swannanoa phase seems to have developed from the earlier Archaic complex by resident populations who adopted ceramics of the basic Northern tradition. The people adopted elements of the South Appalachian ceramic tradition toward the end of the Swannanoa phase when check stamping and simple stamping were introduced. These South Appalachian elements became accentuated, as I have noted, in the succeeding Pigeon phase. The basic conservatism of the mountain folk reasserted itself in the following Connestee phase when the South Appalachian elements were stabilized and blended with the old Northern tradition style of cord marking vessel surfaces.

SAVANNAH RIVER PHASE

This phase was isolated stratigraphically below the Swannanoa midden at Warren Wilson (Bn 29). It also was found in early contexts at both Tuckasegee (Jk 12) and Garden Creek (Hw 2). This complex is composed of large stemmed projectile points (Savannah River Stemmed) and knives, a smaller point which I have termed Otarre Stemmed, steatite bowls, bar gorgets, ground stone grooved axes, large elbow pipes, notched net weights, pitted and pebble hammerstones, large crude bifaces, and flake scrapers.

Fairbanks (1942:223-231) has treated the Savannah River phase in some detail, comparing it with other Archaic complexes in the Middle South and to assemblages as distant as New York. He concluded that the remains on the Savannah, the Tennessee, and the Ohio rivers could be grouped together to form a Southern Shell Mound aspect. Even though there were taxonomic similarities between these and the Lamoka Lake and Brewerton foci of New York, he felt "that two separate traditions are represented with a consequent mingling in certain foci" (Fairbanks 1942:230). I am uncertain how he would have integrated the remains of similar complexes which were not oriented to a shellfish economy.

Although the interareal relationships of the Savannah River phase are beyond the scope of this study, they have been briefly mentioned as another example of the "openness" of the systems involved. Traits which linked the North and South were present throughout most, if not all, of the prehistoric period.

MORROW MOUNTAIN PHASE

This phase was defined by Coe (1964:54) on the basis of his investigations of deeply stratified sites in central North Carolina. Elements of this phase included tapering stemmed points as diagnostics, accompanied by ground stone grooved axes, scrapers, and the other elements it shared in common with the earlier Stanly complex. Since the time of Coe's investigation, little information concerning the complex has been recognized other than a much wider distribution.

The presence of Morrow Mountain I Stemmed points in Zones C and D at Warren Wilson (Bn 29) indicated that the mountain Indians were making projectile points on the same pattern that people on the Piedmont used. Their form and the fact that they occurred below the Savannah River complex are strong indications that these manifestations were contemporary. Morrow Mountain I and Morrow Mountain II Stemmed points were recovered from Garden Creek (Hw 2), but neither type was found at Tuckasegee (Jk 12). Both types occur frequently in surface collections from the Appalachian Summit Area.

EARLIER OCCUPATIONS

Several other projectile point types which, on the basis of typology, represent periods earlier than Morrow Mountain have been noted in the descriptive portions of this study. If Coe's (1964:Fig. 116) estimates are as correct as they seem to be, and the use of "type fossils" is permissible in archaeology, then the Appalachian Summit Area was inhabited by people making finely chipped corner notched points (Palmer Corner Notched) some 9,000 to 9,500 years ago. Even earlier forms, such as the Hardaway types and fluted points, have been found in the area. From this evidence the cultural sequence of the mountains seems to follow the same course of development that occurred on the Piedmont until the earliest South Appalachian elements were introduced during the late Swannanoa phase.

THE CHRONOLOGICAL POSITION OF THE PHASES: RELATIVE AND ABSOLUTE

In this study I have shown that seven distinctive assemblages of aboriginal remains can be identified on the basis of their content and that their relative chronology can be demonstrated by stratigraphy and superposition. It is hoped that finer temporal segments will be isolated someday so that a better understanding of the history of the area can be achieved.

The earliest evidence found of human occupation recovered from any of the sites discussed in detail in this study was the Palmer Corner Notched points at Tuckasegee (Jk 12) and Garden Creek (Hw 2). This occupation was found above the Hardaway occupation at St 4 (Coe 1964). It was followed by the Kirk and Stanly occupations there; these, in turn, were superseded by Morrow Mountain, Guilford, and Savannah River occupations at the Doerschuk site. Beyond the evidence for early occupations in the form of early projectile points in the area, the presence of a Morrow Mountain assemblage at Warren Wilson (Bn 29) was the oldest incontrovertible evidence. Here, above the Morrow Mountain assemblage, Savannah River complex artifacts were found. This complex represented by Savannah River Stemmed and Otarre Stemmed points occurred in Zone C.

Evidence for the temporal priority of the Swannanoa phase over other ceramic phases has been pointed out. Units in Block III at Warren Wilson (Bn 29) were clearly deposited after the end of the Swannanoa period. Furthermore, distributional data at Garden Creek (Hw 2) indicated that Swannanoa ceramics occurred primarily at the base of the premound midden, while Pigeon and Connestee ceramics were found in greater frequencies in the upper two-thirds of the unit. Distributional data at Garden Creek (Hw 2) indicated that Connestee ceramics occurred more frequently in the uppermost one-third of the premound midden; and although the frequency of Pigeon pottery was very high in this part of the midden, evidence from the two mound constructions demonstrated that Connestee pottery was later than Pigeon ceramics. The presence of intrusive Pisgah burials at Garden Creek (Hw 2) indicated that this culture was later than the Connestee phase. The position of Qualla materials at Garden Creek (Hw 1) indicated that this phase followed the Pisgah phase. Furthermore, Qualla phase materials were often associated with Euro-American trade goods. Pisgah materials have never been recovered in such a context.

Absolute dating of the phases is difficult because of the lack of carbon 14 analyses in general for this area. As a consequence, I am forced to offer some guarded estimates based on my interpretation of the relationships the mountain phases have with other units which have been dated. The dates that are offered below are to be considered only as estimates and may have to undergo major revisions, as did my 1972 estimates when more pertinent radiocarbon dates became available.

The latest dates (Table 30) pertinent to the study were obtained from charcoal associated with Qualla phase materials at Garden Creek Mound No. 1 (Hw 1) and Tuckasegee. These dates (A.D. 1775 ± 55, A.D. 1745 ± 65, and A.D. 1730 ± 100) are in line with the observation that historic trade goods were present. I interpret these dates to apply to about the midpoint of the period. Vessels made by Cherokee women in 1880 for the Valentine Museum and in 1908 for Mark R. Harrington (1922:196) could easily be placed into the Qualla series. Vessels most likely made in the late 1600s were recovered at Coweeta Creek (Ma 34) by the writer in the summer of 1970. These are quite similar to those found at Garden Creek (Hw 1), Tuckasegee (Jk 12), and Ce 15. These collections do show some variation, but all were easily classified as a single ceramic complex.

Dickens (1970:78-79) has discussed the radiocarbon age determinations (Table 31) relevant to the Pisgah phase. He accepts these dates as good measurements and brackets the Pisgah period from about A.D. 1000 to A.D. 1550.

Estimates for the absolute dates of the Connestee phase are more difficult to arrive at than those for the Pisgah and Qualla periods. The dates suggested here are based on assemblages which have been dated in Alabama, Georgia, Ohio, and Tennessee. The dates for these assemblages are given in Table 32. The dates represent a time span of approximately five centuries and compare well with the intuitive assessment I had made before I had collected the dates from the literature (Keel 1968). The relationships that I have recognized between the Connestee phase and those from other areas have been made explicit in other sections of this chapter. Consequently, I will not repeat the details here.

The Hopewellian material recovered at Garden Creek (Hw 2) compares very favorably with material recovered from the McGraw

TABLE 30. Radiocarbon dates relative to the Qualla period.

Date and Laboratory No.	Site	Reference
A.D. 1775 ± 55 years GX0593	Tuckasegee, N. C.	J. L. Coe, personal communication
A.D. 1745 ± 65 years GX0729	Garden Creek Mound No. 1, N. C.	Dickens 1970:23
A.D. 1730 ± 100 years GX0596	Garden Creek Mound No. 1, N. C.	Dickens 1970:23

TABLE 31. Radiocarbon dates relative to the Pisgah period.

Date and Laboratory No.	Site	Reference
A.D. 1435 ± 70 years GX0595	Garden Creek Mound No. 1, N. C.	Dickens 1970:78
A.D. 1210 ± 120 years SI-131	Le-17, Va.	Holland 1970:82
A.D. 1120 ± 150 years M-939	Chauga Mound, S. C.	Kelly and Neitzel 1961:64
A.D. 1070 ± 150 years M-933	Chauga Mound, S. C.	Kelly and Neitzel 1961:64

TABLE 32. Radiocarbon dates relative to the Connestee period.

Date and Laboratory No.	Site	Reference
A.D. 605 ± 90 GX2487	Icehouse Bottom, Tenn.	Chapman 1972
A.D. 585 ± 90 GX2154	Icehouse Bottom, Tenn.	Gleeson 1970:132
A.D. 530 ± 150 M-1043	Mandeville, Ga.	Kellar, Kelly, and McMichael 1962:33
A.D. 490 ± 150 M-1045	Mandeville, Ga.	Kellar, Kelly, and McMichael 1961:81
A.D. 481 ± 65 OWU 61	McGraw, Ohio	Prufer 1965:104
A.D. 450 ± 175 ± 826	Russell Cave, Ala.	Faulkner and Grah 1966a:117
A.D. 440 ± 80 UCLA 679c	McGraw, Ohio	Prufer 1965:104
A.D. 435 ± 166 OWU 62	McGraw, Ohio	Prufer 1965:104
A.D. 280 ± 121 UGa.	Tunacunnhee, Ga.	Jefferies 1974:7
A.D. 150 ± 95 UGa.	Tunacunnhee, Ga.	Jefferies 1974:7
A.D. 1335 ± 100 GX2599	McDonald, Tenn.	Schroedl 1973:4
A.D. 1220 ± 95 GX2598	McDonald, Tenn.	Schroedl 1973:4
A.D. 1155 ± 100 GX2601	McDonald, Tenn.	Schroedl 1973:5
A.D. 1145 ± 95 GX2600	McDonald, Tenn.	Schroedl 1973:5

TABLE 32 *(cont.)*. Radiocarbon dates relative to the Connestee period.

Date and Laboratory No.	Site	Reference
A.D. 1100 ± 100 GX2597	McDonald, Tenn.	Schroedl 1973:4
A.D. 1095 ± 95 GX2606	McDonald, Tenn.	Schroedl 1973:6
A.D. 1020 ± 150 M-730	Alford, Tenn.	Faulkner 1967:22
A.D. 920 ± 95 GX2602	McDonald, Tenn.	Schroedl 1973:5
A.D. 890 ± 90 GX0777	Mason, Tenn.	Faulkner 1967:21
A.D. 815 ± 100 GX2596	McDonald, Tenn.	Schroedl 1973:4
A.D. 805 ± 120 GX2605	McDonald, Tenn.	Schroedl 1973:6
A.D. 805 ± 85 GX0593	Garden Creek Mound No. 2, N. C.	Dickens 1970:21
A.D. 800 ± 130 GX2603	McDonald, Tenn.	Schroedl 1973:5
A.D. 770 ± 85 GX0778	Mason, Tenn.	Faulkner 1967:21
A.D. 740 ± 100 I-826	Russell Cave, Ala.	Faulkner and Graham 1966a:118
A.D. 675 ± 105 GX2604	McDonald, Tenn.	Schroedl 1973:5
A.D. 625 ± 105 GX0573	Westmoreland-Barber, Tenn.	Faulkner and Graham 1966a:118

site, Ohio (Prufer 1965), and with similar material from the Mandeville site, Georgia (Kellar, Kelly, and McMichael 1961, 1962), and
Tunacunnhee, Georgia (Jefferies 1974). It seems reasonable to assume that these four manifestations are contemporary since the
similarity is strongest in terms of the whole assemblage rather than
a few isolated objects. Furthermore, the radiocarbon dates (A.D.
530 ± 150 and A.D. 490 ± 150 years) from Mandeville that were
assigned to the Hopewellian material and the dates (A.D. 440 ± 80
years and A.D. 435 ± 166 years) from McGraw overlap in their
1-sigma ranges. The dates from Tunacunnhee of A.D. 280 ± 125
years and A.D. 150 ± 95 do not fit quite so well, but all of the dates
fall with the 2-sigma range of each other except the A.D. 150 date
from Tunacunnhee. The remainder of the dates was taken from
components which shared traits found in the Connestee assemblages
at Warren Wilson (Bn 29), Garden Creek (Hw 2), and Tuckasegee
(Jk 12).

The Russell Cave, Alabama, dates (A.D. 450 ± 175 and A.D.
740 ± 100) are from associations which contained high percentages
of plain ware and low percentages of complicated stamped sherds
(I-826) and later occupational remains where complicated stamping
was more frequent (I-825). At the Westmoreland-Barber site in
southeastern Tennessee a date of A.D. 625 ± 105 years (GX0573)
was obtained from a refuse pit which contained about the same
proportion of brushed, cord marked, simple stamped, and check
stamped pottery that was present at Garden Creek (Hw 2) in Feature 30, although the Tennessee specimens were limestone tempered. This assemblage at Garden Creek (Hw 2) was dated at A.D.
805 ± 85 years, but the feature from which this date was derived
was an intrusive pit and more recent carbon may have been introduced. The Icehouse Bottom dates (A.D. 585 ± 90 and A.D. 605
± 90) were obtained from features which contained Connestee and
Candy Creek series pottery. These seem to apply to Late Connestee. The other dates presented in Table 32 are equally good indicators of a later unnamed phase which, I have suggested, is
characterized by the high frequency of plain and brushed sherds.
The A.D. 770 ± 85 years (GX0778) determination from the Mason
site, Tennessee, seems to be especially good on the basis of the
small triangular projectile points and the predominance of plain
surfaced pottery (Charles H. Faulkner, personal communication).
A second date of A.D. 890 ± 90 (GX0777) years from the Mason
site agrees with the earlier Mason date as well as the Garden Creek

(Hw 2) date. One of the latest dates cited in Table 32 is A.D. 1020 ± 150 (M-730) from the Alford site, Tennessee, a late Hamilton focus site. Faulkner (1967:22) accepts this date as valid for the end of the Hamilton period. The series of Hamilton focus dates with their standard deviations included from the McDonald site (40Rh7), Tennessee, published by Gerald Schroedl (1973) range from A.D. 570 to A.D. 1435. However, the central dates for the initial constructions of Mounds A, B, and D fall between A.D. 800 and A.D. 920. Unfortunately no details of the material recovered from the McDonald mounds have been published. This fact makes it impossible to consider relationships further. These dates, the first in over 20 years from Hamilton burial mounds, support the recently developed idea that Hamilton is quite late in time and cannot be considered contemporary with the Copena Culture (Faulkner 1971; Walthall 1973).

The ceramic assemblage dated from the Alford site (Kneberg 1961:Fig. 5) shows a general similarity to the Connestee assemblage at Garden Creek Mound No. 2 (Hw 2) except that the Alford site collection is devoid of brushed surfaced sherds. This leads me to consider that the Connestee collection at Garden Creek Mound 2 (Hw 2) is much earlier.

In spite of the problems that arise from cross dating, it seems likely the Connestee period began by A.D. 200 and very possibly even earlier. The period probably lasted until about 600 A.D., at which time it had evolved into a transition phase which would develop into the Pisgah phase.

Estimates of absolute age for the Pigeon phase were as hard to arrive at as the solutions to other problems related to this manifestation. Few radiocarbon dates assignable to the Deptford complex have been obtained, and some of those have been rejected. Ford (1969:Table 5) rejected the Deptford date from the Alligator Lake site (Lazarus 1965:83-136) as too early, but gave no reason for this appraisal. I have rejected a date of 890 ± 110 B.C. (Morrell 1960: 106) from the Oakland Mound, Florida, because it was run on material from several proveniences. As Morrell indicated, this date makes it possible to assume only that the mound was built after 890 B.C., because it is not directly applicable to any of the finds from the mound. Dates which have been regarded as acceptable by several investigators are presented in Table 33. These dates show that check stamping was present in Florida, Georgia, and Tennessee prior to the beginning of the Christian era. Furthermore, vessel

TABLE 33. Radiocarbon dates relative to the Pigeon period.

Date and Laboratory No.	Site	Reference
A.D. 200 ± 130 years I-1367	Crystal River, Fla.	Bullen 1966:22
A.D. 80 ± 130 years I-1366	Crystal River, Fla.	Bullen 1966:22
5 ± 150 years B.C. M-1042	Mandeville, Ga.	Kellar, Kelly, and McMichael 1961:81
15 ± 95 years B.C. I-1961	Burtine Island, Fla.	Bullen 1966:20
100 ± 250 years B.C. M-516	Camp Creek, Tenn.	Faulkner 1967:19
154 ± 140 years B.C. M-1116	Booger Bottom, Ga.	Fairbanks 1954
240 ± 140 years B.C. SI-264	Walker Street, Ga.	Radiocarbon 1967:
270 ± 100 years B.C. UGa.-104	Seaside Mound I	Smith 1972:19
335 ± 110 years B.C. GX0780	Brickyard	Faulkner 1967:17-
400 ± 220 years B.C. UGa.-AC3	Seaside Mound I	Smith 1972:19

forms and rim and lip treatments, as well as the form of tetrapodal supports, found in these complexes are identical to those present in the Pigeon series of ceramics. On this basis I offer a temporal span from 300 B.C. to A.D. 100 for the Pigeon phase. In doing this, I find some comfort in the fact that Fairbanks (1962:9) suggested essentially the same range. However, Fairbanks (1965:255) has since extended the beginning to a much earlier date based on the Oakland Mound date. Griffin (1967:177) suggested a time span lasting from a few centuries B.C. up to the beginning of the Christian era. Ford (1969:12) suggested a span from 500 B.C. to A.D. 100. Others, to mention but a few, who have placed the Deptford complex in the same temporal span include Caldwell (1958:Fig. 8), Williams (1968: 322), and Willey (1966:Fig. 5-2).

The dating of the Swannanoa phase relies primarily on radiocarbon dates from Georgia and Tennessee (Table 34). The stratigraphy at Warren Wilson (Bn 29) demonstrates that the Swannanoa phase is not as old as the preceramic Savannah River complex. The priority of the Swannanoa phase over the Pigeon phase was also shown at Warren Wilson (Bn 29) and at Garden Creek (Hw 2).

The debate concerning the earliest ceramics in North America was settled when William A. Ritchie (1962:583-584) acknowledged that the dates for fiber tempered pottery presented by Bullen (1961: 104-106) were correct and preceded the Vinette ceramic dates by 1,500 years. Nonetheless, the initial cord marked and fabric impressed pottery found in the southeastern United States seems to be the product of the same Asiatic tradition which gave rise to other Woodland ceramics (Griffin 1967:180). The dates cited in Table 34 were taken from site components which contained primarily cord marked or fabric impressed pottery and serve as basement dates for the introduction of Northern tradition ceramics into the Southeast. On the basis of the overall similarity of the Swannanoa ceramics and other traits of this phase with the complexes associated with the dates presented in Table 34, I offer a beginning date of about 700 or 600 B.C. and a terminal date of about 200 B.C. for the Swannanoa phase.

The relative age of the Savannah River phase is shown by its position in the stratigraphy at Warren Wilson (Bn 29). Here, as I have stated, the Swannanoa remains were found above those of the Morrow Mountain phase. Radiocarbon assessments of the age of the Savannah River phase are numerous (Table 35), but there are few dates for the Morrow Mountain phase. On the basis of these dates

TABLE 34.   Radiocarbon dates relative to the Swannanoa period.

Date	Site	Reference
150 ± 200 years B.C. I-824	Russell Cave, Ala.	Faulkner and Graham 1966a:114
340 ± 150 years B.C. GX574	Westmoreland-Barber, Tenn.	Faulkner and Graham 1966a:113
540 ± 100 years B.C. M-1117	Mahan, Ga.	Radiocarbon 1963:24(
630 ± 100 years B.C. M-1116	Mahan, Ga.	Radiocarbon 1963:24(
695 ± 300 years B.C. M-31	Newt Cash Hollow, Ky.	Crane 1963:666-664
841 ± 68 years B.C. Y 981	Hunter, N. Y.	Ritchie 1962:584

TABLE 35.   Radiocarbon dates relative to the Savannah River period.

Date	Site	Reference
755 ± 155 years B.C. GX572	Westmoreland-Barber, Tenn.	Faulkner and Graham 1966a:113
1565 ± 140 years B.C. GX2275	Warren Wilson, N. C.	J. L. Coe, personal communication
1780 ± 150 years B.C. M-1278	Stallings Island, Ga.	Bullen and Greene 1970:12
2050 ± 250 years B.C. M-524	Gaston, N. C.	Coe 1964:118
2750 ± 150 years B.C. M-1279	Stallings Island, Ga.	Bullen and Greene 1970:11
2915 ± 280 years B.C. GX2274	Warren Wilson, N. C.	J. L. Coe, personal communication

(Table 35), I suggest that the period of time occupied by the Savannah River phase as it was manifested in North Carolina was from 2500 B.C. until about 800 or 600 B.C. The Savannah River phase was associated with the earliest pottery found in North America. It occurs on the Georgia coast, along the Savannah River, and on the Florida Gulf coast. The fact that cultures without pottery, but otherwise with a Savannah River assemblage, existed had been observed by several writers (cf. Sears 1964).

Joffre Coe (1964:123) felt that there was no basis for assigning a date prior to about 4500 B.C. to the Morrow Mountain complex. This appraisal has been substantiated by Griffin's (personal communication) dates for the Morrow Mountain complex at Russell Cave, Alabama, of 3970 ± 200 B.C. and 4290 ± 190 B.C.

INTRAAREAL DISTRIBUTION OF SITES

In the southern part of the Blue Ridge Province, herein referred to as the Appalachian Summit Area, survey teams of the Research Laboratories of Anthropology had located over 1,400 archaeological sites by the end of 1972. Sites were found along the broad floodplains of the rivers, along the "terraces" or intermountain land between the mountain slopes and the floodplain, on the floors of the coves, along the smaller creeks and branches in the mountains proper, on the ridges, and even on the mountain summits. There seems to have been no microenvironment that was unoccupied for at least a short period of time by each of the cultures discussed in this study.

Although the material collected from the surveys has not been analyzed completely, preliminary studies provide a general impression of the spatial distribution of the phases and complexes discussed in this study.

Historic, Mississippian, Woodland, and Archaic artifact types were found in all parts of the mountains. The major villages of the Pisgah and Qualla phases, which we know cultivated corn, beans, and squash, were located on the floodplains of the rivers. However, we found components of these phases on the other landforms as well. The same generalization holds true for the Connestee, Pigeon, and Swannanoa phases. The use of the total landscape during the Archaic period can be shown by the distribution of materials at Warren Wilson (Bn 29), Garden Creek (Hw 2), Tuckasegee (Jk 12), and Holden's (1966) Transylvania County survey as well as surveys conducted by the author.

It can be demonstrated that all of the landscape was utilized, but the reason for this is not as easily shown. There is clear evidence that, at any one time, the inhabitants of the area were not adapted to any particular topography; instead, the people of all periods used all of the landscape, and the pattern of site distribution reflects ecological considerations. For instance, some berries, e.g., blackberries (*Rubus alleghbeniensis*), growing on the floodplain ripen several weeks prior to those growing on the higher elevations. Frederick J. Ruff (1938) has noted that deer in the Pisgah National Forest while not moving over long distance do make short movements within the area. These movements seem to be controlled by food availability, cover, weather, and seasonal phenomena. During the critical winter period deer congregate at lower elevations in the sheltered hollows and caves. During the early spring, they begin a seasonal movement upslope as browse becomes available, but by late summer they are moving again to lower elevations. By September they are feeding on mast in the oak-chestnut areas of higher elevation, but as winter sets in they begin to return to the lower slopes (Ruff 1938:28-29).

The seasonal variation of availability of wild plant foods coupled with the movements of deer as well as their predators and likely other species may account for the rather high density of sites in the upland areas through the history of aboriginal occupation of the Appalachian Summit Area.

SUMMARY

The identification of at least a segment of historic period Cherokee material culture was accomplished in describing the remains associated with the structure at the Tuckasegee site, Jk 12. Research conducted by Joffre Coe, University of North Carolina, in western North Carolina; Alfred K. Guthe, University of Tennessee, in the Tellico Reservoir; and John D. Combes, University of South Carolina, in the Keowee-Toxaway Reservoir will shed much more light on this period of Cherokee culture history. Undoubtedly, detailed comparative studies between the Underhill towns of South Carolina, the Middle and Valley towns of North Carolina, and the Overhill towns of Tennessee will be made in the near future now that substantial amounts of new data from these areas are becoming available.

The temporal order of the various prehistoric phases has been demonstrated for the Appalachian Summit Area in this study. The method used to achieve this ordering has been largely stratigraphic. Surface finds and the occasional occurrence of early projectile point types in excavated sites have suggested that the Appalachian Summit Area followed the same cultural development during the Archaic period that Joffre L. Coe (1964) discovered on the Carolina Piedmont. At the Warren Wilson site (Bn 29), we found a Morrow Mountain phase level situated below a Savannah River phase midden. This layer predated a Swannanoa midden. Above the Swannanoa zone, in the plow zone, the majority of the remains belonged to the Pisgah phase. However, in this layer there was a small amount of Pigeon and Connestee material. It seemed likely that the Pigeon and Connestee phases were intermediate in time between the Swannanoa phase and Pisgah phase.

Beneath Garden Creek Mound No. 2 (Hw 2), the midden produced a large quantity of Swannanoa, Pigeon, and Connestee remains. Ceramic frequency distributions (Fig. 19b) suggested a sequence of Swannanoa-Pigeon-Connestee. Additionally, the fact that the features contemporary with the mound construction and use contained Connestee materials indicated the Pigeon phase should be placed earlier than the Connestee phase but later than the Swannanoa phase. The chronological position of the Pisgah phase was again suggested by the fact that there were Pisgah materials intrusive into the Connestee period mound stages. Qualla phase items were also found to be intrusive into the Connestee period mounds.

The chronological position of the Qualla phase was established by several lines of evidence. First, European trade goods have been found repeatedly associated with Qualla components but never with any other phase component. Qualla phase items have been shown to postdate the other phases at Tuckasegee (Jk 12). Finally, Qualla remains were clearly later in time than the Pisgah period remains at Garden Creek Mound No. 1 (Hw 1). It might also be added that Cherokee potters continued to make what any archaeologist would regard as Qualla ceramics as late as 1908.

Although this study has established the basic sequence of the cultures in the study area, refinement of dating within the periods is desirable. This can be achieved by at least two methods:

(1) seriation or (2) careful excavation of sites which have substantial midden thickness related to the period in question. The latter method would be preferred.

A detailed investigation of the ecological adaptation of the cultural phases defined in this study would be a substantial project in itself. However, a few comments can be made regarding the economics of these units. The Qualla and Pisgah folk relied to a large degree on agriculture, but they also exploited other vegetal resources. No corn, beans, or squash have been observed for any of the other phases to date. The presence of nut and acorn fragments in numerous Woodland pits implies a great dependence on these foods. The abundance of deer bones in all components is typical of the eastern Woodlands throughout its development. In general, the faunal remains identified from a Pisgah context suggest the use of a wide variety of animals for food or other purposes. More specialized analysis of the floral and faunal remains recovered from these sites remains to be done.

The principal process which ties the cultures of the Appalachian Summit Area to cultures beyond the mountains seems to be diffusion. There is no evidence of any break in the form of cultural growth which cannot be explained in diffusionist terms. Although many of the more obvious traits seem to have their origins outside of the area, the aboriginal peoples there certainly adapted these in terms of their unique environment.

Appendix: *Pottery Descriptions*

CONNESTEE SERIES

CONNESTEE BRUSHED (Plate 45; Fig. 25)

Method of Manufacture: Annular or segmented coils built on a conical, disc, or tabular base. Coils welded by paddle stamping.

Paste: (1) Temper: Very fine to medium-size sand. Occasionally small amounts of crushed quartz added as temper. Fine sand was the predominant form of aplastic and composed 15 to 30 percent of the paste. Sand edges were rounded. Some vessels contained substantial amounts of flake mica which may represent clay sources rather than purposeful additions to the clay.
(2) Texture: Compact, well worked without contortions or laminae, smooth but sandy to the touch.
(3) Color: A wide range of colors present. Tones grade from light tan to very dark brown. Darker colors predominate. Black fire clouds present.

Firing: Vessels fired in both inverted and upright positions in open fire. A reducing atmosphere seems to have been more common than an oxidizing atmosphere. Dark cores were present in a small number of sherds.

Surface Treatment: (1) Exterior: Fine to medium-width parallel lines were scratched into the damp surface by a twig brush or the edge of a sinew-wrapped paddle. Individual brush marks ranged in width from 0.2 to 1.5 mm. The serrations were unevenly spaced, but were usually close together. In depth they varied from slight scratches to 1.5 mm. The orientation of the long axis of the tool marks was most commonly parallel (62.4 percent) to the vessel mouth but was occasionally placed perpendicular (26 percent) or oblique (11.6 percent) to the rim.
(2) Interior: Finished by hand smoothing. Coil joints rarely observed on the interior.

Decoration: A plain band was present between the inflection of the shoulder and the rim on about 10 percent of the rim sherds. Rarely this band was enhanced by a circuit of circular or rectilinear punctations around the shoulder. Only a very small number of incised sherds of the series occurred and at least one of these was of sufficient size to indicate that the vessel

PLATE 45. Connestee Brushed sherds.

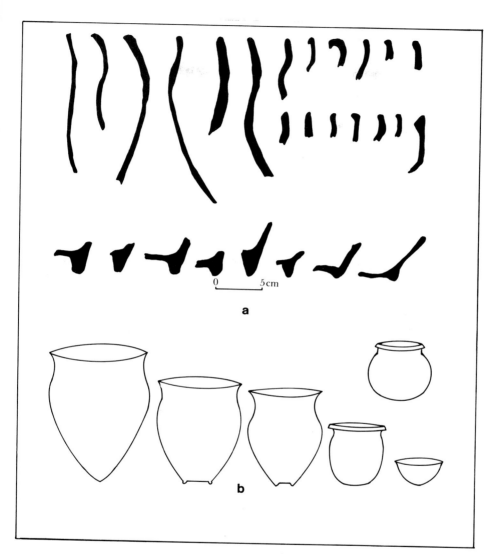

FIG. 25. Connestee series forms: a, rim and base profiles; b, vessel forms.

body had been brushed. Incisions were uniformly narrow. Curvilinear and rectilinear motifs were present. Lips were also decorated; see below.

Form: Conoidal jars, hemispherical bowls, and flat-based jars with tetrapodal supports.
(1) Lip: Three styles of lip were observed and had the following distributions: Rounded, 53 percent; flattened, 41.1 percent; and chamfered, 5.9 percent. Decoration of the lip had the following forms and distribution: notched, 41 percent; brushed, 14.7 percent; and punctated, 2.9 percent. Unmodified lips made up the remaining 41.4 percent of the sample. Thickness averaged 4.5 mm at a point 3 mm from the edge of the lip. The range of thickness at this point was 3 to 6 mm. Decorated lips were slightly thicker than undecorated forms due to the compaction of the lip region produced by the decorative technique.
(2) Rim: Most often flaring (55.8 percent), but straight vertical rims (35.3 percent) and incurved rims (8.9 percent) were present.
(3) Body: Below the shoulder of necked vessels the body was rounded or straight-sided. Conoidal vessels had straight sides. Bowl forms were hemispherical. Body sherds averaged 5.8 mm thick with a range of 3 to 10 mm.
(4) Base: Three basal forms were observed: conical, rounded, and flat. Flat-based jars had appliqued or modeled tetrapodal supports which averaged 13.9 mm long with a range of 8 to 29 mm. Basal thickness ranged from 3 to 11 mm with a mean of 6.9 mm. Tetrapods were rounded or knobby or occasionally pyramidal.

Vessel Size: Estimated. Conoidal jars, rim diameter, 12-40 cm; height, to 45 cm. Bowls, rim diameter, 9-30 cm; height, 10-20 cm. Jars, rim diameter, 16-22 cm; height, 16-35 cm.

CONNESTEE CORD MARKED (Plate 46; Fig. 25)

Method of Manufacture: Same as Connestee Brushed.

Paste: Same as Connestee Brushed.

Firing: Same as Connestee Brushed.

Surface Treatment: (1) Exterior: The exteriors of vessels of this type were completely covered with cord impressions except for a small group (10.5 percent of the rim sherds) which had a plain neck band. The paddle used to stamp the vessels was wrapped with an s-twisted, commonly two-ply, cord that averaged about 2 mm in diameter. The cord impressions were placed perpendicular to the vessel mouth in 92.1 percent of the sample that was studied in detail.
(2) Interior: Same as Connestee Brushed.

Decoration: One percent of the plain band neck sherds had circular punctates.

PLATE 46.   Connestee Cord Marked sherds.

Form: (1) Lip: Same as Connestee Brushed except decorated lips of all types occurred about half as often as frequencies given for Connestee Brushed.
(2) Rim: Flared rims accounted for approximately 70 percent of the sample, whereas straight rims composed about 30 percent of the sample.
(3) Body: Same as Connestee Brushed.
(4) Base: Same as Connestee Brushed except tetrapodal-based vessels were less common and conoidal bases more common.

Vessel Size: Same as Connestee Brushed.

CONNESTEE SIMPLE STAMPED (Plate 47a; Fig. 25)

Method of Manufacture: Same as Connestee Brushed.

Paste: Same as Connestee Brushed.

Firing: Same as Connestee Brushed.

Surface Treatment: (1) Exterior: The entire vessel malleated with a parallel-grooved paddle except for jars with plain neck bands and flat bases. The long axis of the stamp was usually parallel to the mouth of the vessel (69 percent), but occasionally diagonal (23 percent) or rarely perpendicular (8 percent) to the orifice. Grooves averaged 2.6 mm wide and 1.5 mm deep; bands averaged 3.5 mm wide.
(2) Interior: Same as Connestee Brushed.

Decoration: Plain neck bands and shoulder punctates present but rare.

Form: Same as Connestee Brushed. Flat-bottom footed jars seemed more prevalent in the category than in other series types.
(1) Lip: Same forms as Connestee Brushed; however, paddle marked lips occurred on 30 percent of the rims.
(2) Rim: Same as Connestee Brushed. Majority (58.9 percent) of the rims was flaring.
(3) Body: Same as Connestee Brushed. Wall thickness averaged 5.4 mm.
(4) Base: Same as Connestee Brushed.

Vessel Size: Same as Connestee Brushed.

CONNESTEE CHECK STAMPED (Plate 47b; Fig. 25)

Method of Manufacture: Same as Connestee Brushed.

Paste: Same as Connestee Brushed.

Firing: Same as Connestee Brushed.

Surface Treatment: (1) Exterior: Except for plain neck bands and the bases of tetrapodally supported jars the entire surface was covered with a grid pattern produced by a carved paddle. The checks average 5 X 4 mm in size

a

b

PLATE 47.   Connestee sherds; a, Simple Stamped; b, Checked Stamped.

as compared to 9 X 7 mm checks on Swannanoa Check Stamped. Pigeon Check Stamped had the same size range of checks, but paste characteristics make it possible to distinguish between the two types.
(2) Interior: Same as Connestee Brushed.

Decoration: Same as Connestee Brushed.

Form: Same as Connestee Brushed.

Vessel Size: Same as Connestee Brushed.

CONNESTEE PLAIN (Plate 48; Fig. 25)

Method of Manufacture: Same as Connestee Brushed.

Paste: Same as Connestee Brushed.

Firing: Same as Connestee Brushed.

Surface Treatment: (1) Exterior: Well smoothed but not polished or burnished. It was impossible to distinguish between rim sherds of this type and the plain banded neck sherds of other types in the series unless the sherds were very large.
(2) Interior: Same as Connestee Brushed.

Decoration: Same as Connestee Brushed. Some of the incised plain neck band sherds may belong to this type.

Form: Same as Connestee Brushed. Body averaged 5.3 mm thick but had the same range as other types in the series. Bowl forms and globular, necked jars seemed to occur more frequently in the category than in others of the series.

Vessel Size: Same as Connestee Brushed.

CONNESTEE FABRIC IMPRESSED

A small number (less than 100) sherds exhibiting the paste characteristics of the Connestee series and having impressions of a tightly woven twined fabric have been classified as this type. Weft elements of the fabric were tightly twisted two-ply cords between 1.5 and 2.0 mm in diameter, and warp elements were spaced about 5.0 mm apart and were somewhat larger than the weft. It is assumed this minority type exhibits the other general attributes of the series.

PLATE 48. Connestee Plain sherds.

PIGEON SERIES

PIGEON CHECK STAMPED (Plate 49; Fig. 26)

Method of Manufacture: Annular or segmented coils on a conical or tabular base. Coils were firmly welded together by paddle stamping.

Paste: (1) Temper: Crushed quartz or, rarely, crushed felspar. Grain size ranged from 1.5 to 3.5 mm with a mean of 3.0 mm. Rarely large pieces of quartz with a mean up to 6.0 mm were present. Temper constituted from 15 to 35 percent of the paste. A 10X magnification showed temper particles to be quite angular.
(2) Texture: Compact and even. Weathered specimens are gritty to the touch, but unweathered sherds are quite smooth.
(3) Color: Light brown, light to dark gray, and red to orange. Lighter colors more common.

Firing: Apparently some vessels were fired upright and others were inverted. Dark cores were occasionally present.

Surface Finish: (1) Exterior: Entire surface, except flat-bottomed tetra-podally supported jars, covered with checkered pattern produced by stamping with a carved paddle. Rectangular checks that average 4 X 5 mm and ranged from 2 X 4 to 9 X 7 mm in size more frequent than square checks that average 4 X 4 mm and ranged from 3 X 3 mm to 6 X 6 mm in size.
(2) Interior: Well smoothed and often polished. The iridescent sheen produced by rubbing with a steatite pebble on the interior of Pigeon ceramics was one of the easiest recognizable attributes of the series.

Decoration: None; however, see lip treatment.

Form: Simple open bowls, straight-sided conoidal jars, jars with slightly restricted necks, and flat bases with large tetrapodal supports.
(1) Lip: Rounded or flattened. Compressed and thickened by paddle stamping of lip, which was not a common practice, occurring on only 19 percent of the rim sherds. Incipient folded or everted-appearing lips were produced by lip paddling.
(2) Rim: Straight or slightly flaring.
(3) Body: Straight-sided or with slight shoulders. Thickness ranged from 4 to 8 mm and had a mean of 5.3 mm.
(4) Base: Commonly flat and supported by large tetrapods. Rounded and conical bases were also present. Tetrapods were large, ranging up to 45 mm long with a mean of 26.7 mm, or approximately double the length of Connestee tetrapods (mean = 13.9 mm). Basal thickness ranged from 3.5 to 11 mm with a mean value of 6.1 mm. Tetrapods were conical or wedge-shaped.

PLATE 49.   Pigeon Check Stamped sherds.

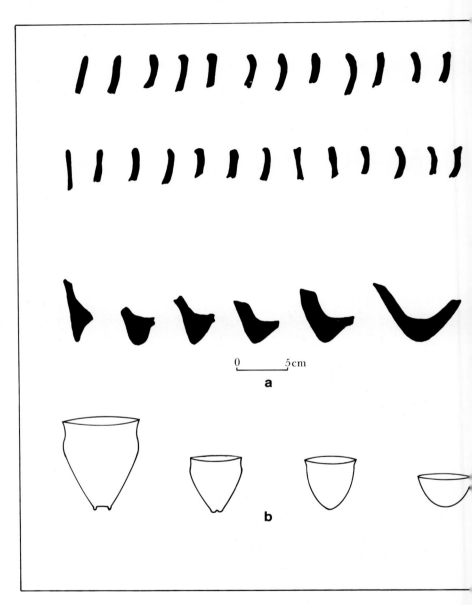

FIG. 26.   Pigeon series forms: a, rim and base profiles; b, vessel forms.

Vessel Size: Estimated. Bowls, rim diameter, 9-25 cm; height, to 14 cm. Conoidal jars, rim diameter, 9-46 cm; height, to 50 cm. Tetrapodal jars, rim diameter, 14-40 cm; height, to 40 cm.

PIGEON SIMPLE STAMPED (Plate 17f)

Method of Manufacture: Same as Pigeon Check Stamped.

Paste: Same as Pigeon Check Stamped.

Firing: Same as Pigeon Check Stamped.

Surface Treatment: (1) Exterior: Placement of parallel impressions from a carved paddle covered the same area as described for Pigeon Check Stamped. Bands were from 2 to 3.5 mm wide and grooves from 2 to 3 mm wide and about 1 mm or less deep. In most cases the pattern of bands and grooves was parallel to the mouth of the vessel on the upper portion of the vessel but rotated to the vertical near the base of conoidal jars.
(2) Interior: Same as Pigeon Check Stamped.

Decoration: Same as Pigeon Check Stamped.

Form: Same as Pigeon Check Stamped.

Vessel Size: Same as Pigeon Check Stamped.

PIGEON PLAIN (Plate 6n)

Method of Manufacture: Same as Pigeon Check Stamped.

Paste: Same as Pigeon Check Stamped.

Firing: Same as Pigeon Check Stamped.

Surface Finish: (1) Exterior: Well smoothed and usually characterized by an iridescent sheen except on weathered sherds. Ceramics having this characteristic sheen have been experimentally produced by polishing bone-dry vessels with a piece of steatite prior to firing.
(2) Interior: Same as Pigeon Check Stamped.

Decoration: None.

Form: Same as Pigeon Check Stamped.

Vessel Size: Same as Pigeon Check Stamped.

PIGEON BRUSHED

This type has been recognized only at Garden Creek Mound No. 2, where it made up 1.7 percent of the series. Brushing was fine, 0.5 to 1.5 mm in width, and was placed vertically or diagonally to the mouth of the vessel.

PIGEON COMPLICATED STAMPED (Plate 17d, e)

This is another minority type found in the series. At excavated sites it had the following frequencies in the series: Tuckaseegee, 21.5 percent; Garden Creek Mound No. 2, 0.20 percent; and Warren Wilson, 20.1 percent. Rectilinear motifs similar to Napier Stamped predominated, but curvilinear Swift Creek-like motifs were also present.

SWANNANOA SERIES

SWANNANOA CORD MARKED (Plate 50, Fig. 27)

Method of Manufacture: Coiled on conoidal or disc-shaped base. Some bases have a central nipple-like protrusion.

Paste: (1) Temper: Heavily tempered with crushed quartz (56 percent) or coarse sand (44 per cent). Temper makes up to 40 percent of the paste. The size of the crushed quartz had a mean of 4.6 mm and ranged from 3 to 19 mm. Individual pieces of temper as large as 17 X 12 X 7 mm have been noted. The mean sand grain size was 2.1 mm with a range of 1.5 to 3.0 mm.
(2) Texture: Compact, sandy or gritty to the touch.
(3) Color: Red, reddish brown, and light brown.

Firing: Inverted or upright in open fire.

Surface Treatment: (1) Exterior: Entire vessel surface malleated with a cord wrapped paddle. The long axis of the cords usually were placed vertically to the rim and rotated to the diagonal at the base. Cordage was two- or three-ply S-twisted with a range of diameters from 1.0 to 3.5 mm and a mean of about 2.4 mm. The majority of the paddles were wrapped closely, but some had a space of 5 mm between individual cords.
(2) Interior: Hand smoothed, gritty or sandy to the touch.

Decoration: Extremely rare shallow X's or parallel lines were incised over the cord marked surface. Fewer than 10 of the more than 5,000 Swannanoa sherds studied from the Warren Wilson collection were incised.

Form: Large- to medium-sized conoidal jars and hemispherical bowls.
(1) Lip: Rounded, 69 percent, or flattened, 31 percent. Notching of lips was rarely practiced (5 percent), and about 7 percent of the lips were cord marked.
(2) Rim: Vertical or slightly incurved.
(3) Body: Straight-sided or slightly barrel-shaped jars and hemispherical bowls. Body thickness averaged 8.1 mm and had a range of 6 to 12 mm.
(4) Base: Conical; conical with nipple-like protrusion; or jars, rounded or slightly flattened on bowls. Basal sherds were often 20 mm thick.

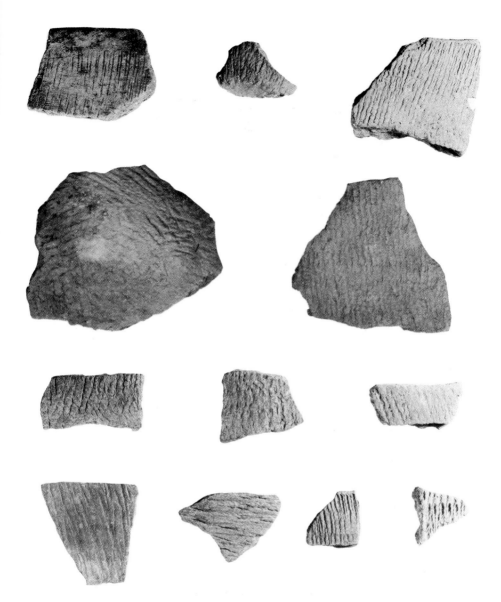

PLATE 50. Swannanoa Cord Marked sherds.

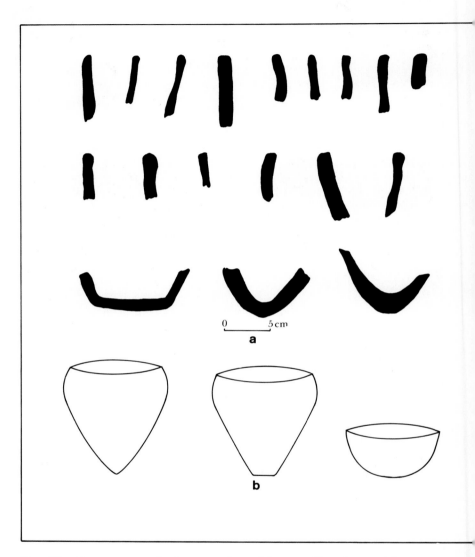

FIG. 27. Swannanoa series form: a, rim and base profiles; b, vessel forms.

Vessel Size: Estimated. Jars, rim diameter 16-45 cm; height, to 60 cm. Bowls, rim diameter, 9025 cm; height, 10-20 cm.

SWANNANOA FABRIC IMPRESSED (Plate 51; Fig. 27)

Method of Manufacture: Same as Swannanoa Cord Marked.

Paste: Same as Swannanoa Cord Marked.

Firing: Same as Swannanoa Cord Marked.

Surface Treatment: (1) Exterior: Entire vessel covered with impressions of a twined fabric. Warp elements ranged in size from 5 to 15 mm with a mean of 8.9 mm. Weft diameters were somewhat smaller, ranging from 5 to 9 mm with a mean of 6.9 mm. A few sherds appeared to have been finished with untwisted fibers or sinew, since no clear cord twists could be seen.
(2) Interior: Same as Swannanoa Cord Marked.

Decoration: None.

Form: Same as Swannanoa Cord Marked.

Vessel Size: Same as Swannanoa Cord Marked.

SWANNANOA PLAIN (Plate 52a; Fig. 27)

Method of Manufacture: Same as Swannanoa Cord Marked.

Paste: Same as Swannanoa Cord Marked.

Firing: Same as Swannanoa Cord Marked.

Surface Finish: (1) Exterior: Hand smoothed over the entire vessel.
(2) Interior: Same as Swannanoa Cord Marked.

Decoration: None.

Form: Hemispherical bowls seemed to have been more frequently represented than jar forms in the collections from excavated sites.

Vessel Size: Same as Swannanoa Cord Marked.

SWANNANOA SIMPLE STAMPED (Plate 52b; Fig. 27)

Method of Manufacture: Same as Swannanoa Cord Marked.

Paste: Same as Swannanoa Cord Marked.

Firing: Same as Swannanoa Cord Marked.

Surface Treatment: (1) Exterior: Vessel covered with carelessly applied simple stamping. Lands up to 7 mm wide, but averaged about 2.5 mm in width. Grooves were of similar size as the lands and were relatively deep, up to

PLATE 51. Swannanoa Fabric Impressed sherds.

PLATE 52.   Swannanoa sherds; a, Plain; b, Simple Stamped.

2.5 mm but averaging 1.5 mm. Many sherds appeared to have been purposely cross-stamped.

(2) Interior: Same as Swannanoa Cord Marked.

Decoration: None.

Form: Same as Swannanoa Cord Marked.

Vessel Size: Same as Swannanoa Cord Marked.

SWANNANOA CHECK STAMPED

Method of Manufacture: Same as Swannanoa Cord Marked.

Paste: Same as Swannanoa Cord Marked.

Firing: Same as Swannanoa Cord Marked.

Surface Treatment: (1) Exterior: Vessel surface covered with large shallow checks ranging in size from 6 X 8 mm to 7 X 10 mm with a mean of 7 X 9 mm. Usually poorly executed.

(2) Interior: Same as Swannanoa Cord Marked.

Decoration: None.

Form: Same as Swannanoa Cord Marked.

Vessel Size: Same as Swannanoa Cord Marked.

Bibliography

Adair, James. 1940. *Adair's History of the American Indians*, ed. Samuel Cole Williams. Watauga Press, Johnson City, Tenn.

Bartram, William. 1940. *The Travels of William Bartram*, ed. Mark Van Doren. Dover Publications, New York.

Binford, Lewis R., and Sally R. Binford (eds.). 1968. *New Perspectives in Archaeology*. Aldine Publishing Co., Chicago.

Brown, Jack, and Richard A. Gould. 1964. Column chromatography and the possibility of carbon-lens migration. *American Antiquity* 29:387-389.

Broyles, Bettye J. 1967. Bibliography of pottery type descriptions from the eastern United States. *Southeastern Archaeological Conference*, Bull. 4.

_____. 1968. St. Albans site, West Virginia. *Newsletter, Southeastern Archaeological Conference* 11 (1):10-11.

Bullen, Ripley P. 1961. Radiocarbon dates for Southeastern fiber-tempered pottery. *American Antiquity* 27:104-106.

_____. 1963. The earliest pottery in the Southeastern United States, 2000-1000 B.C. and its case as an independent invention. *VIe Congress International des Sciences Anthropologiques et Ethnologiques 1960* 2(1): 363-367. Paris.

_____. Burtine Island, Citrus County, Florida. *Contributions of the Florida State Museum, Social Sciences*, No. 14. Gainesville.

Bullen, Ripley P., and H. Bruce Greene. 1970. Stratigraphic tests at Stallings Island, Georgia. *Florida Anthropologist* 23:8-28. Gainesville.

Caldwell, Joseph R. 1947. Appraisal of the archaeological resources, Allatoona Reservoir in Bartow, Cobb, and Cherokee counties, Georgia. Mimeographed. River Basin Surveys, Smithsonian Institution, Washington, D.C.

_____. 1950. A preliminary report on excavations in the Allatoona Reservoir. *Early Georgia* 1. Athens.

_____. 1952. Archaeology of eastern Georgia and South Carolina. In *Archeology of the Eastern United States*, ed. James B. Griffin. Univ. of Chicago Press, Chicago.

_____. 1953a. Appraisal of the archaeological resources, Buford Reservoir in Hall, Forsyth, Dawson, and Gwinnett Counties, northern Georgia. Mimeographed. River Basin Surveys, Smithsonian Institution, Washington, D.C.

_____. 1953b. Appraisal of the archaeological resources of Hartwell Reservoir, South Carolina and Georgia. Mimeographed. National Park Service, Richmond.

Caldwell, Joseph R. 1954. The Old Quartz industry of Piedmont Georgia and South Carolina. *Southern Indian Studies* 5:37-39. Chapel Hill, N.C.

_____. 1955. Cherokee pottery from northern Georgia. *American Antiquity* 20:277-280.

_____. 1958. Trend and tradition in the prehistory of the eastern United States. *Memoirs of the American Anthropological Association*, No. 88.

_____. 1970. Chronology of the Georgia coast. Paper presented at the 27th Southeastern Archaeological Conference, Columbia.

_____. n.d. Survey and excavations in the Allatoona Reservoir, northern Georgia. Unpublished ms on file, Dept. of Anthropology, University of Georgia, Athens.

Caldwell, Joseph R., and Robert L. Hall (eds.). 1964. Hopewellian studies. *Illinois State Museum Scientific Papers*, Vol. XII. Springfield.

Caldwell, Joseph R., Charles E. Thompson, and Sheila K. Caldwell. 1952. The Booger Bottom Mound, a Forsyth period site in Hall County, Georgia. *American Antiquity* 17:319 and 328.

Caldwell, Joseph R., and Antonio J. Waring, Jr. 1939a. Coastal Georgia pottery type descriptions. *Newsletter, Southeastern Archaeological Conference* 1 (5 and 6).

_____. 1939b. The use of a ceramic sequence in the classification of aboriginal sites in Chatham County, Georgia. *Newsletter, Southeastern Archaeological Conference* 3:6-7.

Cambron, James W., and David C. Hulse. 1969. *Handbook of Alabama Archaeology*, Part 1, Point types. Archaeological Research Association of Alabama, Inc., Birmingham.

Carney, C. B., A. V. Hardy, and C. H. M. van Bavel. 1963. *Weather and Climate in North Carolina*. North Carolina Agricultural Experiment Station, Raleigh.

Chang, K. C. 1967. *Rethinking Archaeology*. Random House, New York.

_____. 1968. Toward a science of prehistoric society. In *Settlement Archaeology*, ed. K. C. Chang. National Press Books, Palo Alto, Calif.

Chapman, Jefferson. 1972. Hopewell elements in lower valley at the Little Tennessee River. Paper presented at the 1971 Southeastern Archaeological Conference, Macon, Ga.

_____. 1973. The Icehouse Bottom site 40Mr23. M.A. thesis, Dept. of Anthropology, Univ. of North Carolina, Chapel Hill.

Claflin, William H., Jr. 1931. The Stalling's Island Mound, Columbia County, Georgia. *Papers of the Peabody Museum*, Vol. 14, No. 1

Clarke, David L. 1968. *Analytical Archaeology*. Methuen and Co., Ltd., London.

Cochran, David. 1962. *The Cherokee Frontier: Conflict and Survival 1740-62*. Univ. of Oklahoma Press, Norman.

Coe, Joffre L. 1952. The cultural sequences of the Carolina Piedmont. In *Archeology of the Eastern United States*, ed. James B. Griffin, Univ. of Chicago Press, Chicago.

Coe, Joffre L. 1961. Cherokee archaeology. In Symposium on Cherokee and Iroquois culture, ed. William N. Fenton and John Gulick. *Bureau of American Ethnology,* Bull. 180.

_____. 1964. The formative cultures of the Carolina Piedmont. *Transactions of the American Philosophical Society,* N.S., 54 (Pt. 5).

_____. 1968. Cherokee archaeology: 1964-1967. Paper presented at the 33rd Annual Meeting of the Society for American Archaeology, Santa Fe, N.M.

_____. 1969. Shaft and chamber burials of the 16th century Cherokee. Paper presented at the 34th Annual Meeting of the Society for American Archaeology, Milwaukee.

Coe, Joffre L., and Bennie C. Keel. 1965. Two Cherokee houses in western North Carolina. Paper presented at the 30th Annual Meeting of the Society for American Archaeology, Urbana, Ill.

Coe, Joffre L., and Ernest Lewis. 1952. Certain eastern Siouan pottery types. In *Prehistoric Pottery of the Eastern United States,* ed. James B. Griffin. Univ. of Michigan Press, Ann Arbor.

Crabtree, Don E. 1968. Mesoamerican polyhedral cores and prismatic blades. *American Antiquity* 33:446-478.

Crabtree, Don E., and Earl H. Swanson, Jr. 1968. Edge-ground cobbles and blade-making in the Northwest. *Tibiwa* 11:50-58. Pocatello, Idaho.

Crane, H. R. 1963. University of Michigan radiocarbon dates. *Science* 124: 665.

Davis, William M. 1889. The rivers and valleys of Pennsylvania. *National Geographic* 1:183-253.

de Baillou, Clemens. 1965. A test excavation of the Hollywood Mound (9Ri1), Georgia. *Southern Indian Studies* 17:3-11. Chapel Hill, N. C.

Deetz, James. 1965. The dynamics of stylistic change in Ankara ceramics. Univ. of Illinois Press, Urbana, Ill.

_____. 1967. *Invitation to Archaeology.* Natural History Press, Garden City, N. Y.

DeJarnette, David L., Edward Kurjack, and James Cameron. 1963. Stanfield-Worley bluff-shelter excavations. *Journal of Alabama Archaeology* 8. University, Ala.

DeJarnette, David L., Edward Kurjack, and Bennie C. Keel. 1973. Archaeological investigations of the Weiss Reservoir of the Coosa River in Alabama, Parts I and II. *Journal of Alabama Archaeology* 14:(1 and 2). University, Ala.

Dickens, Roy S., Jr. 1964. The Stone Mountain salvage project, DeKalb and Gwinnett counties, Georgia, Part I. *Journal of Alabama Archaeology* 10: 43-49. University, Ala.

_____. 1965. The Stone Mountain salvage project, DeKalb and Gwinnett counties, Georgia, Part II. *Journal of Alabama Archaeology* 11:123-132. University, Ala.

Dickens, Roy S., Jr. 1967. The route of Rutherford's expeditions against the
    North Carolina Cherokees. *Southern Indian Studies* 19:3-24. Chapel Hill,
    N. C.
_____. 1969. The Pisgah Culture: a preliminary statement on a late pre-
    historic manifestation in the Southern Appalachians. Paper presented at the
    34th Annual Meeting of the Society for American Archaeology, Milwaukee.
_____. 1970. The Pisgah Culture and its place in the prehistory of the
    Southern Appalachians. Ph.D. dissertation, Dept. of Anthropology, Univ.
    of North Carolina, Chapel Hill.
_____. 1974. A processual approach to Mississippian Origins on the
    Georgia piedmont. Paper presented to the 31st Annual Southeastern
    Archaeological Conference, Atlanta.
Egloff, Brian J. 1967. An analysis of ceramics from Cherokee towns. M.A.
    thesis, Dept. of Anthropology, Univ. of North Carolina, Chapel Hill.
Egloff, Keith T. 1971. Methods and problems of mound exploration in the
    Southern Appalachian area. M.A. thesis, Dept. of Anthropology, Univ. of
    North Carolina, Chapel Hill.
_____. 1972. Archaeological survey of Mills River Reservoir, North
    Carolina. Report submitted to the National Park Service by the Research
    Laboratory of Anthropology, Univ. of North Carolina, Chapel Hill.
Fairbanks, Charles H. 1942. The taxonomic position of Stallings Island,
    Georgia. *American Antiquity* 7:223-231.
_____. 1950. A preliminary segregation of Etowah, Savannah, and Lamar.
    American Antiquity 16:142-151.
_____. 1952. Creek and pre-Creek. In *Archeology of the Eastern
    United States,* ed. James B. Griffin. Univ. of Chicago Press, Chicago.
_____. 1954. 1953 excavations at site 9H164 Buford Reservoir, Georgia.
    Florida State University Studies 16:1-26. Tallahassee.
_____. 1956. Archaeology of the Funeral Mound, Ocmulgee National
    Monument, Georgia. *Archaeological Research Series* 3. National Park
    Service, Washington, D.C.
_____. 1961. Comment on Joffre L. Coe's "Cherokee Archaeology." In
    Symposium on Cherokee and Iroquois culture, ed. James N. Fenton and
    John Gulick. *Bureau of American Ethnology,* Bull. 180.
_____. 1962. The check stamped series. *Newsletter, Southeastern
    Archaeological Conference* 8:9-19.
_____. 1965. Excavations at the Ft. Walton temple mound, 1960.
    Florida Anthropologist 18:239-264. Tallahassee.
Faulkner, Charles H. 1967. Tennessee radiocarbon dates. *Tennessee Archae-
    ologist* 23(1):12-30. Knoxville.
_____. 1968a. A review of pottery types in the eastern Tennessee Valley.
    Proceedings of the Southeastern Archaeological Conference, Bull. 8:23-35.
_____. 1968b. *Archaeological Investigations of the Tims Ford Reservoir,
    Tennessee, 1966.* Dept. of Anthropology, Univ. of Tennessee, Knoxville.

Faulkner, Charles H. 1971. Adena and Copena: A Case of Mistaken Identity. In *Adena: The Seeking of an Identity*, ed. B. K. Swartz, Jr., Ball State University, Muncie.

Faulkner, Charles H., and J. B. Graham. 1965. Excavations in the Nickajack Reservoir: season I. *Tennessee Archaeological Society, Miscellaneous Paper*, No. 7. Knoxville.

_____. 1966a. *Westmoreland-Barber Site (40Mi11), Nickajack Reservoir, Season II*. Dept. of Anthropology, Univ. of Tennessee, Knoxville.

_____. 1966b. *Highway Salvage in the Nickajack Reservoir*. Dept. of Anthropology, Univ. of Tennessee, Knoxville.

_____. 1967. Plant remains on Tennessee sites: a preliminary report. *Southeastern Archaeological Conference*, Bull. 5:36-40.

Fenneman, N. M. 1938. *Physiography of Eastern United States*. McGraw-Hill, New York.

Ferguson, Leland G. 1971. South Appalachian Mississippian. Ph.D. dissertation, Dept. of Anthropology, Univ. of North Carolina, Chapel Hill.

Ford, James A. 1938. A chronological method applicable to the Southeast. M.A. thesis, Dept. of Anthropology, Univ. of Michigan, Ann Arbor.

_____. 1954a. Comments of A. C. Spaulding, "Statistical techniques for the discovery of artifact types." *American Antiquity* 19:390-391.

_____. 1954b. On the concept of types: the type concept revisited. *American Anthropologist* 65:42-57.

_____. 1954c. Spaulding's review of Ford: I. *American Anthropologist* 56:109-112

_____. 1969. A comparison of formative cultures in the Americas. *Smithsonian Contributions to Anthropology*, Vol. 11.

Ford, James A., and Gordon R. Willey. 1941. An interpretation of the prehistory of the eastern United States. *American Anthropologist* 43:325-363.

Fowler, Melvin L. 1957. Ferry site in Hardin County, Illinois. *Illinois State Museum Scientific Papers*, No. 9. Springfield.

_____. 1959. Summary report of Modoc rockshelter—1952, 1953, 1955, 1956. *Illinois State Museum, Report of Investigations*, No. 8. Springfield.

Gearing, Fred. 1962. Priests and warriors. *Memoirs of the American Anthropological Association*, No. 93. Menasha, Wisc.

Gleeson, Paul F. 1970. Archaeological investigations in the Tellico Reservoir, interim report. *Report of Investigations*, No. 8. Dept. of Anthropology, Univ. of Tennessee, Knoxville.

_____. 1971. (ed.) Archaeological investigations in the Tellico Reservoir, interim report, 1970. *Report of Investigations*, No. 9. Dept. of Anthropology, Univ. of Tennessee, Knoxville.

Graham, J. B. 1964. *Archaeological Investigations of Moccasin Bend (40Ha63), Hamilton County, Tennessee*. Dept. of Anthropology, Univ. of Tennessee, Knoxville.

Griffin, James B. 1943. *The Fort Ancient Aspect, Its Cultural and Chronological Position in Lower Mississippi Valley Archaeology.* Univ. of Michigan Press, Ann Arbor.

_____. 1945. The ceramic affiliations of the Ohio Valley Adena Culture. In The Adena People, ed. W. S. Webb and C. E. Snow, *Publications of the Department of Anthropology,* No. 6, Univ. of Kentucky, Lexington; rpt. 1974, Univ. of Tennessee Press, Knoxville.

_____. 1958. The chronological position of the Hopewell culture in the eastern United States. *Anthropological Papers,* No. 12. Museum of Anthropology, Univ. of Michigan, Ann Arbor.

_____. 1961. Some correlations of climatic and cultural change in eastern North American prehistory. *Annals of the New York Academy of Science* 96:710-717. Albany.

_____. 1967. Eastern North American archaeology: a summary. *Science* 156:175-191.

Griffin, James B., Richard E. Flanders, and Paul F. Titterington. 1970. The burial complexes of the Knight and Norton mounds in Illinois and Michigan. *Memoir of the Museum of Anthropology,* No. 2. Univ. of Michigan, Ann Arbor.

Guthe, Alfred K. 1965. Agriculture and ecology: the Tennessee River. Paper presented at the 22nd Southeastern Archaeological Conference, Macon, Ga.

Hally, David J. 1970. *Archaeological Investigations of Pott's Track Site (9Mu103) Carters Dam, Murray County, Georgia.* Dept. of Sociology and Anthropology, Univ. of Georgia, Athens.

Harrington, Mark R. 1922. Cherokee and earlier remains on upper Tennessee River. *Indian Notes and Monographs,* No. 24. Museum of the American Indian-Heye Foundation, New York.

Harwood, Charles R. 1959. Quartzite points and tools from the Appalachian highland. *Tennessee Archaeologist* 15:89-95. Knoxville.

Heye, George G. 1919. Certain mounds in Haywood County, North Carolina. *Contributions from the Museum of the American Indian-Heye Foundation* 5:35-43. New York.

Heye, George C., Frederick W. Hodge, and George H. Pepper. 1918. The Nacoochee Mound in Georgia. *Contributions from the Museum of the American Indian-Heye Foundation* 2. New York.

Hodge, Frederick W. 1916. The Nacoochee Mound in Georgia. *Smithsonian Institution, Field Work and Explorations for 1915, Miscellaneous Collections,* Vol. 66; pp. 75-82.

Holden, Patricia Padgett. 1966. An archaeological survey of Transylvania County, North Carolina. M.A. thesis, Dept. of Anthropology, Univ. of North Carolina, Chapel Hill.

Holland, C. G. 1955. An analysis of projectile points and large blades. In A ceramic study of Virginia archaeology, ed. Clifford Evans. *Bureau of American Ethnology,* Bull. 160:165-191.

Holland, C. G. 1970. An archaeological survey of southeast Virginia. *Smithsonian Contributions to Anthropology*, No. 12.

Holmes, William Henry. 1884. Etowah Mounds. *Science* 3:437.

_____. 1903. Aboriginal pottery of the eastern United States. *Bureau of American Ethnology*, 20th Annual Report for 1898-1899.

Hoyt, W. G., and W. B. Langbein. 1955. *Floods*. Princeton Univ. Press, Princeton, N. J.

Jefferies, R. W. 1974. A Hopewellian burial complex in Dade County, Georgia. Paper submitted to Dept. of Anthropology, Univ. of Georgia, Athens.

Jennings, Jesse D. 1968. *Prehistory of North America*. McGraw-Hill, New York.

Jennings, Jesse D., and Charles H. Fairbanks. 1939. Type descriptions of pottery. *Newsletter, Southeastern Archaeological Conference* 1.

_____. 1940. Type descriptions of pottery. *Newsletter, Southeastern Archaeological Conference* 2.

Jennings, Jesse D., and Edward Norbeck (eds.). 1964. *Prehistoric Man in the New World*. Univ. of Chicago Press, Chicago.

Keel, Bennie C. 1963. An archaeological survey of the Wilkesboro (W. Kerr Scott) Reservoir. Report submitted to the National Parks Service. Ms. on file at Chapel Hill, N. C.

_____. 1964. A historic Cherokee house. Paper presented at the 30th Annual Meeting of the Archaeological Society of North Carolina, Chapel Hill.

_____. 1965. Archaeology and ecology of the Coosa River, Alabama and the Cherokee Area of North Carolina. Paper presented at the 22nd Southeastern Archaeological Conference, Macon, Ga.

_____. 1967. Garden Creek mound, Hw 2, Haywood County, North Carolina. Paper presented at the 32nd Annual Meeting of the Society for American Archaeology, Ann Arbor, Mich.

_____. 1968. Recent archaeological investigations in the Cherokee area of North Carolina. Paper presented at the 21st Annual Meeting of the Northwest Anthropological Conference, Portland.

_____. 1970. The Cane Creek site, Ml 3, Mitchell County, North Carolina. Unpublished ms. on file at the Research Laboratories of Anthropology, Univ. of North Carolina, Chapel Hill.

_____. 1972. Woodland phases of the Appalachian Summit Area. Ph.D. dissertation, Dept. of Anthropology, Washington State Univ., Pullman.

_____. 1974. Hopewellian influence in the Appalachian Summit Area. Ohio Archaeological Society, Delaware, Ohio.

Keel, Bennie C., and Jefferson Chapman. 1972. The cultural position of the Connestee phase in Southeastern prehistory. Paper presented at the 37th Annual Meeting of the Society for American Archaeology, Miami, Fla.

Keeler, Robert W. 1971. An archaeological survey of upper Catawba River valley. Undergraduate honors thesis, Dept. of Anthropology, Univ. of North Carolina, Chapel Hill.

Kellar, James H., A. R. Kelly, and E. V. McMichael. 1961. Final report to the National Parks Service, Mandeville site, Georgia (1961). Dept. of Sociology and Anthropology, Univ. of Georgia, Athens.

_____. 1962. The Mandeville site in southwestern Georgia. *American Antiquity* 27:336-355.

Kellenberg, John M. 1963. Chert and "flint" of the Tennessee area. *Tennessee Archaeologist* 19:1-7. Knoxville.

Kelly, Arthur R. 1938. A preliminary report on archaeological excavations at Macon, Georgia. *Bureau of American Ethnology*, Bull. 119, Anthropological Papers, No. 1.

Kelly, Arthur R., and Clemens de Baillou. 1960. Excavation of the presumptive site of Estatoe. *Southern Indiana Studies* 12:3-30. Chapel Hill, N. C.

Kelly, Arthur R., and R. S. Neitzel. 1961. The Chauga site in Oconee County, South Carolina. *University of Georgia, Laboratory of Archaeology Series*, No. 3. Athens.

Kichline, Herbert E. 1941. Climate of the states—North Carolina. *Agricultural Yearbook 1941*, pp. 1035-1044. U.S. Dept. of Commerce, Washington, D. C.

Kneberg, Madeline D. 1952. The Tennessee area. In *Archeology of the Eastern United States*, ed. James B. Griffin. Univ. of Chicago Press, Chicago.

_____. 1956. Some important projectile point types found in the Tennessee area. *Tennessee Archaeologist* 12:17-28. Knoxville.

_____. 1957. Chipped stone artifacts of the Tennessee Valley area. *Tennessee Archaeologist* 13:55-66.

_____. 1961. Four Southeastern limestone-tempered pottery complexes. *Newsletter, Southeastern Archaeological Conference* 7:3-14.

_____. 1962. Woodland fabric marked ceramic system. *Newsletter, Southeastern Archaeological Conference* 8.

Krieger, Alex. 1944. The typological concept. *American Antiquity* 9:271-288.

_____. 1960. Archaeological typology in theory and practice. In *Men and Cultures. Selected Papers of the Fifth International Congress of Anthropological and Ethnological Sciences. Philadelphia, September 1-9, 1956*, ed. Anthony F. C. Wallace. Univ. of Pennsylvania Press, Philadelphia.

Kroeber, Alfred L. 1963. Cultural and natural areas of native North America. *University of California Publications in American Archaeology and Ethnology*, Vol. 38 (fourth printing). Univ. of California Press, Berkeley.

Larson, Lewis. 1959. Middle Woodland manifestation in northern Georgia. *Newsletter, Southeastern Archaeological Conference* 6:54-58.

Lazarus, William C. 1965. Alligator Lake. *Florida Anthropologist* 28:83-124.

Lee, William D. 1955. The soils of North Carolina. North Carolina Agricultural Experiment Station, Raleigh.

Leonhardy, Frank C. 1970. Artifact assemblages and archaeological units at Granite Point Locality I (42WT41) southeastern Washington. Ph.D. dissertation, Dept. of Anthropology, Washington State Univ. Pullman.

Lewis, Thomas M. N. 1943. Late horizons in the Southeast. *Recent Advancements in American Archaeology, Proceedings of the American Philosophical Society* 86:304-312.

Lewis, Thomas M. N., and Madeline D. Kneberg. 1941. The prehistory of the Chickamauga Basin in Tennessee. *Tennessee Anthropological Papers,* No. 1. Univ. of Tennessee, Knoxville.

_____. 1946. *Hiwassee Island: An Archaeological Account of Four Tennessee Indian Peoples.* Univ. of Tennessee Press, Knoxville.

_____. The Camp Creek site. *Tennessee Archaeologist* 13:1-48.

Longacre, William A. 1970. Archaeology as anthropology: a case study. *Anthropological Papers of the University of Arizona,* No. 17, ed. Mark P. Leone. Univ. of Arizona Press, Tucson.

McCollough, Major C. R., and Charles H. Faulkner. 1973. Excavation of the Higgs and Doughty sites. I-75 Salvage Archaeology. *Tennessee Archaeological Society Miscellaneous Paper,* No. 12. Project conducted and reported in accordance with Tennessee Dept. of Highways, State Agreement No. 0144, I-75—2 (16) 72, 53002-117-44.

McKern, Will C. 1939. The Midwestern taxonomic method as an aid to archaeological culture study. *American Antiquity* 4:301-313.

McMichael, Edward V. 1960. The anatomy of a tradition: a study of Southeastern stamped pottery. Ph.D. dissertation, Dept. of Anthropology, Univ. of Indiana, Bloomington.

Maxwell, Moreau S. 1951. The Woodland cultures of southern Illinois. *Logan Museum Publications in Anthropology, Bulletin,* No. 7. Beloit College, Beloit.

Michalek, Daniel D. 1969. Fan-like features and related periglacial phenomena of the southern Blue Ridge. Ph.D. dissertation, Dept. of Geology, Univ. of North Carolina, Chapel Hill.

Miller, Carl F. 1949. The Lake Spring site, Columbia County, Georgia. *American Antiquity* 15:38-51.

Mooney, James. 1889. Cherokee mound building. *American Anthropologist* 2:167-171.

_____. 1891. The sacred formulas of the Cherokees. *Seventh Annual Report of the Bureau of Ethnology,* pp. 301-397.

_____. 1900. Myths of the Cherokee. *Bureau of American Ethnology, 19th Annual Report,* Pt. 1.

Moore, Clarence B. 1915. Aboriginal sites on Tennessee River. *Journal of the Academy of Natural Sciences of Philadelphia,* 2nd ser., 16 (Pt. 3):431-487.

Morrell, L. Ross. 1960. Oakland Mound (Je 53), Florida, a preliminary report. *Florida Anthropologist* 13:101-108. Tallahassee.

Perino, Gregory. 1968. Guide to the identification of certain American Indian projectile points. *Oklahoma Anthropological Society, Special Bulletin,* No. 3. Norman.

Phelps, David S. 1965. The Norwood series of fiber-tempered ceramics. *Proceedings of the 20th Southeastern Archaeological Conference,* Bull. 2:65-69.

Phillips, Philip, James A. Ford, and J. B. Griffin. 1951. Archaeological survey in the lower Mississippi alluvial valley, 1940-47. *Peabody Museum Papers,* Vol. 25.

Pi-Sunyer, O. 1965. The flint industry. In The McGraw site: a study in Hope-wellian dynamics, ed. Olaf H. Prufer. *Scientific Publications of the Cleve-land Museum of Natural History*, N. S., Vol. 3, pp. 60-89. Cleveland.

Polhemus, Richard R. Ms. Fieldnotes on sites and excavations, Caldwell County, North Carolina. Ms. on file, Research Laboratories of Anthro-pology, Univ. of North Carolina, Chapel Hill.

Polhemus, Richard R., and James H. Polhemus. 1966. The McCullough Bend site. *Tennessee Archaeologist* 22:13-24. Knoxville.

Prufer, Olaf H. 1964. The Hopewell complex of Ohio. In Hopewellian studies, ed. Joseph R. Caldwell and Robert L. Hall. *Illinois State Museum Scientific Papers*, Vol. XII, pp. 35-84. Springfield.

_____. 1965. The McGraw site: a study in Hopewellian dynamics. *Scien-tific Publications of the Cleveland Museum of Natural History*, N. S., Vol. 3. Cleveland.

_____. 1968. Ohio Hopewell ceramics—an analysis of extant collections. *Anthropological Papers*, No. 33. Museum of Anthropology, Univ. of Michi-gan, Ann Arbor.

Prufer, Olaf H., and Douglas M. McKinzie. 1965. Ceramics. In The McGraw site: a study in Hopewellian dynamics, ed. Olaf Prufer. *Scientific Publica-tions of the Cleveland Museum of Natural History*, N. S., Vol. 3, pp. 18-59. Cleveland.

Radiocarbon. 1963. University of Michigan Radiocarbon dates, Vol. 5, p. 240. Yale Univ. Press, New Haven, Conn.

_____. 1967. University of Michigan Radiocarbon dates, Vol. 9, p. 373. Yale Univ. Press, New Haven, Conn.

Reed, Nelson A. 1969. Monks and other Mississippian mounds. In Explora-tions into Cahokia Archaeology, ed. Melvin L. Fowler. *Illinois Archaeologi-cal Survey, Inc.*, Bull. 7:31-42. Urbana.

Reid, J. Jefferson. 1965. A comparative statement of ceramics from the Hollywood and Town Creek mounds. *Southern Indian Studies* 17:13-25. Chapel Hill, N. C.

_____. 1967. Pee Dee pottery from the mound at Town Creek. M.A. thesis, Dept. of Anthropology, Univ. of North Carolina, Chapel Hill.

Reid, J. Jefferson, and Valetta Canouts. 1969. Fieldnotes, 1969 excavations at Bn 29, North Carolina. Ms. on file at Research Laboratories of Anthro-pology, Univ. of North Carolina, Chapel Hill.

Richards, Horace G., and Sheldon Judson. 1965. The Atlantic Coastal Plain and the Appalachian Highlands in the Quaternary. In *Quaternary of the United States*, ed. H. E. Wright, Jr., and David G. Frey, pp. 129-136. Princeton Univ. Press, Princeton, N. J.

Ritchie, William A. 1962. The antiquity of pottery in the Northeast. *Ameri-can Antiquity* 27:583-584.

Rowe, Chandler W. 1952. Woodland cultures of eastern Tennessee. In *Archeology of Eastern United States*, ed. James B. Griffin, pp. 199-206. Univ. of Chicago Press, Chicago.

Rouse, Irving. 1939. Prehistory in Haiti: a study in method. *Yale University Publications in Anthropology,* No. 21. New Haven, Conn.

Ruff, Frederick J. 1938. The White-tailed deer on the Pisgah National Game Preserve, North Carolina. United States Department of Agriculture, Forest Service. Asheville.

Salley, A. S., Jr. 1917. George Hunter's map of the Cherokee country and the path thereto in 1730. *Bulletin 4, Historical Commission of South Carolina,* Columbia.

Salo, Lawr V. (ed.). 1969. *Archaeological Investigations in the Tellico Reservoir, Tennessee, 1967-1968, an interim report.* Dept. of Anthropology, Univ. of Tennessee, Knoxville.

Sanford, Patricia P. 1970. An ethnobotanical study of the Fawcette site. Honors thesis, Dept. of Anthropology, Univ. of North Carolina, Chapel Hill.

Schroedl, Gerald F. 1973. Radiocarbon dates from three burial mounds at the McDonald site in East Tennessee. *Tennessee Archaeologist* 29(1). Knoxville.

Scully, Edward G. 1951. Some central Mississippi Valley projectile point types. Mimeographed. Publication of the Museum of Anthropology, Univ. of Michigan, Ann Arbor.

Sears, William H. 1950. Preliminary report on the excavation of an Etowah Valley site. *American Antiquity* 16:137-142.

_____. Ceramic development in the South Appalachian Province. *American Antiquity* 18:101-110.

_____. 1955. Creek and Cherokee culture in the 18th century. *American Antiquity* 21:143-149.

_____. 1958. The Wilbanks site (9Ck5), Georgia. *Bureau of American Ethnology,* Bull. 169:129-194.

_____. 1960. Ceramic systems and Eastern archaeology. *American Antiquity* 25:324-329.

_____. 1962. The state in certain areas and periods of the prehistoric southeastern United States. *Ethnohistory* 9:109-125.

_____. 1964. The southeastern United States. In *Prehistoric Man in the New World,* ed. Edward Norbeck. The Univ. of Chicago Press, Chicago.

Setzler, Frank M. and Jesse D. Jennings. 1941. Peachtree mound and village site. *Bureau of American Ethnology,* Bull. 131.

Shelford, Victor E. 1963. *The Ecology of North America.* Univ. of Illinois Press, Urbana.

Shetrone, H. C. and E. F. Greenman. 1931. Explorations of the Seip group of prehistoric earthworks. *Ohio State Archaeological and Historical Quarterly,* No. 40, pp. 343-509. Columbus.

Smith, Betty Anderson. 1972. An analysis of regional variations of Deptford pottery. M.A. thesis, Dept. of Anthropology, Univ. of Georgia, Athens.

Smith, D. C., and Frank M. Hodges, Jr. 1968. The Rankin site, Cocke County, Tennessee. *Tennessee Archaeologist* 24:36-91. Knoxville.

Spaulding, Albert C. 1953a. Statistical techniques for the discovery of artifact types. *American Antiquity* 18:305-313.

Spaulding, Albert C. 1953b. Review of "Measurements of some prehistoric de-
    sign developments in the Southeastern states," by James A. Ford. (Anthro-
    pological Papers of the American Museum of Natural History, Vol. 44, 1952.)
    American Anthropologist 55:588-591.
_____. 1954a. Reply to Ford. *American Anthropologist* 56:122-124.
_____. 1954b. Reply to Ford. *American Antiquity* 19:391-393.
Steward, Julian H. 1942. The direct historical approach to archaeology.
    American Antiquity 7:337-343.
Struever, Stuart. 1964. The Hopewellian interaction sphere in riverine western
    Great Lakes culture history. In Hopewellian studies, ed. Joseph R. Caldwell
    and Robert L. Hall. *Illinois State Museum Scientific Papers,* Vol. XII, pp. 85-
    106. Springfield.
Stuckey, Jasper Leonidas. 1965. *North Carolina: Its Geology and Mineral Re-
    sources.* Dept. of Conservation and Development, Raleigh.
Swanton, John R. 1932. Ethnological value of the DeSoto narratives. *Ameri-
    can Anthropologist,* N. S., 34:570-590.
_____. 1946. The Indians of the southeastern United States. *Bureau of
    American Ethnology,* Bull. 137.
Swartz, B. K., Jr. (ed.). 1971. *Adena: The Seeking of an Identity.* Ball State
    University, Muncie, Indiana.
Thomas, Cyrus. 1887. Work in mound exploration of the Bureau of Ethnology.
    Bureau of American Ethnology, Bull. 4.
_____. 1891. Catalogue of prehistoric works east of the Rocky Moun-
    tains. *Bureau of American Ethnology,* Bull. 12.
_____. 1894. Report on the mound explorations of the Bureau of
    Ethnology. *Bureau of American Ethnology, 12th Annual Report.*
Thornbury, William D. 1965. *Regional Geomorphology of the United States.*
    John Wiley & Sons, New York.
Timberlake, Henry. 1927. *Lieut. Henry Timberlake's Memoirs,* ed. Samuel C.
    Williams. Watauga Press, Johnson City, Tenn.
United States Geological Survey. 1949. Floods of August 1940 in the South-
    eastern States. *U.S. Geological Survey Water Supply Paper* 1066. Washing-
    ton, D. C.
Valentine Mann S. et al. Ms. A. Notes taken in North Carolina, 1880s. Photo-
    copy on file at Research Laboratories of Anthropology, Univ. of North
    Carolina, Chapel Hill.
_____. Ms. B. Records relating to the affairs of the Valentine brothers'
    collection. Typescript copy on file at Research Laboratories of Anthro-
    pology, Univ. of North Carolina, Chapel Hill.
_____. Ms. C. Memo—Jan. 29, 1880. Photocopy on file at Research
    Laboratories of Anthropology, Univ. of North Carolina, Chapel Hill.
Valentine Museum. 1898. Catalogue of collections. The Valentine Museum,
    Richmond.
Walthall, John A. 1973. Copena: A Tennessee Valley Middle Woodland cul-
    ture. Ph.D. dissertation, Dept. of Anthropology, University of North Caro-
    lina, Chapel Hill.

Waring, Antonio J., Jr. 1968. A history of Georgia archaeology to World War II. In The Waring papers, ed. Stephen Williams. *Papers of the Peabody Museum,* Vol. 58.

Wauchope, Robert. 1948. The ceramic sequence in the Etowah drainage, northwest Georgia. *American Antiquity* 13:201-209.

_____. 1950. The evolution and persistence of ceramic motifs in northern Georgia. *American Antiquity* 41:16-22.

_____. 1953. Unusual Lamar variant of the filfot cross. *American Antiquity* 18:391-392.

_____. 1956. (Ed.) Seminars in archaeology. *Memoirs of the Society for American Archaeology,* No. 11.

_____. 1966. Archaeological survey of northern Georgia. *Memoirs of the Society for American Archaeology,* No. 21.

Webb, William S. 1938. An archaeological survey of the Norris Basin in eastern Tennessee. *Bureau of American Ethnology,* Bull. 118.

Webb, William S., and David L. DeJarnette. 1942. An archaeological survey of the Pickwick Basin in the adjacent portions of Alabama, Mississippi, and Tennessee. *Bureau of American Ethnology,* Bull. 129.

Weigland, Phil C. 1970. Huichol ceremonial reuse of a fluted point. *American Antiquity* 35:365-367.

White, Anta M. 1963. Analytic description of the chipped-stone industry from the Snyders site, Calhoun County, Illinois. In Miscellaneous studies in typology and classification, ed. Anta M. White, Lewis R. Binford, and Mark L. Papworth. *Anthropological Papers* No. 19. Museum of Anthropology, Univ. of Michigan, Ann Arbor.

_____. 1968. The lithic industries of the Illinois Valley in Early and Middle Woodland periods. *Anthropological Papers* No. 35. Museum of Anthropology, Univ. of Michigan, Ann Arbor.

Whiteford, Andrew H. 1952. A frame of reference for the archaeology of eastern Tennessee. In *Archeology of the Eastern United States,* ed. James B. Griffin. Univ. of Chicago Press, Chicago.

Willey, Gordon R. 1939. Ceramic stratigraphy in a Georgia village site. *American Antiquity* 5:140-147.

_____. 1949. Archaeology of the Florida Gulf Coast. *Smithsonian Miscellaneous Collections,* Vol. 113.

_____. 1966. *An Introduction to American Archaeology, Volume I, North and Middle America.* Prentice-Hall, Englewood Cliffs, N. J.

Willey, Gordon R. and Philip Phillips. 1958. *Method and Theory in American Archaeology.* Univ. of Chicago Press, Chicago.

Williams, Stephen (ed.). 1968. The Waring papers. *Papers of the Peabody Museum,* Vol. 58.

Williams, Stephen and James B. Stoltman. 1965. An outline of southeastern United States prehistory with particular emphasis on the Paleo-Indian era. In *The Quaternary of the United States,* ed. H. E. Wright and David G. Frey, pp. 669-683. Princeton Univ. Press, Princeton, N. J.

Willoughby, Charles C. 1922. The Turner group of earthworks, Hamilton County, Ohio, with notes on the skeletal remains by Ernest A. Hooton. *Papers of the Peabody Museum*, Vol. 8.

Wing, Elizabeth S. 1970. Appendix II, Faunal remains from the Warren Wilson site. In The Pisgah Culture and its place in the prehistory of the Southern Appalachians, by Roy S. Dickens, Jr., pp. 294-299. Ph.D. dissertation, Dept. of Anthropology, Univ. of North Carolina, Chapel Hill.

Winters, Howard Dalton. 1970. *The Riverton Culture, a second millenium occupation in central Wabash Valley. Report of Investigations*, No. 13. Illinois State Museum, Springfield.

Wright, Robert J. 1942. Underfit meanders of the French Broad River, North Carolina. *Journal of Geomorphology* 5(3):183-190.

Yarnell, Richard A. 1970. Appendix I, Floral remains from the Warren Wilson site. In The Pisgah Culture and its place in the prehistory of the Southern Appalachians, by Roy S. Dickens, Jr., pp. 283-293. Ph.D. dissertation, Dept. of Anthropology, Univ. of North Carolina, Chapel Hill.

Index